Soviet Politics in Transition

Soviet Politics in Transition

Joan DeBardeleben
McGill University

D. C. Heath and Company   Lexington, Massachusetts / Toronto

Address editorial correspondence to

D. C. Heath
125 Spring Street
Lexington, MA   02173

Book Design: David Ford
Cover Design: Terrence M. Fehr

Published simultaneously in Canada.

Printed in the United States of America.

International Standard Book Number: 0-669-28676-1

10 9 8 7 6 5 4 3 2 1

Preface

When I recently spoke to a Soviet diplomatic official about this textbook, he said, "It is impossible to write a completely accurate account of Soviet politics now. Things are changing too quickly and developments are too contradictory." Five days later, on August 19, 1991, an unexpected coup attempt by hard-line military and security forces temporarily ousted Mikhail Gorbachev from his post as president of the USSR, a seeming confirmation of the diplomat's warning. That event demanded yet another set of revisions for this text; one of the several probable future scenarios discussed in the previous draft of the book had already become history.

The confusing and unpredictable course of events in the USSR in the late 1980s and early 1990s made this book a challenge to write, but also provided the rationale for its structure and content. I have tried to pose fundamental questions about the reform process in the USSR so that transitory phases of development will not date the underlying analysis. Thus, although specific material may be superseded by subsequent developments, I believe the book will continue to provide a framework for understanding fundamental conflicts and possibilities.

Unlike many other books on recent Soviet politics, the first two sections of this text place the post-1985 reform period in a broad historical context, going back to the prerevolutionary tsar-

ist period and up to the end of the Brezhnev era. This background material makes the student aware of both the sources of and likely limitations on the reform process. The historical sections, however, are not only descriptive, but they also encourage the student to reflect on important questions of historical interpretation. Why did the first successful revolution by a Marxist party occur in a backward country like Russia rather than in more advanced areas that Marx had expected? Did Russia's backwardness pose insurmountable obstacles to the realization of the Marxist project? Had some of the operative precepts of Leninism undermined the very achievement of Lenin's larger goals? What explains the rise of Stalinism? How was the Communist Party transformed from a revolutionary force to a conservative oligarchical party in power? What was the basis of regime stability following Stalinism? To what extent did it rest on coercion and to what extent on an implicit social contract with the population? How could a reformer like Gorbachev emerge out of an entrenched, bureaucratic party structure? Questions such as these draw out the significance and continuing relevance of the historical material.

The bulk of the book examines the post-1985 period in detail. Chapter 3 provides a succinct chronological account of the Gorbachev period, right up through the aftermath of the failed coup of August 19–21, 1991. It also explores the "contested principles" of the reform movement. This section thus gives the student a clear understanding of the historical progression that produced the present crises and the issues that divide the major protagonists in the present period. It analyzes debates over key concepts such as "democratization," "rule of law," "sovereignty," and "*glasnost'*," clarifying Leninist and non-Leninist roots of the various positions, as well as the political interests involved in the debates. This analysis will help the student link debates in the Soviet context to larger issues in the field of comparative politics and to understand the parameters of conflict, even if the outcomes in particular skirmishes are contradictory and fluid.

The fourth chapter explores the "nuts and bolts" of the Soviet system but emphasizes that the study of rapidly changing political institutions requires an understanding of the evolving political environment in which they have emerged. The chapter provides a thorough description of the new and evolving state institutions and their relationship to the larger social and political forces (including the Communist Party). Problems of local politics and conflict over decentralization of economic and political power are also discussed. The demise of the Communist Party of the Soviet Union is viewed against the backdrop of its former dominant role and Gorbachev's unfulfilled aspiration to make the Party the leading instrument of reform. Finally, I provide an overview of and framework for understanding new political forces and parties that have emerged since the 1989. Numerous organizational charts and illustrative materials enhance the discussion.

The last chapter covers the social and economic roots of the present crisis in Soviet politics and society. It first focuses on the origin and nature of the economic collapse, exploring dilemmas and conflicts surrounding various approaches to economic reform. The potential for working class unrest is also explored. The second half of the chapter examines the nationality

problem; students learn about the complex nature of the issues, as well as their destabilizing (but at the same time facilitating) effect on the entire reform process. The chapter clarifies reasons behind the broad demands for national sovereignty and independence articulated by various national groups, as well as the complex linkages between the political, national, and economic crises. Finally the chapter discusses possible future scenarios for Soviet politics—including the likelihood of continued democratization and economic reform, national disintegration, or dictatorship.

I have written the text assuming that students have no prior background in Soviet politics and thus have emphasized clarity of style and explanation. Important concepts are defined in a straightforward manner, and illustrative materials provide vivid evidence of developments and trends outlined in the text. This textbook may be particularly useful in two settings: first, as a basic textbook for courses on Soviet politics; second, as an overview of Soviet politics for courses that have a more comparative focus (e.g., introduction to comparative politics, European politics, and comparative communism). The book is sufficiently short and succinct to allow assignment in its entirety and in this way it provides the student with an overview of developments in Soviet politics as a foundation for comparative analysis. At the same time, the book is comprehensive in coverage (both historically and thematically), so that it provides a firm foundation for an in-depth study of Soviet politics itself.

I wish to express my gratitude to the specialists who reviewed parts or all of the manuscript. Their suggestions and comments were essential. I especially thank Alec Nove, University of Glasgow (who read an earlier version of the book); Lars Lih, Wellesley College; and Victoria Zinde-Walsh, McGill University; as well as the series editors, Joel Krieger, Wellesley College, and Mark Kesselman, Columbia University, who offered constant encouragement and guidance. My research assistants, Keith Geral Martin and Brian Haynes, were very helpful in preparing illustrative materials; I am especially indebted to Ivar Tallo for his generous commitment of thought and energy to the project, and for his attention to nuance and detail as he commented on the manuscript. Adam Jones' skill, patience, and speed in preparing the manuscript made feasible the constant revisions that were required. I am also highly appreciative of the flexibility and top-quality work provided by the outstanding professional staff at D. C. Heath, especially Paul Smith, Lyri Merrill, Gary Crespo, Shira Eisenman, and Heather Garrison.

And finally I stand in awe and respect before the thousands of reformers and activists all over the former USSR who have made a formerly rather dull field of study into the most dynamic and intriguing subject matter one could possibly imagine.

J.D.

Contents

Soviet Politics in Transition

C H A P T E R

1

The Emergence of
the Soviet State

The Russian Revolution in October 1917 ush-ered in not only a radical change in Russian government but also a new force in the inter-national political system. For the first time in history, a Marxist party took the reins of state power. Some seventy-odd years later, the Soviet Union approached another period of revolution-ary change involving a fundamental challenge to Soviet Marxist principles. After taking office as Communist Party leader in March 1985, Mik-hail Gorbachev instituted a reform process that took on an increasingly radical character over time. Under the slogan of *perestroika* (restruc-turing), Gorbachev encouraged *glasnost'* (open-ness), *demokratizatsiia* (democratization*), and halting moves toward a market economy. On August 19, 1991, forces seeking preservation of key elements of the old system attempted a coup d'état, temporarily removing Gorbachev from the leadership post. The defeat of that effort resulted in a further acceleration of the already dizzying pace of reform, reinforcing powerful centrifugal forces and toppling the Communist Party from power. When this chapter went to press in the fall of 1991, one could not, with assurance, even speak of the "Soviet Union" anymore. Commentators called the region "the former Soviet Union," as some regions were realizing their long-standing goal of national independence and others were groping their way toward defining new forms of cooperation and governance. The region had moved from reform to revolution. But intertwined political, eco-nomic, and social crises left observers and par-ticipants alike nervous about the outcome of the revolutionary process.

The goal of this section is to set the historical context for present-day Soviet politics and to elucidate the problems confronting the system as it faces this historic juncture. Although some of the specific facts or details may change, the underlying dynamics that push reform forward, and also frustrate, its realization are more con-stant.

Note: The map on pp. 2–3 represents the internationally recognized borders of the USSR as of November 15, 1991. As of the same date, official documents still referred to the country as the Union of Soviet Socialist Republics. However, new names for the altered union have been suggested, such as Union of Sovereign States or Union of Soviet Sovereign Republics. The name of the country, as well as its present borders, may change by the time this book is printed. The independence of Estonia, Latvia, and Lithuania was officially recognized by the Soviet government on September 6, 1991, following recognition by several other countries (including most of the countries of Western Europe and North Amer-ica). Most of the other Soviet republics had declared inde-pendence as well by October 1, 1991, but, of these, only Moldova and Georgia did not participate in the post-coup discussions for development of transitional central struc-tures.

* We will use the Russian word *demokratizatsiia* throughout to stress that we should not assume, at the outset, that the Soviet version of "democratization" parallels our Western understanding of the term.

U.S.S.R.

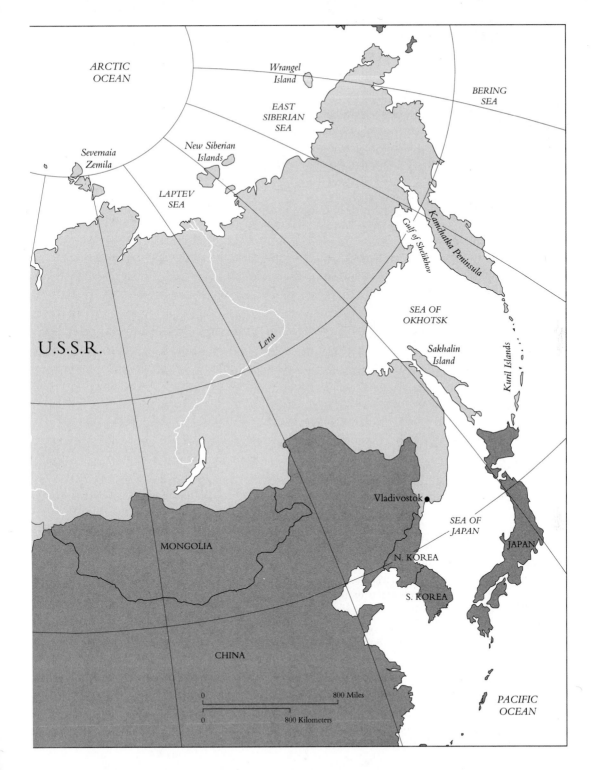

The Principles of Soviet State Formation

To understand contemporary politics of the region, we must first turn back to the 1917 revolution. This event laid the groundwork for the entire Soviet period. While motivated by Marxist theory, this revolution did not occur, as Karl Marx and Friedrich Engels had expected, in an industrial country of Western Europe, such as Germany, France, or England. Rather, it shook Russia, a country where some 80 percent of the population were peasants, most tilling the soil for a subsistence living.

The victorious Marxist group, the Bolsheviks, faced many problems as they attempted to construct a socialist and, finally, a communist society. Some resulted from the backwardness of the country at the time of the revolution. For example, Marx and Engels had assumed that a socialist revolution would be carried out by a strong urban proletariat (working class), which would first revolt against the exploitive and inhumane working conditions in capitalist factories. The proletariat would replace the bourgeoisie (the capitalist ownership class) as the ruling class and would proceed to construct a more equitable and democratic society. For Marx and Engels, socialism would be a first step on the road to communism; it would be democratic because both political and economic power would rest in the hands of the majority— namely, the working class. Society as a whole, rather than private capitalists, would own the means of production (e.g., factories, machines, and land). Thus, political democracy would be reinforced by economic democracy in an industrial society. In Russia, however, the working class was small, as factory workers made up only about 5 percent of the population in 1917. If this class held power, it would rule as a minority over recalcitrant elements from other social classes, such as the peasantry, the old gentry, and the bourgeoisie. Furthermore, it was not clear whether the small and immature working class

could direct the necessary social changes to transform society. Rather, this class was to be led by a party that included only a minority of the proletariat and that was headed not by workers, but by a progressive component of the intelligentsia.

Although Marx did not provide much guidance on what should follow the revolution, his writings suggest that once the power of the proletariat was secure, the next step would be the elimination of class divisions. All citizens would be equal working participants in communist society, sharing both the burdens and the benefits of labor, for communist society would be a classless society. The elimination of class conflict depended, however, on material abundance. Capitalism itself, according to Marx and Engels, would have laid the economic and technological foundation for overcoming material scarcity. Marx and Engels recognized that capitalism, despite its social injustices, could be highly efficient and productive. Yet Russian capitalism in 1917 was certainly not developed enough to provide the material foundation for a future socialist or communist society.

Despite the rapid industrial takeoff of the late 1800s and early 1900s, industrial output in Russia was still far below that in most Western European countries; levels of literacy, especially in the countryside and among women, were low; and, by almost any measure, the Russian standard of living was well below that of Western Europe. Thus, before the Bolsheviks could hope to build a society free of class competition, they would have to overcome the economic backwardness inherited from the previous period. They might have to fill in for the capitalists, at least for a time, to progress to the next stage. Could this be done without resorting to coercion? Who would bear the costs and burdens of the industrialization effort, which the working class had largely borne during industrialization under capitalism? If the relative backwardness of Russia in 1917 proved a difficult starting point for the Bolsheviks, why did they ground their revolution in a theory that, on the face of it, seemed of little direct relevance to an agrarian peasant society? How could power fall into the hands of such a group, when even in Western Europe, where conditions seemed so much more propitious, no Marxist party had been able to win power? We address these questions in this chapter as we explore some of the unique conditions in prerevolutionary Russia that paved the way for the Bolshevik Revolution of 1917 and some of the problems that ensued from the revolution.

If some of the problems confronting the Bolshevik Party were rooted in the particular circumstances facing Russia in 1917, others might have faced any Marxist party in any country. The new leaders were forced to conduct their social experiment with little theoretical or practical guidance. How could *social* ownership of economic resources be made genuine? Would it simply be *state* ownership? If so, would a new class of bureaucrats, running the state-owned industries and farms, simply replace the former capitalist and tsarist elite? Furthermore, would it be possible to construct a society that was at once both socialist and democratic? Questions such as these surfaced again in the late 1980s, as Soviet reformers sought to redefine the nature of socialism and democracy. Present-day reformers look to Soviet history both for guidance and to understand past errors underlying present problems.

The Old Order

Up until the Bolshevik Revolution of 1917, Russia had taken a separate developmental path from Western Europe, which may account for the different political outcomes in the twentieth century. In Russia, social classes were able to wield much less autonomous power in relation to the state, and the state took on a much more extensive role in furthering industrialization. Certain cultural patterns, such as collectivism

(an emphasis on group over individual values) and a continuing close link between the Russian Orthodox Church and the tsarist state, also differentiated Russia from Western Europe. Finally, the political leadership had suffered repeated setbacks in the international sphere, partly because Russia's domestic structures were too weak to support a successful foreign policy. Foreign policy debacles in turn sparked domestic unrest; for example, Russia's involvement in World War I became the final catalyst for the fall of the tsarist regime.

The State and Social Classes

In prerevolutionary Russia, all social classes had developed in dependence on the strong tsarist state. In the sixteenth century, the tsar Ivan the Terrible began the process that finally subordinated the nobility to the state. By the reign of Peter I (1682–1725), every nobleman was required to perform lifetime service in the military corps or state bureaucracy in exchange for the right to exploit land and labor. Thus, the landed class also became an administrative class. Not until 1762, during the reign of Peter III, were the nobles formally freed from compulsory state service. However, the *dvorianstvo* (Russian nobility) still did not become a strong political force, and they were dependent on the state for control of the labor force, the serfs, who were in servitude to their masters. (The holdings of the nobility were scattered, and many nobles lived in virtual poverty.) Serfdom, which had developed gradually over the previous centuries, was fully developed by the middle of the seventeenth century. In most regions, the *dvorianstvo* did not develop an entrepreneurial spirit to improve and commercialize agriculture but was able to live off the labor of the dependent peasant class.

In 1861, Tsar Alexander II emancipated the serfs, but this was a mixed blessing. The peasant became a legal person, free from the landlord's authority. But the freed peasants were obligated to pay redemption fees to the state for forty-nine years to gain ownership of the land (the state had compensated the previous landowners). They also remained bound to the land and to the *mir* (peasant commune), which still engaged in periodic repartition of land among families in the community. The *mir* also had legal ownership of the land and was collectively responsible for the redemption payments, as well as for providing military recruits for the government. Only wealthy peasants could buy their freedom. Not until 1907, with the Stolypin reforms, were redemption payments abolished and measures taken to replace the peasant commune by private cultivation. Peter Stolypin, president of the tsar's Council of Ministers, hoped that a more truly independent and prosperous peasant class would soon take on the attributes of a conservative petite bourgeoisie in the countryside. As beneficiaries of the tsarist reforms, this class was to provide a stable foundation of political support for the regime and help to improve agricultural productivity. World War I interrupted this process in 1914, and the regime was so severely shaken by the international crisis that revolutionary forces were able to topple it in 1917, before Stolypin's blueprint had a chance to prove itself.

Might Russia have followed a path similar to that of Western Europe had the war not intervened? This is a question we will never be able to answer definitively, but there was no substantial bourgeoisie or other social base to provide a political foundation for constitutional government and liberalism, as had developed in most Western European countries. Once the tsarist government fell in February 1917, the peasants contributed to the revolution by seizing the land remaining in large estates.

Meanwhile, in the late nineteenth century, industrialization was taking off in Russia. From the beginning, the key impetus came not from an indigenous bourgeois class, but from the state itself and from heavy injections of foreign (especially French, English, German, and Belgian) capital in the form of joint-stock companies and

foreign debt incurred by the tsarist government. For example, about 75 percent of the output of coal and pig iron depended on French capital. In 1900, over 70 percent of capital invested in industrial joint-stock companies in mining, metallurgy, engineering, and machinery was of foreign origin. Percentages were lower in other sectors of the economy but still above 25 percent in lumber; chemicals; leather processing; and cements, ceramics, and glass.

The large role of state and foreign capital in the Russian industrialization effort had significant social consequences. Although many workers were employed in small private workshops, on the whole, factories were larger than in Western Europe or North America. In 1914, over 40 percent of the workers were employed in factories with one thousand workers or more (as compared to just over 30 percent in 1901).[1] Many of these factories were run by absentee owners who did not develop personal relations with their workers. A small but restless working class was developing in the cities. Meanwhile, in the countryside, traditional patterns still survived. It seemed that Russia suffered the injustices of two worlds—the constraints on and dependence of the peasantry, and the inhumane and impersonal oppression of the large capitalist factories. Many members of the small working class retained their link to the countryside. They were worker-peasants, often making their way back to the village on weekends or holidays to help out with the harvest, supplementing family income with their factory earnings.

The tsarist state did not legalize trade unions until 1906, and then their activities were carefully circumscribed. By 1914, they were largely ineffectual, but the absence of strong trade unions did not imply a passive working class. At the end of the nineteenth century, there was increasing evidence of worker discontent in the form of numerous illegal strikes, especially in the large urban centers. In 1905, worker discontent produced a major state crisis, with widespread strikes in the cities and uprisings in rural areas. The tsar responded by establishing a constitutional monarchy, with an elected legislative branch. However, the powers of the Duma, the elected assembly, were gradually restricted in the following years. Through increasing repression, the tsarist state was able to maintain its dominance over Russian society.

Russian Political Culture

Just as patterns of economic development set Russia off from Western Europe, so also was the country's political culture less conducive to liberal democratic development. Autocracy, collectivism, and a close link between religious and political authority characterized the Russian cultural heritage. These prerevolutionary values were to find continued expression under the new Soviet regime as well.

Russia was converted to Orthodox Christianity in 987. The Russian Orthodox Church took on an increasingly independent status after Constantinople (Byzantium), the center of Orthodoxy, fell to the Turks in 1453. The tsarist state was intimately connected with the Russian Orthodox Church, which provided a kind of official religion or ideology for tsarism. As early as the sixteenth and seventeenth centuries, the notion spread in influential circles that Russia was the Third Rome, meaning that only in Russia was true Christianity still embodied in the Church's doctrine and rituals; Russia was the rightful world center of Christianity, as the Roman and Byzantine churches (the First and Second Romes) had been corrupted by heretical doctrines.

In the 1660s, a schism shook the Russian Orthodox Church, as its head, Patriarch Nikon, sought to reform church rituals and statutes. The Old Believers, who had followers among both peasants and rich merchant families, rejected the reforms as embodiments of the anti-Christ, thus alienating the official Orthodox Church from broad segments of the Christian population. Nonetheless, the tradition of an of-

ficial state religion was firmly entrenched in Russian history and may bear some resemblance to the Soviet state's traditional monopoly on correct political doctrine.

Russian political culture also was firmly linked to autocracy, which legitimized the strong dependence of social classes on the state and the right of the state to intervene in a broad range of social affairs. The tsar's secret police waged a repressive campaign against the secret societies that demonstrated fledgling opposition to the regime in the nineteenth century, and strict censorship was imposed. At the same time, a series of popular uprisings, which had been a feature of Russian history since the seventeenth century, reflected the alienation of the peasantry from the prevailing patterns of authority.

Russian patriotism, embodied in the idea of Moscow as the Third Rome, also was important. By the nineteenth century, tsarist control extended into central Asia (bordering on what is now Iran, Iraq, and Afghanistan) and to the Pacific coast in the north and east, and it also included a part of present-day Poland and the Baltic states (see the map on pages 514 and 515). The empire included a mosaic of diverse ethnic groups: Russians were the dominant population group, and a significant proportion was Slavic (e.g., Polish, Ukrainian, or Belorussian). The official commitment to nationalism implied both Russian dominance and justification of expansionism in the national interest.

Another important element of traditional Russian culture was collectivism, reflected most clearly in the *mir*, which regulated the most important aspects of the peasant's everyday life. *Mir* in Russian means both "world" and "peace," exemplifying the association in the peasant's mind between the security of the immediate social environment and the whole world. The state supported the formation of the peasant commune in the eighteenth century in part because the *mir* facilitated collection of taxes from the peasantry. The *mir* periodically redistributed strips of land within the commune, depending on changes in family circumstances. This served as an obstacle to the improvement of agriculture, for the peasant family felt little inclination to make sacrifices for land with which it would soon part. The commune reinforced preindustrial values and survived until Stalin's industrialization campaign in 1929.

International Pressures

Standing relatively unprotected between Europe and Asia, Russia had been subject to repeated intrusions and challenges for centuries. The Mongol invasion of 1237 led to about 250 years of subjugation. From the late 1400s, the principality of Moscow had engaged in expansion by conquest. Land hunger and a desire for geopolitical security, as well as for access to seaports and trade routes, were important motives. By the seventeenth century, the Russian empire extended east to the Pacific coast in Siberia (see the map on page 521). Russia's defeat in the Crimean War (1854 to 1856) helped to convince tsarist officials that Russia's inferior military position could be rectified only if Russia were strengthened economically. Serfdom was holding back Russia's development, for it bound the peasants to a backward form of agrarian subsistence and allowed the nobility to maintain its old lethargic life-style. The state's desire to remain an international power compelled the regime to consider emancipation of the serfs, even if the nobility opposed the reform.

Despite the industrial takeoff in the late nineteenth century, the Russo-Japanese War of 1904–05 strained the system, as did the failed revolution of 1905. Russia also entered World War I ill-prepared, which caused widespread food shortages and rising prices in both the countryside and the city. Further, the Russian army suffered repeated setbacks at the hands of the Germans, triggering disillusionment among the soldiers. Soldiers of peasant background rubbed shoulders with more politicized urban recruits. In this way, some of the peasants came

into contact with the revolutionary ideas circulating among factory workers.

War was clearly a catalyst for revolution (as in later communist revolutions, such as in China and Yugoslavia). World War I bared the weak spots in the tsarist economic and political structures, and the incompetence of the regime in handling the war left a power vacuum into which revolutionary forces could enter. The bourgeois and liberal forces, which had dominated the evolution of Western European polities, proved too weak and inflexible to fill the gap in Russia. To understand why a Marxist party should come out on top, we need to examine the revolutionary movement as it had developed in the nineteenth century.

The Revolutionary Movement

The Russian revolutionary movement of the nineteenth century had roots among certain elements of the nobility. Following their emancipation from state service in 1762, the gentry had the leisure to travel frequently to Europe, where they came into contact with the ideas of German idealism and the French Enlightenment. Sons and daughters of the gentry were educated in Russian universities and were exposed to new ideas through intellectual circles and journals. Some began to question their own place in society, giving rise to the classic "superfluous man" portrayed so frequently in Russian literature of the time. The superfluous man found no purpose or place for himself in society and often drifted into lethargy and stagnation. Other offspring of the nobility worked with the *zemstvo* (an organ of local government), which, ,among other things, engaged in various social-welfare activities. Finally, some responded by commitment to revolutionary ideologies and organizations, seeking to alter the backward and oppressive Russian institutions. In time, these individuals came to form the basis of the Russian revolutionary intelligentsia, which was linked

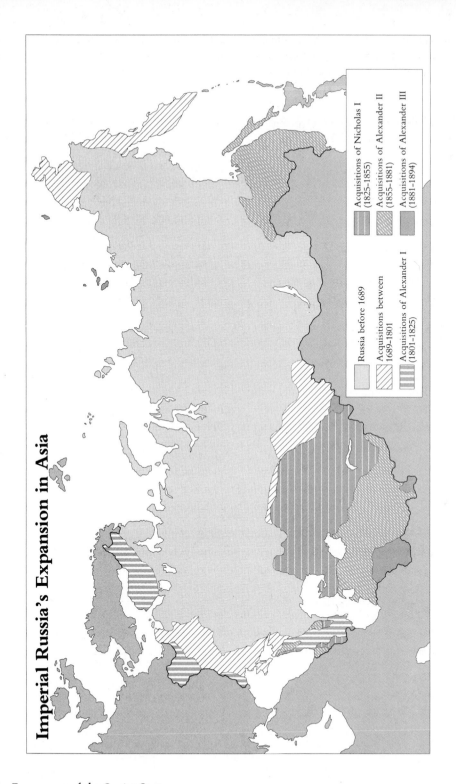

Imperial Russia's Expansion in Asia

Russia before 1689

Acquisitions between
1689–1801

Acquisitions of Alexander I
(1801–1825)

Acquisitions of Nicholas I
(1825–1855)

Acquisitions of Alexander II
(1855–1881)

Acquisitions of Alexander III
(1881–1894)

more by attitudes than social background, although most had studied for at least some period of time at a university. Sons and daughters of peasants, artisans, clergy, and civil servants also joined the ranks, and by the mid-1800s the intelligentsia, which was to form the core of the revolutionary movement in Russia, was made up of *raznochintsy* (individuals of diverse social class rank), united by their disillusionment with the injustices of the existing order.

From Populism to Marxism

Initially, the revolutionaries were not Marxists. In fact, Marx's and Engels's writings did not receive much attention (from revolutionaries or the tsarist censors) until the last decades of the nineteenth century. The earliest uprising of the gentry, the December movement of 1825, was based in the military corps and involved demands for a constitutional monarchy. Indeed, throughout the nineteenth century and up to 1917, the "liberal" intelligentsia, including elements of the small bourgeois class and gentry, continued to voice such demands. This element, however, was too weak to set the tone for the revolutionary movement.

Most revolutionaries of the 1840s to 1880s were populists. Populism was a diverse movement, united by its faith in the peasantry and in the *mir* as a unique and indigenous basis for building socialism in Russia. Some elements in the populist movement felt that only conspiratorial action, assassination, and terrorism could topple the tsarist order before the communes were destroyed by the incipient capitalism that was gradually beginning to disrupt traditional relations in the countryside. Drastic action by a revolutionary elite might be required. Members of these revolutionary circles often exhibited a fanatical and total commitment to the cause, disavowing all other values. Contrary to their expectations, however, even the assassination of Tsar Alexander II in 1881 elicited neither a peasant rebellion nor a collapse of the old order.

Rather, many peasants had a romantic attachment to the tsar as their protector. The new tsar, Alexander III, simply responded to the attack with increased repression.

Other populists took a different approach: they wanted to educate the peasants to realize the necessity of revolution. To do this, hundreds of students went to the villages to bring their revolutionary message directly to the peasantry during the "To the People" movement of the 1870s. The peasants were suspicious of these strangers, however, and the young intelligentsia became disillusioned with possibilities for a peasant-based revolution. Nonetheless, populist ideas received continued expression in the Socialist Revolutionary Party, which was founded in 1900. Even Lenin's older brother had participated in a (failed) plot to assassinate the tsar and was sentenced to death. The young Lenin disavowed these methods and embraced Marxism.

As the intrusion of capital and Western values seemed increasingly inevitable, many revolutionaries turned to Marxism. The first Marxist organization, the Emancipation of Labor Group, was formed in 1883. Unlike the populists, the Marxists placed their hope for revolution in the urban proletariat. They had little faith in terrorism and assassination; rather, they sought to lead a full-scale revolution in the socioeconomic foundation of society. They saw removal of individual leaders as a superficial measure. As the assassination of Alexander II had demonstrated, the ruling class would simply install new leaders to replace those who had been eliminated. The Marxists wanted to turn ownership and control of the factories over to the workers as a whole. The working class, however, was a small minority in tsarist Russia. Thus, a role for the revolutionary intelligentsia in the movement would be assured, for they would best understand the demands of revolutionary change.

Marxism may have been attractive to parts of the intelligentsia for other reasons as well. Marxism recognizes the inevitability and desirability of social change and industrialization; this ensures the necessity of science and education, endeavors appreciated by the intelligentsia. In embracing Marxism, some Russian intellectuals also expressed their ambivalence toward Western culture. In many ways, the intelligentsia saw the West as more progressive and advanced than Russian society, with its backward and oppressive institutions, but in other ways, they felt repulsed by the inhumane factory conditions that Western capitalism had spawned. They had a certain hope for Russia's potential, for a socialist revolution might allow Russia to become an example for Western Europe. If a workers' revolution were to occur in Russia, however, some alterations would have to be made in the interpretation of Marxism.

Leninism

Marxism did not seem to be directly and immediately applicable to Russia. The working class was small, and capitalism was only beginning to push out feudal relations in the countryside. Yet some elements of the intelligentsia were attracted to the theory. Some workers, introduced to Marxism by political activists, may have found the radical tenor in the party appealing. The Marxist party, the Russian Social Democratic Labor Party (RSDLP), formed in 1898, was soon riddled with conflict over the correct application of Marxism in Russia. The two major factions in the party, the Bolsheviks and the Mensheviks, emerged with independent newspapers and largely separate organizations by 1917, despite repeated efforts at reunification. The most influential Marxist revolutionary by 1917 was Vladimir Ilich Lenin (born Ulianov), the leader of the Bolshevik organization, which was finally to take power. Lenin reinterpreted key elements of Marxist theory so that they better fit Russian reality.

How and why should a workers' revolution occur in a country with such a small proletariat? Normally, according to Marxist theory, a bourgeois democratic revolution should precede a socialist workers' revolution. But because the indigenous Russian bourgeoisie was so weak, Lenin believed that the working class, with the help of the peasantry, would have to take on a greater role in toppling the tsarist government and in struggling for "bourgeois" rights. Once a bourgeois democratic revolution had occurred, the working class must realize that its interests were no longer congruent with those of the capitalist class, which would want to take as much profit from the workers' hands as possible. At this point, the working class must step forward and push the revolution to its next stage: dismantling private capitalist ownership patterns and replacing them with collective working-class control.

Russian Marxists disagreed about the actual timing of these two phases of the revolution. Some, like Leon Trotsky, felt that the two revolutions, the bourgeois democratic and the proletariat socialist, could and should be telescoped into one, producing a situation of permanent revolution to extend beyond Russia to other countries. The Mensheviks generally took a more gradualist approach, believing that there must be two distinct phases. Lenin seemed to stand somewhere in the middle, impatient with and distrustful of the bourgeoisie, but also skeptical of Trotsky's outline for the revolution. When 1917 came and the tsarist regime was toppled, Lenin saw that mass discontent made an almost immediate grasp for power feasible. He seemed to adopt, in practice, Trotsky's notion of telescoping the bourgeois and proletarian revolutions into virtually one phase, separated in time by only a few months. For Lenin, the revolutionary coalition initially had to include the peasantry, for they suffered from both the remnants of feudalism in the countryside and the incipient effects of capitalist intrusion into peasant markets.

Lenin also argued that international conditions facilitated a workers' revolution in a backward country like Russia. Following the ideas of theorists such as Rosa Luxemburg, John A. Hobson, and Rudolf Hilferding, Lenin developed his famous *theory of imperialism*. He believed that the more advanced capitalist countries of Western Europe had been forced to invest capital in the more backward capitalist countries (such as Russia) and in overseas colonies to ensure continuing profit levels. These profits, extracted from imperialist ventures, could be used by the owners in the more advanced capitalist systems to buy off their own working classes through improved working conditions and wages. The Western European working classes, therefore, had lost some of their revolutionary fervor, and the social democratic parties that represented them had become increasingly reformist, abandoning social revolution for simple amelioration of conditions.

Meanwhile, backward capitalist countries such as Russia suffered the effects of imperialism. Factories were large and conditions oppressive. Because the indigenous Russian bourgeoisie was weak, it had not been able to push forward basic democratic reforms such as genuine constitutionalism and freedom of political expression and organization. The bourgeoisie also had not been able to consolidate its power as effectively as its counterparts in Western Europe. Therefore, the apparatus of legitimation— that is, the mechanisms to bring the population to accept the existing order of things—had not been fully developed. Despite some legal reforms, there was little real amelioration in working conditions. Lenin concluded that Russia was the weakest link in the capitalist chain: the oppression was particularly severe, but control by the capitalist class was less firmly embedded in society. The bourgeoisie had to rely on the tsar's crude instruments of political repression to inhibit organization of the working class. Revolution could come more easily in Russia than in Western Europe, and once it did, according to Lenin, it would stimulate the German working class to follow the Russian example. Russia would experience the first revolution, but

it would spark further revolutions in Western Europe. Subsequently, the newly established proletarian governments in Western Europe could offer material assistance to their Russian comrades, who still would have to cope with a backward, largely agrarian economy.

The Revolutionary Party

On a more practical level, revolution required a revolutionary party. In 1902, Lenin laid the groundwork for Bolshevik Party organization in his famous work *What Is to Be Done?*, in which he supported the idea that "the history of all countries shows that the working class, exclusively by its own efforts, is able to develop only trade union consciousness."[2] That is, without appropriate ideological leadership, the proletariat would not see the systemic source of its repression—namely, the whole ownership and control system of capitalism. Rather, workers might focus on the particular factory owner or seek simple material improvements in working conditions, such as shorter hours, better pay, or improved safety conditions.

Western European experience seemed to confirm Lenin's conviction that the working class needed a conscious vanguard to lead it to a proper revolutionary understanding. This vanguard would necessarily include many members of the intelligentsia, for they had the capability and opportunity to perceive the broader sources of exploitation more clearly than the worker, who, however revolutionary his or her sentiment might be, had only a limited view of the situation as a whole. Lenin's vanguard notion suggested that all party members must possess a superior political awareness. Thus, the party would not be an open, broad-based organization (as would the trade unions) but would be limited to those who had made an active commitment to the cause and who understood revolutionary dynamics. This pattern was to continue after the revolution and into Soviet rule. Substance, not procedure, was emphasized, and it became more important to hold the correct viewpoint than to resolve disputes through established democratic procedures. There was some disagreement between the two major factions in the party, the Mensheviks and the Bolsheviks, over how strict membership requirements should be for the party, but essentially both groups concurred in endorsing a vanguard concept.

Did introduction of the vanguard party concept represent a rejection of democratic principles? It certainly involved an abrogation of simple majority rule. The Canadian political theorist C. B. Macpherson explains the dilemma facing revolutionaries who wish to transform society democratically:

> What makes a period revolutionary is a more or less widespread belief that the existing system of power, the existing system of power relations between people, is somehow thwarting their humanity. . . . If you believe . . . that the very structure of society, the dominant power relations in it, have made people less than fully human, have warped them into inability to realize or even to see their full human potentiality, what are you to do? How can the debasing society be changed by those who have themselves been debased by it? . . . The debased people are, by definition, incapable of reforming themselves *en masse*.[3]

Lenin's solution was, of course, that the vanguard party would lead the people to realize their own true interests—interests they might not recognize themselves. How different this is from the liberal view, which defines people's interests as the people themselves see them. Macpherson poses the question "Can a vanguard state properly be called a democratic state?" His answer underscores the ambiguity of the term *democracy*:

> If democracy is taken in its narrow sense as meaning simply a system of choosing and authorizing governments, then a vanguard state cannot be called democratic. A vanguard state may be a government *for* the people, but it is not government *by* the people, or even by the choice of the people.[4]

But in a broader sense, Macpherson points out, "Democracy has very generally been taken to mean something more than a system of government. Democracy in this broader sense has always contained an ideal of human equality, . . . such an equality as could only be fully realized in a society where no class was able to dominate or live at the expense of others."[5] In this sense, then, a vanguard party may be a legitimate instrument for achieving an otherwise unrealizable goal of democracy.

Repressive political conditions in Russia certainly required a tightly knit organization that generally had to work underground. As Lenin himself suggests in *What Is to Be Done?*:

> "Broad democracy" in party organization, amidst the gloom of autocracy and the domination of the gendarmes, is nothing more than a *useless and harmful* toy. . . . It is a harmful toy, because any attempt to practice the "broad principles of democracy" will simply facilitate the work of the police in making big raids; it will perpetuate the prevailing primitiveness, divert the thoughts of the practical workers from the serious and imperative task of training themselves to become professional revolutionists to that of drawing up detailed "paper" rules for election systems.[6]

To prevent tsarist agents from infiltrating the party and thus exposing party activists to arrest or exile, strict controls had to be maintained over intraparty organization. These repressive conditions were a major impetus for the development of the party's internal political procedure, the principle of *democratic centralism*. Based on this principle, party cells at the base level did not have contact with one another but were linked through a hierarchical structure. In this way, if one cell were compromised, its members would not be able to betray their colleagues in other cells. The basic principle of democratic centralism, which guided the party's internal political structure, was freedom of discussion until a decision was taken; following that, strict discipline and unity were required in carrying out the action. Discussion initially was to take place in all party cells, with the views of lower bodies being transmitted through elected delegates to higher organs in the party hierarchy. Finally, the Central Committee or Party Congress made the decision, which was to be strictly adhered to by all party members.

Elections of party leaders were held within the same hierarchical structure. Elected delegates from party cells (which might be formed in factories, soldiers' contingents, or universities) represented the cell at the next highest party organ in the hierarchy. This organ (perhaps a district or city committee) likewise elected delegates to the next highest organ in the hierarchy, until finally the composition of the highest elective body, the Central Committee, was determined. Delegates were accountable to their constituencies, but once the Central Committee determined a certain path, the minority must submit to the majority. In this way, the party could act effectively in a highly precarious political environment.

Nonetheless, party organizations were repeatedly decimated by arrests. As Lenin stated in January 1903, "We do not know whether people are alive or not; we are compelled, simply compelled, to consider them almost nonexistent."[7] Lenin himself had been arrested in 1895 and exiled to Siberia for three years in 1897. At the time of the collapse of the tsarist government in February 1917, he was carrying out his revolutionary activities from a base in Switzerland and returned to Russia only two months later. Under these conditions, it is perhaps understandable that the party should take such extraordinary measures to protect the anonymity of the revolutionary cells.

In his famous piece *State and Revolution*, written in 1917 before the Bolshevik Revolution, Lenin presents his understanding of the relationship between democracy and socialism:

In capitalist society we have a democracy that is curtailed, wretched, false; a democracy only for the rich, for the minority. The dictatorship of the proletariat, the period of transition to communism, will for the first time create democracy for the people, for the majority, along with the necessary suppression of the minority—the exploiters. Communism alone is capable of giving really complete democracy, and the more complete it is the more quickly will it become unnecessary and wither away of itself.[8]

Lenin cites the example of the Paris Commune (a popular revolutionary regime that ruled Paris for two months in 1871) to elucidate some of the characteristics of democratic proletarian rule: all privileges for officials will be abolished; representatives of the working people will be subject to immediate recall by the people; remuneration of all state officials will be at the level of workers' wages. Finally, once class enemies had been brought under control, Lenin foresaw the withering away of the state. The special apparatus of control and repression would be unnecessary; human freedom would be complete. The division between mental and manual labor would be overcome, and the principle of "from each according to his ability, to each according to his needs" would prevail. Clearly, Lenin's vision for communist society was "for the people" and contained an ideal of human equality, as Macpherson suggests, even if it does not correspond to the Western concept of liberal democracy or to a narrower definition of rule "by the people." But could Lenin's vision become reality, or would it be undermined by the very means he proposed to realize it?

The Revolution and Its Dilemmas

There were actually two revolutions in 1917: the first toppled the tsarist regime, and the second put the Bolsheviks in power. In February, the tsarist regime was overthrown, and the provisional government, which eventually involved a coalition of bourgeois and socialist forces (the Bolsheviks did not participate), took control.

Dual power emerged: alongside the provisional government, workers' and soldiers' soviets (councils) represented the working elements of the population more directly. Initially, the Mensheviks and Socialist Revolutionaries were more heavily represented in the soviets than the Bolsheviks, but by October the Bolsheviks had a majority in many of the most important soviets.

The provisional government hesitated in addressing the major issues that had moved the masses to rebellion. Despite widespread disillusionment with the faltering war effort, the government was not prepared to withdraw (which would, in fact, have meant surrender to Germany), nor was the government willing to address the land issue at once. Rather, the leaders of the provisional government planned to wait until late in 1917, when the problem could be thoroughly investigated and elections to the Constituent Assembly could be held, before making any major policy decision regarding redistribution of land. The elected Constituent Assembly, they felt, would be a more appropriate body to address this controversial question.

Meanwhile, soldiers were deserting and returning to their villages. Peasants were beginning to seize control of large landed estates. When Lenin arrived by train in Petrograd (previously St. Petersburg, subsequently Leningrad, and now St. Petersburg again[9]) in April of 1917, he recognized the revolutionary potential of the situation. After several months of increasing mass radicalization, he persuaded his Bolshevik colleagues (with the exception of Grigorii Zinoviev and Lev Kamenev) that the time was ripe to seize power. The Bolshevik slogan "Land, Bread, Peace" addressed the major issues troubling the population. On October 25, 1917 (November 7 by the new Western calendar adopted by the revolutionary regime in February 1918), the revolutionary forces took over the winter palace in Petrograd, overthrowing the provisional government and replacing it with a government of soviets headed by the Bolsheviks.

Although power was secured quickly in the capital and in Moscow, three to four years of civil war ensued before the Bolsheviks were able to subdue major areas of the countryside.

The Bolsheviks gave immediate recognition to the peasants' demands for land. In November 1917, they went ahead with the elections to the Constituent Assembly but, to their disappointment, won only 136 seats as compared to 237 for the Socialist Revolutionaries, who were better known and respected in the rural areas, even though they balked at immediate resolution of the land question. The Bolsheviks responded in quick order by disbanding the Constituent Assembly following a one-day meeting in January 1918. They believed that the peasants were ill-informed about the actual land policies of the two parties and therefore were not able to make a choice in their true interests.

The reasons for the Bolsheviks' initial success are clear. The provisional government inadequately filled the vacuum left by the tsar. The Bolsheviks, especially Lenin, saw the people ripe for revolt and were prepared to act quickly, basing themselves in the workers' and soldiers' soviets. The Bolsheviks' program ("Land, Bread, Peace") expressed the sentiments of the population better than that of the provisional government or any of the other socialist parties. These factors probably did more together to ensure the Bolshevik victory than did the organizational structure of the party.

Problems of Rulership

Following the October 1917 revolution, a new government was formed under the leadership of the Bolshevik organization, renamed the Russian Communist Party (Bolsheviks) in 1918 and the Communist Party of the Soviet Union (CPSU) in 1952. (Hereafter we capitalize *Party* when referring to the CPSU to emphasize its monopoly position in Soviet society until the late 1980s and to distinguish it from other political parties that emerged in the Soviet Union in 1989.) On December 30, 1922, four constituent republics (the Russian, Transcaucasian, Ukrainian, and Belorussian republics) formally joined to constitute the Union of Soviet Socialist Republics (USSR), henceforth referred to as the Soviet Union. Following 1922, additional constituent republics were added to the Union.

Once in power, the Bolsheviks were quick to learn that it is easier to criticize than to rule. They soon felt compelled to take extraordinary measures to ensure the survival of the regime. The initial challenge was an extended civil war for control of the countryside and outlying regions. The civil war (1918 to 1921) had negative repercussions for the new Soviet state. Many of the most loyal and committed activists, especially from the working class, were killed, thus weakening even further the Party's base in the population. The Cheka, the internal security arm of the regime, was strengthened to control harmful political tendencies, and the power of the elected soviets was greatly restricted in an effort to retain central control over the war effort.

The Party faced other difficulties once it achieved power. Making good on its promise of peace meant virtual surrender to the Germans. After heated debate within the Party leadership, the Soviet regime finally accepted the unfavorable terms of the Brest-Litovsk Treaty. As a result, Germany took, among other things, large sections of Ukraine, the Baltic states, and Belorussia. Only the defeat of Germany by Russia's former allies (the United States, Britain, and France) reversed some of these concessions. However, these countries were hardly pleased with internal developments in Russia. Not only did the revolution mean expropriation of foreign holdings and Russia's withdrawal from the war effort, it also represented the first successful challenge to the capitalist order. As a result, the former allies sent material aid and troops to oppose the new Bolshevik government in the civil war period.

Notwithstanding some humanitarian (famine) aid provided in 1921–22, the Soviet Union benefited little from Western assistance or investment. The most severe blow was the failure of the German workers' revolution in 1918. The entire premise of Lenin's strategy had been proven faulty: the struggling new Soviet state found no socialist revolution in Western Europe to aid it. The new leaders had to find ways to address Russia's economic backwardness without outside assistance. Furthermore, they found no previous models of socialist construction. Marx and Engels themselves had had little to say about the process of building a socialist society. The Bolshevik leaders were forced to undertake their vast, bold experiment with no real historical or theoretical precedents.

Controlling the Opposition

It is hard to overstate how precarious was the situation facing the fledgling Soviet government in the early 1920s. Its survival was by no means assured. The Party had only a narrow base in the population, and the tenuousness of its power made the Bolshevik leaders increasingly intolerant of dissent. They first dismantled the Constituent Assembly, as noted previously. Gradually, restrictions were placed on other socialist parties, until by 1921, they were effectively banned. Then came limits on intra-Party democracy.

At the Tenth Party Congress in March 1921, a conflict over the demands of the so-called Workers' Opposition led to acceptance of the antifactionalism rule. The Workers' Opposition, under the leadership of the prominent Bolshevik figures Aleksandra Kollantai and Aleksandr Shliapnikov, demanded more autonomy for trade unions and a greater role for the unions in representing workers' interests in industrial management. Furthermore, the Workers' Opposition wanted Party members to be bound by the decisions of higher trade union organs, rather than vice versa, which was the prevailing pattern. After extensive debate in 1920 and 1921, the ideas of the Workers' Opposition were firmly condemned by the Party's Central Committee as a deviation from Marxism. Under Lenin's guidance, the trade unions were instructed to emphasize their educational role in bringing the workers to support Party initiatives in the economy. They were given no independent role in economic administration, although they were to safeguard certain workers' rights in the factory.

More significant than the defeat of the opposition plank was the imposition of the antifactionalism rule. It forbade groups from meeting to develop platforms in advance of Party meetings, on the grounds that this could lead to the growth of divisive factions, solidify lines of conflict in the Party, and interfere with Party discipline. Theoretically, however, individual Party members could still raise problems or make proposals at the Party meeting itself, in line with the precepts of democratic centralism. The Central Committee was authorized to penalize members for factionalism, and penalties included expulsion from the Central Committee itself on a two-thirds vote of all members and alternates.

Adoption of the antifactionalism rule by the Tenth Party Congress followed shortly upon the Kronstadt Rebellion of March 1921, an unsuccessful uprising of sailors at a naval base near Petrograd. The sailors demanded democratization of the soviets and criticized their domination by the Bolsheviks. The Party leadership no doubt felt particularly vulnerable at this time. Despite the fact that the antifactionalism rule was initially viewed as a temporary measure to address a crisis situation, after Lenin's death it was applied even more rigidly, to control any form of opposition within the Party. Aspiring leaders stigmatized their opponents for engaging in factionalism, but in so doing, they gradually undermined a basic premise of democratic centralism itself: that minority viewpoints should

be permitted up to the point where a decision was taken.

In the mid- to late 1920s, as Josef Stalin consolidated his support in the Party bureaucracy, he was able to defeat his opponents by charging them with factional activity. By 1929, open dissension within the Party was almost eliminated. Major figures who might offer an alternative view, including Leon Trotsky, Nikolai Bukharin, Grigorii Zinoviev, and Lev Kamenev, had all been expelled from the highest Party organs. Trotsky had been forced into exile. None of them had felt confident enough of Soviet power to appeal for mass support when they came under attack. Apparently each believed that the survival of Party rule was of greater importance than the preeminence of his individual viewpoint. In 1924, Trotsky himself expressed this view: "My party—right or wrong . . . I know one cannot be right against the party . . . for history has not created other ways for the realization of what is right."[10]

The Peasant Problem and Industrialization

The peasantry posed both economic and political problems for the Bolsheviks, as Lenin himself emphasized the importance of an alliance with the peasantry. Indeed, in 1917 recognition of the peasants' desire for control of the land represented a political compromise for the Bolsheviks, whose long-term goal was a socialized economy. Once the civil war was under way, economic demands led the Bolsheviks to introduce the policy of War Communism, which sought to ensure the supply of materials necessary for the war effort. In the industrial sphere, this involved direct state control of the larger productive facilities; in the agricultural sector, the peasants were allowed to maintain control over the land, but grain was forcibly requisitioned to supply the army and cities. By 1921, the leadership recognized the potential political costs of the War Communism policy, which effectively negated many of the benefits the peasants had gained from the revolution. The leadership feared that the peasants' resentment of the forced requisitioning of grain would continue to grow and ultimately undermine the very goals the regime was trying to pursue.

The New Economic Policy (NEP), initiated at the Tenth Party Congress in March 1921, brought concessions for the peasantry. The new policy created greater incentives for them by abolishing forced requisitioning of grain and replacing it with a tax in kind. Once the tax was paid, peasants could dispose of their surplus as they saw fit—by raising food for their own consumption or by selling it in the free market or to state agencies. In other sectors of the economy, private enterprise and trade also were revived. The state, however, retained control of large-scale industry.

The NEP posed new dilemmas for the Bolsheviks. First, it strengthened private property and a market economy, which contradicted the Bolsheviks' long-term goal of socialization of the economy. Second, the NEP made it more difficult to achieve rapid industrialization, which the Bolsheviks saw as necessary. The growth of industry would strengthen the Soviet state in dealing with external challenges. It also would be an important step in the construction of socialism by developing a large working class, which would be the political base of socialist society. But industrialization required capital. Where was this capital to come from? The small industrial sector could hardly generate enough capital for its own rapid expansion. This left the agricultural sector. If adequate grain could be produced for export, the industrialization drive could be funded. Further, if the regime were able to extract foodstuffs from the countryside at low prices, the cost of maintaining the industrial work force would be reduced. The NEP, however, limited the state's ability to extract capital from the rural sector.

The NEP was, then, a political compromise. The peasantry was allowed a greater measure of independence in production as long as taxes were paid. The government would then buy additional grain at established prices. At the same time, a relatively free market was allowed to reign in the countryside, giving rise to the ignominious NEP men, whom the Bolsheviks viewed as speculators seeking a profit. By the mid-1920s, the economy had been restored to its prewar level of production and doubts were surfacing in the Party over whether the NEP should be altered. Some elements were impatient with the slow pace of industrialization; others were concerned that the present course might allow the growth of a new rural capitalist class as the *kulaks* (rich peasants) were allowed to accumulate wealth. A major debate developed in the Party over economic policy.

In the mid-1920s, the strongest supporter of the NEP was Nikolai Bukharin, who seemed at the time to be expressing the views of Stalin as well. Bukharin argued that the peasants would lose the incentive to make their farms more productive if further restrictions were imposed. He concluded, "We must say to the whole peasantry, to all its strata: enrich yourselves, accumulate, develop your economy."[11] Bukharin believed that if the peasants were allowed to flourish, they would come to accept the new socialist order and the existing agrarian policy could serve as an adequate framework for industrialization.

Another group of Bolsheviks, including first Trotsky and then Zinoviev and Kamenev, accepted the basic framework of the NEP but felt that too many concessions had been made to the peasantry. Rapid industrialization was of paramount importance, requiring some alterations in present policy. Expressing the sentiment of this so-called Left opposition in the Party, Trotsky's ally, Evgenii Preobrazhensky, put forth his theory of primitive socialist accumulation. In short, it was necessary to pursue policies that could more effectively extract from the nonsocialized agricultural sector a surplus, which could then be used to finance industrialization. To achieve this, prices for agricultural commodities should be lowered and taxes on the peasantry increased. Trotsky believed that poor peasants should, however, be helped and given incentives to join rural cooperatives. In this way, the socialist sector would be strengthened as the poor peasants benefited from government assistance. These measures also would inhibit the growth of an exploitive capitalist class in the countryside. Meanwhile, rich peasants should be taxed more heavily. In any case, unless industry was developed more quickly, the peasantry would lose its incentive to work, since there would be few goods for the peasants to purchase with their income.

By late 1924, Trotsky was being sharply criticized by other Party leaders. He was vilified for lack of faith in the peasantry, for his earlier concept of permanent revolution, and for his failure to believe in the possibilities of building socialism in one country. These were mere pretexts to undermine Trotsky's standing in the Party. Although Kamenev and Zinoviev were to voice criticisms of the NEP similar to Trotsky's, their strong dislike for him led them to demand his expulsion from the Party. Stalin opposed this extreme measure. Instead, Trotsky was removed as head of the army and condemned by the Central Committee in January 1925.

Before long, Zinoviev found his base of power in the Party threatened by Stalin's growing ambitions. In 1926, he, Kamenev, and Trotsky finally joined other dissident elements to form a united opposition to Stalin's growing power, but it was too late. In August of 1927, Stalin's support was strong enough to expel Trotsky and Zinoviev from the Central Committee. By November 14, they were expelled from the Party, and in January 1928, Trotsky was exiled from the Soviet Union. In 1940, he was assassinated in Mexico by Stalinist agents.

Bukharin cooperated with Stalin in removing the so-called Left opposition (Trotsky, Zinoviev, and Kamenev) and in so doing helped legitimize methods that would later lead to his own removal from the leadership. In 1928, the country faced a major grain procurement crisis: the peasants refused to sell their grain to the government. This seemed to trigger Stalin's reversal in position. He began to emphasize the need for a change that would speed industrialization and more effectively mobilize the agricultural surplus to that end. In late 1929, a policy of rapid collectivization of agriculture was instituted. Although the process was allegedly voluntary, the peasants were actually forced to give up their land, tools, and livestock and join government-established collectives or state farms. In November 1929, Bukharin, the most prominent figure in the so-called Right opposition, was expelled from the Politburo, by then the top policy-making body in the Party.

By 1929, virtually all internal opposition within the Party had been eliminated, and Stalin's power was secure. Stalin's rivals apparently did not realize that Lenin's emphasis on Party discipline could be twisted to suppress all debate in the Party. Furthermore, Stalin's rivals had been reluctant to appeal to the broad masses of the people for support, fearing that this might mobilize popular sentiment against Party rule itself. Although members of the Left opposition had held some demonstrations in factories in 1926, they later admitted that, in so doing, they had violated Party discipline. It seems that most Bolshevik leaders accepted Trotsky's conviction of "my party—right or wrong."

Leadership Succession and Bureaucratization

The struggles over economic policy were closely linked to the struggle for the top leadership position. Lenin's premature death in 1924 (at the age of fifty-four) resulted in competition at the top, which reinforced the difficulties facing the regime in consolidating its rule.

In 1919, the Party had formed several executive bodies, which were to administer Party policy between Central Committee meetings. One of these was the Politburo, which gradually emerged as the leading policy-making organ of the Party. Likewise in 1919, the Party Secretariat had been formed to fulfill largely secretarial functions—that is, keeping records and doing paperwork for the Party. A third body, the Orgburo, was formed to handle organizational matters. (It was abolished in 1952.) In 1922, Stalin, who was the only member of the Politburo to sit on the Orgburo, was chosen as head of the Secretariat. Over time, the Secretariat took on much greater importance than was originally anticipated. It was a key factor in Stalin's personal consolidation of power and eventually came to head the Party's extensive administrative bureaucracy.[12]

The Secretariat was staffed with full-time, paid Party workers, who along with other full-time paid Party workers came to be known as the *apparatchiki*. They were often in a better position to command influence than the elected delegates to Party committees, who might hold jobs elsewhere. The *apparatchiki* had greater access to information and more time to devote to Party work. At each level in the Party organization (in larger cells or primary Party organizations, or at the city, district, and regional levels), Party secretaries were elected to perform functions similar to those of the Secretariat at the central level. These individuals became the most powerful Party figures at the local and regional levels.

As head of the Secretariat, Stalin was able to wield increasing influence over appointments at lower levels of the Party. Because democratic centralist tenets mandated strict Party discipline in supporting decisions made by the Central Committee, it was necessary to maintain some central overview of policies being pursued by subordinate Party committees. If Party leaders at lower levels in the hierarchy were deviating from established central policy, measures had to be taken to reexert Party discipline by transferring local officials to other work or replacing them. Despite formal election procedures, the Party center (primarily through the Secretariat) began to direct the selection of candidates for Party office, and during the 1920s, election procedures became more and more formalistic.

A pattern developed that Western Sovietologists have subsequently dubbed a circular flow of power: the central Party Secretariat was able to influence election of local Party officials and delegates from lower Party organs, ultimately playing a large role in determining the composition of the Central Committee itself; the Central Committee, whose members were beholden to the Secretariat for their positions, in turn lent support to the Secretariat and its head (Stalin); and the Secretariat in turn continued to strengthen its control over selection of officials at lower Party levels. It was a self-perpetuating system, a type of massive political machine that ensured the head of the Secretariat support throughout the Party structure. As early as 1923, over 50 percent of the delegates to the Party Congress were *apparatchiki*. By 1924, at the Thirteenth Party Congress, this figure had risen to 65.3 percent.

Critics within the Party claimed that the apparatus of the Secretariat was gaining control over the election process. At the same time, debate within the Party over economic policy provided a pretext for Stalin's hard line against any remaining political challengers. By 1929, the Central Committee was packed with individuals who were beneficiaries of Stalin's goodwill. The lack of emphasis on procedural guarantees for democratic decision making (such as an independent judiciary, rights for an organized opposition, separation of powers, or limits on the tenure of top leaders) was taking its toll.

The Transition to Stalinism

The year 1929 was a turning point in Soviet history. The initial goals of the revolution were in danger: the worker-peasant alliance was weak, the soviets were powerless, intra-Party debate was greatly restricted, and a bureaucratic apparatus was growing in the Party. In 1929, Stalin introduced radical changes that further undermined socialist democracy and popular control. He embarked upon a Third Revolution (the first two being the February and October revolutions of 1917), allegedly to remove class enemies but, in practice, directed in an arbitrary manner even against loyal Bolsheviks. While Stalin justified the policies of the 1930s as necessary to advance socialism, their effect was to further compromise many of the initial revolutionary goals, such as social equality, power to the soviets, creative fulfillment of the individual, and the withering away of the state. Instead, Stalin set the course for rapid industrialization and the aggrandizement of his own personal power. While the industrialization campaign may have seemed necessary to provide the economic foundation for socialism, the methods used to achieve economic advances were in some ways counterproductive and also made realization of the other goals more difficult.

The Rise and Fall of Stalinism

The Stalinist period subjected Soviet society to major political, economic, and social upheavals that betrayed many of the initial Bolshevik goals. In some ways, Stalin's Third Revolution also restored some dominant themes of the tsarist period: personal dictatorship, a strong state structure, and appeals to Russian nationalism. From 1929 to 1953, one man, Josef Stalin, dominated the Soviet Union; by 1953 every semblance of Soviet democracy had been destroyed. Although the groundwork for Stalinism was laid in an earlier time, these developments were not inevitable. Other outcomes were both conceivable and possible. Western scholars have put forth varying explanations for the rise of Stalinism, and since 1986, Soviet commentators have openly joined the debate.

The Basic Features of Stalinism

The Third Revolution was a revolution from above, imposed on an often resistant population. All sectors of Soviet society felt the effects of Stalin's rise to power. But from 1929 to 1934, the most dramatic changes were economic, and they had the most impact in the countryside. The decision to pursue the forced collectivization of agriculture brought immediate results. Near the end of 1928, only an estimated 195,000 peasant families were members of collective or state farms. By June 1929, this number had increased some fivefold, and by the beginning of March 1930, it was over 14 million (see Table 1.1). This was hardly due to a spontaneous mass movement, as the Central Committee claimed in November 1929, but resulted from a process of coercion and intimidation, enforced by arrests and deportations (to Siberia and the Far East). Stalin justified collectivization as necessary to eliminate the *kulaks*, a group that allegedly was threatening to become an entrenched and exploitive class in the countryside. *Kulak* was an ambiguous term in itself, since these peasants were not that distinct from their less fortunate neighbors. Further, the *kulaks* were not the only targets of the collectivization campaign; less affluent peasants (the so-called middle and poor peasants) also were forced to give up control of their land and livestock to join the collective and state farms. To resist was to risk being labeled a *kulak* or class enemy oneself, subject to the same reprisals of arrest or deportation. Official Stalinist dogma justified the campaign with revolutionary rhetoric: far from being eliminated, class conflict was intensifying with the construction of socialism, and this required drastic action from the Party.

Historical evidence indicates that social inequality in the countryside was hardly as extreme as Stalin implied. The historian Moshe Lewin estimates that in the 1920s, most peasants classified by the regime as *kulaks* had only mod-

Table 1.1 Collectivization (in percent)

	1930	1931	1932	1933	1934	1935	1936
Peasant households collectivized	23.6%	52.7%	61.5%	64.4%	71.4%	83.2%	89.6%
Crop area collectivized	33.6	67.8	77.6	83.1	87.4	94.1	—

Note: State farm area and households included.

Source: *Sotsialisticheskoe stroitel'stvo SSSR* (1936), p. 278.

est resources—perhaps three or four cows and one paid worker. Some engaged in occasional "speculation" by holding grain to sell at a propitious moment, but peasants of this type were a small minority—4 percent of peasant households, according to various estimates.[13] The majority of the peasantry generally did not hire laborers regularly or hire out their own labor. These middle peasants (a broad and vaguely defined category) were more important in terms of grain production. Along with the poor peasants (those who often had to hire out their own labor), they also suffered severe repercussions from the Stalinist collectivization campaign. By July 1938, over 90 percent of the peasantry was brought into the sphere of the collective and state farms.

Industry also was affected by Stalinization. The state took over almost all industrial operations and introduced central economic planning in the form of five-year economic plans, which, until recently, sought to guide almost all Soviet economic production. The First Five-Year Plan (1929 to 1933) set unrealistic production targets for both agriculture and industry. The result was neglect of low-priority sectors, such as agriculture and consumer goods production, and emphasis on heavy industry, including machine building, hydroelectric dams, and steel mills. Actual production often bore little relation to plan indicators, so the plan itself was little more than a spur to achieve the highest output possible.

"Shock methods" were intense campaigns to increase output in key sectors. The Stakhanovite movement was an effort to increase labor productivity by emulating the miner Aleksei Stakhanov, who reportedly exceeded his work norm by fourteen times. During the Stakhanovite movement, model workers who produced the most in the shortest time received state honors. The Stalinist economic machine also was supported by an extensive network of labor camps, which, at various times, are estimated to have held between 10 and 15 million prisoners.[14] The opening of new archival materials may, in the coming years, allow scholars to make a more definitive estimate of the scope of these camps. Among other things, the infamous Gulag system provided the labor power to construct cities, canals, and railways. Conditions in the camps, documented most graphically by Aleksandr Solzhenitsyn, generally were harsh and often inhumane.[15]

Stalin's economic campaigns did succeed in boosting industrial output. Earlier estimates by the Western economist Alexander Gerschenkron, correcting to some extent for the inflation in Soviet estimates, suggested an increase in industrial output of around 14 to 16 percent annually in the period from 1928 to 1939.[16] Recent Soviet reassessments suggest, however, that earlier official estimates of growth in the 1930s vastly overstated increases in the physical volume of production and understated the growth rate in prices. Thus, Gerschenkron's figures may still be too high, according to the research of Soviet economists Nikolai Shmelev and Vladimir Popov. Agricultural production actually declined in the 1930s, even though extraction of grain from the countryside and exports increased.[17] Nonetheless, the Stalinist economic strategy did have some positive payoffs in moving the Soviet Union quickly toward becoming a highly industrialized society. But during the 1930s, industrial production lacked balance and was often of mediocre quality. Further, benefits to the working class were limited. Many had, indeed, experienced a sort of upward social mobility as they were able to move from subsistence agriculture to steady industrial jobs in urban areas, but the supply of consumer goods increased little, housing was short, and wage levels were low. The benefits of socialist construction would have to wait until the economic foundation was stronger.

The political sphere also was revolutionized in the 1930s. In the early 1930s, those most affected by Stalinization were the peasants. Once collectivization had been essentially achieved in the mid-1930s, Stalin turned his attention to other sectors of the population as well. The Party, as a viable political institution, was decimated. Open opposition was impossible, and the secret police, answerable to Stalin himself through the minister of internal affairs, replaced the Party as the most powerful institution in Soviet society. Stalin engineered competition and duplication of duties between various Party and state institutions to make them all ineffective. No Party Congress was convened between March 1939 and October 1952.

A series of purges (in Russian, *chistka*, "cleansing"), accompanied by wide-ranging terror, swept all levels of society in the mid- to late 1930s. At first, large numbers of people were expelled from the Party, but by 1937 arrests, torture, and even executions had become widespread. Central and provincial Party officials, military officers, and intellectuals (writers, academics, and engineers) were most affected. All the individuals mentioned by Lenin as possible successors, with the exception of Stalin himself,

were targeted. Nikita Khrushchev, a beneficiary of the purges, notes in his memoirs that Stalin's closest advisers were uncertain of their own fate. Seventy percent of the Central Committee members died during the purges, as did many high-ranking military officers. It often was unclear why an individual was victimized. Charges of treason, for example, were often clearly trumped up, and the victim might finally confess only under psychological pressure, torture, or threats against his or her family.

Overall, an estimated 5 percent of the Soviet population was arrested at one point or another. Some of the victims were executed; others were condemned to labor camps or prisons. Some were exiled to Siberia, forced to relocate, denied access to education, or removed from their posts. Because the purges seemed to be arbitrary, reflecting Stalin's paranoia or perverse political reasoning, they can best be described as terror.

The beneficiaries of the purges were those who experienced upward social mobility by filling the spots vacated by the victims or created by the process of rapid industrialization. A whole new generation came into the top Party posts, changing the complexion of the Party elite. These were the very individuals who would fill the major leadership positions after Stalin's death. All were implicated in the purges in some way, even if only by their silence and compliance with Stalin's wishes. At lower levels in the Party as well, thousands of sons (and some daughters) of peasants and workers replaced former Party officials. The new *apparatchiki* were beholden to Stalin for their positions; this helped ensure their political loyalty. The revolutionary leaders who had guided the Party through 1917 and the difficult years that followed were replaced by leaders of a different social class, no longer from the intelligentsia but from working-class and peasant origins. Individuals from these groups also rose to respectable positions as engineers, managers, administrators, and the like. Vera Dunham calls this group the Soviet middle class and believes that these people were the real support for the Stalinist system as it emerged after World War II.[18]

Soviet culture also changed. In the 1920s, experimentation in art, literature, education, and family life had been widespread. In the 1930s, state control in the cultural sphere was enforced, while in some regards there also was a return to traditional values. New laws reinforced the nuclear family, making divorce more difficult and abortion illegal. Stalin appealed to Russian patriotism. This was even more marked in the 1940s, when World War II became known as the Great Patriotic War, evoking images of Russian nationalism rather than socialist internationalism. Education emphasized technical skills, and wage differentiation increased. While the rhetoric was revolutionary, the style of politics harked back to the days of the tsar. There was to be no withering away of the state in the foreseeable future; rather, the state must be strengthened to further socialist construction. As in tsarist times, social classes were made dependent on state power, and strong central control was glorified. Economic development was state led, and the figure of Stalin dominated the political scene. Although the Stalinist state preached atheism, it saw itself, like the tsarist state, as the guardian of correct dogma.

By 1938, the "revolutions from above" were over and were supplanted by what Seweryn Bialer calls "mature Stalinism." During World War II, the main concern was national self-defense, which inspired an appeal to traditional patriotic sentiments. From 1945 to 1953, many features of the Stalinism of the 1930s remained intact: the reliance on terror, Party purges, the weakness of the Party, and the lack of clear jurisdictions among political institutions. Many veterans of World War II who had spent time in German prison camps or were deemed to have had too much exposure to Western European life were imprisoned on their return to the Soviet Union, out of fear that they might be conduits for subversive foreign ideas. In the late 1940s and early 1950s, an "anticosmopolitan" campaign victimized Soviet Jews (many were arrested, and some were shot), stigmatizing them as disloyal to the Soviet Union. Nonetheless, major social transformations, such as collectivization, did not occur at this time; rather, as Bialer writes, "the key goal of the regime was the reproduction of existing relations."[19] Not until after Stalin's death in 1953 were patterns of governance questioned.

Why Stalinism?

One of the major themes of discussion in the Soviet Union since 1985 has been Stalinism—its causes, its character, and its legacy. The Stalinist system subjected Soviet society to major trauma; barely a single Soviet family escaped its violent excesses in the form of collectivization, purges, forced labor camps, or executions. Under the policy of *glasnost'*, censorship in the media has been sharply curtailed, and Soviet writers, journalists, and critics have become increasingly bold in their efforts to address openly the nature of that era. Literary works depicting the revolutionary and the Stalinist periods, which were previously forbidden publication in the Soviet Union (but were often available in the West), have appeared or are scheduled to appear in the Soviet Union (including Solzhenitsyn's novels, Boris Pasternak's *Doctor Zhivago*, Vasilii Grossman's *Life and Fate*, and Anatolii Rybakov's *Children of Arbat*). Questions such as the following have become usual topics of conversation: Why did the Soviet system take such a radical turn in the late 1920s? What were the causes of Stalinism? Does a Leninist revolution necessarily result in Stalinist-type terror? How can Soviet society purge itself of the effects of Stalinism? Indeed, there are vocal defenders of Stalin and his policies. The dominant trend, however, has been a critical examination of the Stalinist past in an effort to supersede it.

On the seventieth anniversary of the Bolshevik Revolution (November 2, 1987), Mikhail Gorbachev himself issued his own assessment of the Stalinist period. Although the speech was more moderate than some liberal intellectuals had hoped, it went far beyond Khrushchev's charges in 1956. Gorbachev strongly defended Lenin's approach but criticized the excesses of collectivization, calling them "a departure from Lenin's policy towards the peasantry." He went on to condemn Stalin's repressive political methods and said they were made possible by "the absence of a proper level of democratization in Soviet society." He noted, "Many thousands of people inside and outside the party were subjected to wholesale repressive measures. Such, comrades, is the bitter truth."[20]

On August 13, 1990, Gorbachev took a giant step forward when he issued a far-reaching presidential decree that rehabilitated all of the victims of political repression from the 1920s to the 1950s (but not war criminals). The decree acknowledged that

> the repression in the 1920s to 1950s carried out in relation to the peasants during the period of collectivization and also in relation to other citizens in regard to political, social, national, religious, or other motives was illegal and antithetical to the basic civil and socio-economic rights of man.[21]

Numerous other assessments and depictions of Stalin, until recently often more radical than Gorbachev's own, have appeared in Soviet literature and the Soviet press. Statements by Soviet leaders and intellectuals also include a positive evaluation of the NEP. Shmelev and Popov write that the "NEP is an extremely rich source of experience that can guide the implementation of today's reform, offering hope that perestroika will succeed."[22] This statement seems to reflect Gorbachev's view as well. In 1988, the Politburo of the CPSU established a special commission to examine new facts and documents related to the Stalinist period. Even before the 1990 decree, many victims of Stalinism were posthumously rehabilitated, acquitted of guilt for alleged crimes, and reinstated in the Party. Some of the most prominent figures here include Nikolai

Bukharin, Lev Kamenev, Grigorii Zinoviev, and members of the Workers' Opposition. The list of little-known Soviet citizens included in the group is long.

In January 1989, the Soviet public was even informed that Leon Trotsky was assassinated under the direction of an agent of the Soviet secret police (the People's Commissar of Internal Affairs, or NKVD) in 1940 in Mexico City,[23] and in August 1989 excerpts from Trotsky's writings were published in a Soviet magazine for the first time since his exile in the late 1920s.[24] Public organizations, such as Memorial, formed all over the USSR to push forward the rehabilitation of Stalinist victims. In this way, the previously official history of the USSR is being reconsidered. Western scholarly studies, such as Stephen Cohen's sympathetic study of Bukharin, also are being published in the USSR. The extent of this revolution in historiography is symbolized by the cancellation of history exams for students in 1988, since old textbooks were no longer reliable and new ones not yet available.

A question of long-standing concern in the West and now in the USSR involves the origins and causes of Stalinism. We examine some of the most common explanations in the following sections.

Economic Backwardness. One group of scholars sees the roots of Stalinism in the attempt to bring socialism to an economically backward country: economic necessity demanded the brutal collectivization of agriculture, and this in turn engendered the need for Stalin to find scapegoats to divert attention away from the debacle. In other words, collectivization was the only effective means of ensuring that enough surplus could be squeezed from the agricultural sector to fund the industrialization drive. Once the rural economy was brought under state control, grain and other produce could be extracted easily and cheaply. Presumably, mechanization would proceed more quickly, and the benefits of scale would improve productivity. The state could mobilize labor more effectively and would gain increased political control over the work force as an added benefit. According to this thesis, the political purges of the mid- to late 1930s were required to divert attention from the real problem (a disastrous and unpopular agrarian policy) to imagined traitors; at the same time, fear would restrain open opposition.

Despite the strength of this argument, many scholars question whether forcible collectivization of agriculture was the only way to extract enough surplus from the countryside to support industrialization. This assumption has been forcefully attacked by some Soviet scholars in recent years. Shmelev and Popov maintain that a continuation of the NEP could have brought better economic results without imposing the high costs of collectivization and forced labor camps.[25] Indeed, many leading Bolsheviks (including both the Right and Left oppositions) *rejected* Stalin's coercive measures and proposed alternatives, even if by 1929 they could no longer do so publicly. Both Bukharin and Evgenii Preobrazhensky supported a continuance of the NEP, but they emphasized different goals. Bukharin proposed continued concessions to the peasantry, which would involve a slower pace of industrialization and some greater stratification of income in the countryside. With some controls, however, this need not have implied the emergence of a new rural bourgeois class. Preobrazhensky proposed turning the terms of trade against the peasant, which might have been a feasible method to allow the state to buy agricultural produce at low cost if prices had been lowered on *all* agricultural goods. As it happened, prices for grain were kept low relative to livestock prices, and the peasants withheld their grain to feed the livestock. (In retrospect, the Bolsheviks were not likely to be shrewd in managing market prices, given their training and antimarket inclinations.) The fact that intelligent leaders in Stalin's time offered these proposals suggests that there were realistic alternatives to forced collectivization.

Stalin's agrarian policy was hardly a booming success. It had immense economic, as well as human, costs. Many peasants resisted turning their livestock over to the collective and state farms; they slaughtered them instead, which caused severe and long-lasting damage to Soviet agriculture. In the early 1930s, famine ravaged the countryside, especially in Ukraine and the northern Caucasus region, resulting in a loss of lives (and labor power) estimated in the millions. The famine was caused in large part by the disorganization that ensued from the rapid collectivization campaign and from state efforts to extract excessive amounts of grain. Apparently, in the 1930s, the state was able to obtain more grain from the countryside to sell abroad than it had in the 1920s (see Tables 1.2 and 1.3). However, production overall did not increase; some of the exported grain was available precisely because the livestock slaughtered by the defiant peasantry no longer required it as feed. James Millar argues that the agricultural sector did not make a significant contribution to industrialization from 1928 to 1932; rather, resources flowed from the industrial sector to agriculture, since peasants could charge high prices for goods produced on private plots and the state needed to provide tractors to replace livestock.[26]

Had the state been more adept at using positive incentives (market or otherwise) to encourage the production and sale of the commodities it required, industrialization could have been spurred without the drastic economic and human costs of the collectivization campaign. The pace of industrialization might have been slower, but the distance between the regime and the agrarian population might have been smaller. Then, in turn, the dramatic political repression of the mid- to late 1930s might not have seemed necessary to bolster the regime's stability. Undoubtedly, economic backwardness produced strains for the leadership, particularly in the face of international isolation, but it did not *mandate*

Table 1.2   State Grain Procurements (Millions of tons)

1928	1929	1930	1931	1932	1933
10.8	16.1	22.1	22.8	18.5	22.6

Source: Malafeev, *Istoriia tsenoobrazovaniia v SSSR* (Moscow: 1964), pp. 175, 177.

Table 1.3   Grain Exports (Millions of tons)

1927–28	1929	1930	1931	1932	1933
0.029	0.18	4.76	5.06	1.73	1.69

Source: Soviet trade returns.

the extreme measures embraced by Stalin in both the economic and the political spheres.

Leninism and Stalinism. This school of thought seeks the roots of Stalinism in Lenin's thought and policies. It focuses on the vanguard party concept and the centralized Party structure. Once the Party leaders perceived themselves as the vessels of correct theory, it was easy to defend the elimination of those who held false, or counterrevolutionary, viewpoints and to justify control in molding consciousness. Furthermore, according to this view, the centralized Party structure could suppress minority viewpoints by demanding adherence to Party decisions. The antifactionalism principle and demands for Party discipline enabled Stalin to cement his own position at the head of a powerful bureaucratic hierarchy. Supporters of this view note that Lenin himself had frequently used harsh methods to deal with his opponents, and during the civil war and NEP periods, the Party oppressed even socialist critics of the regime.

While this theory was not permitted expression in the Soviet Union prior to *glasnost'*, in 1989 criticism of Lenin, as well as Stalin, became increasingly common in the Soviet media. Already in 1988, Vasily Selyunin suggested that the policies introduced under Lenin's leadership during War Communism set a precedent for Stalin's later economic strategy.[27] In a November 1989 article, the Soviet philosopher Aleksandr Tsipko asked, "Doesn't the idea of a revolutionary vanguard lead to new forms of social inequality?"[28] Posthumous publication in June 1989 (in the magazine *Oktiabr'*) of Vasilii Grossman's novella *Everything Flows* allowed the Soviet reader to reflect on Lenin's historical role and the relationship between Leninism and Stalinism. Some Communists interpreted the proposal to restore Leningrad to its old name (St. Petersburg) as an affront and insult to Lenin's memory. Following the failed coup d'état in August 1991, the attack on Leninist symbols intensified; statues and monuments of Lenin and other Bolshevik figures all over the USSR were dismantled under public pressure. The mayor of Leningrad (renamed St. Petersburg shortly thereafter) proposed that Lenin's body be removed from the mausoleum outside the Kremlin walls and that Lenin be buried "with all due honors."

Despite this growing criticism of Lenin in the USSR, a direct link between Stalinism and Leninism is questionable. Stalin may have used certain Leninist precepts and ideas to justify his policies, but Lenin's doctrine was hardly congruent with Stalin's policy of forced collectivization of agriculture. Lenin had supported the NEP and had always emphasized an *alliance* with the peasantry. Bukharin's reasoned defense of the NEP was firmly rooted in the Leninist commitment to the peasant-worker alliance. Despite some resemblance to the economic policy of the Left opposition (i.e., in favoring more rapid industrialization and greater controls on the *kulaks*), Stalin's forced collectivization policy was far more coercive than the system of incentives, taxes, and price policy advocated by Trotsky and Preobrazhensky. Mainstream Bolshevik thought, therefore, did not necessarily lead to the economic strategy embraced by Stalin in 1929.

The measures taken against Party opponents under Lenin's leadership also were less radical than Stalin's purges and executions. Likewise, Lenin was not always able to impose his will on the Party. When Kamenev and Zinoviev broke Party discipline by making public their disagreement with the Bolsheviks' decision to grasp state power in 1917, Lenin did advocate their expulsion from the top Party organs (although certainly not their execution, as Stalin might have done for a similar violation in the 1930s), but the Central Committee did not concur. When the Workers' Opposition, which demanded a greater role for trade unions, was censured in 1921, its two most prominent leaders, Aleksandra Kollantai and Aleksandr Shliapnikov, were allowed to remain in the Central Committee. Thus, Lenin's tolerance for dissent was far greater than Stalin's in the 1930s.

It is, of course, impossible to know what Lenin would have done had he lived longer, but there are ample indications that Lenin saw extreme methods as justified only under the most extreme conditions. Stalin certainly saw conditions in the 1930s as extreme enough to justify his excesses, but was the Soviet regime in fact as vulnerable then as it had been during the civil war period and in the early 1920s? The answer to this question is almost certainly no. In the years following the revolution, an actual civil war gripped the country, foreign and domestic opposition threatened to topple the government, and the country was in economic shambles. By the time of Stalin's Third Revolution in 1929, Party rule was secure, prewar levels of economic production had been regained, and the Soviet Union was not under military attack. Although Party rule was much more precarious in Lenin's time, he did not resort to Stalinist-type terror. Although some political executions did occur, the victims were generally real opponents of Bolshevik power rather than imagined enemies, and the scale did not approach that of the Stalinist purges. To draw a direct linkage between Leninism and Stalinism overlooks the particular circumstances and pressures that allowed Stalin to emphasize only certain elements of Leninist thought, at the expense of some of the more participatory, democratic strains.

Cultural Continuity. A third theory explaining the rise of Stalinism points to its cultural roots. Many elements of Stalinism are reminiscent of traditional Russian patterns of rulership. The previous theory links Stalinism to revolutionary Leninism; the cultural explanation emphasizes the continuity from tsarism to Stalinism. The cultural theory asks, for example, whether collectivization was merely a new form of serfdom (some peasants called it the second serfdom) and the purges another way of asserting the dominance of the state over a potentially powerful social stratum (the intelligentsia). Strong state authority had long-standing precedents in Russian history. Perhaps the active private market and cultural renaissance of the 1920s, rather than Stalinism, represented the more dramatic break with traditional political culture. Certainly, the renewed appeal to nationalism in the 1930s and 1940s resembled the official patriotism of the tsarist period. Stalin also revived many national heroes of the prerevolutionary period. [29]

Cultural explanations of Stalinism also are being raised in contemporary Soviet discussions.

For example, in 1989, Tsipko examined critically the cultural heritage of the Russian intelligentsia and laid at its feet part of the blame for Stalinism:

> I believe that had it not been for the Russian intelligentsia's traditional contempt for daily life and for what we to this day contemptuously call "the ordinariness of everyday life," Stalin would not have succeeded in convincing the Party of the need to close down the NEP and of the possibility of building socialism on an empty belly without everyday comforts of any sort.[30]

With a somewhat different focus, Roy Medvedev, a leading Soviet historian and former dissident, sees the backward and superstitious mentality of the Russian peasantry as providing fertile ground for Stalinism.[31]

However, in other ways, Stalinism did represent a truly revolutionary break from traditional patterns: atheism replaced orthodoxy as the official state religion; the *mir*, which had survived the 1920s fairly intact, was finally destroyed; traditional social authorities (the family, the *mir*, and the church) in the countryside were replaced by a new breed of Party bureaucrats; and industrial and technical values replaced superstition and religious beliefs. Although Stalinism resembled tsarist rule, the form of political control was much more extreme.

Stalin's Personality. A fourth group of scholars emphasizes the key role of Stalin himself in shaping Soviet history. Until 1987, official post-Stalinist interpretations from Moscow, including Khrushchev's Secret Speech, placed the blame on Stalin as an individual, clearing Marxism and the Party of any responsibility for the purges and political violence of the 1930s. In the opinion of most Marxists, however, this explanation is inadequate because it attributes too great an influence to a single individual, overlooking the underlying social and economic dynamics that allowed Stalin to exercise power.

Some scholars have suggested psychological reasons for Stalin's behavior. Ethnically, Stalin was a Georgian, not a Russian, and he may have felt a need to compensate by embracing extreme Russian nationalism. In addition, he had little exposure to Western culture or ideas. Stalin also may have had a strong psychological need to prove himself a true revolutionary in the Leninist tradition. By carrying out the Third Revolution in 1929, he demonstrated his revolutionary credentials. Perhaps Stalin simply suffered from clinical paranoia. The definitive psychobiography of Stalin may never be written, due to the difficulty of unearthing the intimate detail required for this type of analysis.[32]

Unquestionably, however, Stalin's personality traits contributed to the extreme methods he used. Had another person taken over the leadership post in 1924, Soviet history probably would have taken a somewhat different turn. Medvedev writes, "It was an historical accident that Stalin, the embodiment of the worst elements of the Russian revolutionary movement, came to power after Lenin, the embodiment of all that was best."[33] Emphasis on Stalin's personality, however, begs the question of why such a paranoid and dangerous man was able to rise to power. Therefore, we must return to an examination of the cultural, economic, and political environment in which Stalin was able to make his bid for power.

The Force of Circumstances. None of the preceding theories, taken alone, is fully adequate to explain the rise of Stalinism. No doubt all of these factors, as well as some others, contributed to Stalin's ascendance. Circumstances worked together to produce a situation conducive to Stalin's rule: Lenin's early death, the failure of the Party to dismantle the secret police (Cheka) established during the civil war, the economic problems that developed in the late 1920s, and the presence of a shrewd politician (Stalin) who could take advantage of these circumstances. In addition, the Bolshevik leaders were unable to practice the politics of compromise and bargaining; their skills, perceptions, and responses were profoundly influenced by the repressive cultural and political environment of tsarism. In many ways, the Leninist Party structure had to mirror this environment to survive. Hierarchy, secrecy, and discipline were required to prevent subversion by tsarist agents. Even exposure to Western European ideas and politics could not make up for the lack of a democratic, participatory tradition at home.

The Soviet experience does not represent a prototype for every socialist experiment. The outcome of a Marxist revolution, or even a Leninist revolution, might be quite different under other circumstances. But then, such revolutions have not occurred in countries with strong liberal democratic traditions, so we cannot know what the outcome would be. Perhaps a Leninist party would not be able to achieve power in such an environment. As subsequent Soviet leaders have struggled to forge a new foundation of political support following Stalin's death, they have revived other elements of Leninist and socialist thought to justify and explain their policies. At the same time, the weak liberal tradition of the prerevolutionary period is being augmented by a vitalization of liberal thought among many contemporary Soviet intellectuals.

Notes

1. M. E. Falkus, *The Industrialization of Russia, 1700–1914* (London: Macmillan, 1972), pp. 72, 83.

2. V. I. Lenin, *What Is to Be Done?* (New York: International Publishers, 1929), pp. 32–33.

3. C. B. Macpherson, *The Real World of Democracy* (New York: Oxford University Press, 1972), pp. 18–19.

4. Ibid., p. 20.

5. Ibid., p. 22.

6. Lenin, *What Is to Be Done?*, p. 130.

7. V. I. Lenin, quoted in Marcel Liebman, *Leninism Under Lenin* (London: Merlin Press, 1975), p. 28.

8. V. I. Lenin, "State and Revolution," in *Essential Works of Marxism*, ed. Arthur P. Mendel (New York: Bantam Books, 1961), p. 172.

9. On June 12, 1991, voters in Leningrad supported a proposition to restore Leningrad to its earlier name of St. Petersburg by a vote of about 55 percent. The change was confirmed by the Russian parliament in September 1991.

10. Leon Trotsky, quoted in Leonard Schapiro, *Communist Party of the Soviet Union*, 2d ed. (New York: Vintage Books, 1971), p. 288.

11. N. I. Bukharin, quoted in Stephen F. Cohen, *Bukharin and the Bolshevik Revolution: A Political Biography, 1888–1928* (New York: Vintage Books, 1975), pp. 176–177.

12. This and the discussion that follows draw heavily on the analysis in Jerry Hough and Merle Fainsod, *How the Soviet Union Is Governed* (Cambridge, Mass.: Harvard University Press, 1979), pp. 124–133.

13. M. Lewin, *Russian Peasants and Soviet Power* (London: George Allen & Unwin, 1968), pp. 72–78.

14. Nikolai Shmelev and Vladimir Popov, *The Turning Point: Revitalizing the Soviet Economy* (New York: Doubleday, 1989), p. 64.

15. See, for example, Aleksandr Solzhenitsyn, *The Gulag Archipelago 1918–1956: An Experiment in Literary Investigation*, 3 vols. (New York: Harper & Row, 1974–1978).

16. Alexander Gerschenkron, cited in David Lane, *State and Politics in the USSR* (Oxford: Basil Blackwell, 1985), pp. 69–70.

17. Shmelev and Popov, *The Turning Point*, pp. 37–40, 54–56, 62–65.

18. Vera Dunham, *In Stalin's Time: Middleclass Values in Soviet Fiction* (Cambridge: Cambridge University Press, 1976), chapter 1.

19. Seweryn Bialer, *Stalin's Successors: Leadership, Stability, and Change in the Soviet Union* (Cambridge: Cambridge University Press, 1980), p. 10.

20. "Revolution's Road from 1917 to Now: The

Leader Takes Stock," *New York Times*, 3 November 1987, p. A12.

21. *Izvestiia*, 14 August 1990, p. 1.

22. Shmelev and Popov, *The Turning Point*, p. 21.

23. *Literaturnaia gazeta*, 4 January 1989.

24. "Trotsky Works Printed in a Soviet Magazine" *The New York Times*, 18 August 1989.

25. Shmelev and Popov, *The Turning Point*, pp. 44–63.

26. James Millar and Alec Nove, "A Debate on Collectivization: Was Stalin Really Necessary?" *Problems of Communism* (July–August 1976), pp. 53–55.

27. Vasily Selyunin, "Sources," *Novyi mir*, no. 5 (1988), trans. in Isaac J. Tarasulo, ed., *Gorbachev and Glasnost': Viewpoints from the Soviet Press* (Wilmington, Del.: Scholarly Resources, 1989), pp. 11–27.

28. A. Tsipko, "The Roots of Stalinism," *Nauka i zhizn'*, no. 11 (November 1989), trans. in *Current Digest of the Soviet Press* (hereafter *CDSP*) 41, no. 10 (1989), p. 4.

29. For an explication of this type of argument, see Zbigniew Brzezinski, "Soviet Politics: From the Future to the Past?" in Paul Cocks, Robert V. Daniels, and Nancy Whittier Heer, eds., *The Dynamics of Soviet Politics* (Cambridge, Mass.: Harvard University Press, 1976), pp. 337–351.

30. A. Tsipko, "The Roots of Stalinism," *Nauka i zhizn'*, no. 1 (January 1989), trans. in *CDSP* 41, no. 12 (1989), p. 21.

31. Roy Medvedev, *Let History Judge: The Origins and Consequences of Stalinism* (New York: Vintage Books, 1973), pp. 364–365, 428. A revised version of Medvedev's book was issued in 1989, published under the same title by Columbia University Press (New York).

32. However, see Robert C. Tucker's excellent books on Stalin, *Stalin as Revolutionary 1879–1929: A Study in History and Personality* (New York: W. W. Norton and Co., 1973) and *Stalin in Power: The Revolution from Above 1928–1941* (New York: W. W. Norton and Co., 1990). See also Dmitrii Antonovich Volkogonov, *Triumf i tragediia: politicheskii portret I. V. Stalina*, 2 vols. (Moscow: Novosti, 1989).

33. Medvedev, *Let History Judge*, p. 362.

C H A P T E R

2

Attempts at
De-Stalinization: From Stalin
to Gorbachev

The era of Stalin's rule had far-reaching effects on Soviet society. Despite the efforts of Stalin's successor, Nikita Khrushchev, to de-Stalinize Soviet society, many of its fundamental organizational, psychological, and economic features have survived. Indeed, one of the major tasks proclaimed by the Gorbachev leadership has been to reveal and reverse the negative aspects of Stalinism. As we saw in the last chapter, since 1986 social critics in the USSR have sought to unravel the roots and nature of Stalinism. Most observers interpret the Brezhnev era, which extended from 1965 to 1982, as a retrenchment from Khrushchev's de-Stalinization initiatives. Some Soviet émigrés have even argued that Soviet politics under Brezhnev maintained the fundamental traits of the Stalin period. Although there was significant continuity, a major transition *did* occur with the death of Stalin. In this chapter, we discuss the nature and extent of the changes that followed Stalin's death.

The Legacy of Stalinism

Stalin's death on March 5, 1953, came as a shock to the Soviet population. His "cult of the personality" (personal usurpation of power) and the epic upheavals of his long reign had made him

nearly a sacred object. With Stalin's death, the remaining leaders also faced major problems. How should Stalin's legacy be dealt with? No clear procedures for a change of leadership had been established, and in some thirty-six years of Soviet rule, Party leaders had faced this problem only once before. Should Stalin's policies and style of politics be continued? Even Stalin's closest comrades had been subject to insecurity in their positions. Should such an unpredictable system be allowed to remain, or should some attempt be made to introduce greater regularity? If changes did occur, how could they be explained to the Soviet people? If the Party reduced its reliance on political repression, wouldn't some greater accommodation with the population have to occur?

The legacy of Stalinism was felt in all spheres of life. Economically, the Stalinist strategy left the Soviet Union weak in the agricultural and consumer goods sectors; the Stalinist economic structures, now referred to in the Soviet Union as the *command-administrative system*, embedded an inefficient and highly centralized system of production that emphasized the development of heavy industry. Investment in agriculture was low, and effective management methods were virtually ignored. Stalin's support for T. D. Lysenko, an agronomist who suggested that living organisms (in this case, plants) could adapt to environmental change during the course of their lifetimes, damaged agricultural production in the Soviet Union for years thereafter. Lysenko's theory sanctioned inappropriate planting decisions, with disastrous consequences for agricultural output.

The chaos produced by the rapid collectivization of agriculture and the continued resistance of the peasantry forced Stalin (and his successors) to accept the existence of small, private agricultural plots as early as 1933. Production on these plots proved to be more efficient than on the collective and state farms, producing a significant proportion of the fresh produce and meat available to Soviet consumers. This concession to private initiative and efforts by Khrushchev and Brezhnev to raise the priority of agriculture were not sufficient to overcome the deficiencies in agricultural production. Shortages of basic food items have continued to plague the Soviet economy, and the Soviet leadership has, in recent years, relied on large grain imports from the West to feed its population.

Following Stalin's death, Soviet authorities also had to address the earlier neglect of consumer goods production. In the 1930s and after World War II, housing was in short supply and consumer services (restaurants, laundries, and recreational facilities) were grossly inadequate in the burgeoning urban centers. Individual consumer items, including meat and fresh produce, clothing, and household goods, often were unavailable or of such low quality as to be of little use. From the late 1950s to the present, an increasing level of investment has been devoted to production of consumer items, which has placed strains on other investment sectors. By 1990 under *perestroika*, shortages in the consumer sector had reached crisis proportions.

The Stalinist period left its political mark as well. Stalin's successors were the survivors of the purges, filling the posts vacated by Stalin's victims. Their apprenticeship in the 1930s shaped their attitudes, and they have only gradually modified the secretive, closed style of politics that characterized the Stalinist period. After Stalin's death, more information on policy debates (at least in less-sensitive policy arenas) was made public and greater institutional stability developed. Until recently, however, the actual functioning of top state and Party bodies (such as the Politburo, Central Committee, and Council of Ministers) was shrouded in mystery. High officials were rarely criticized in public, and when they retired or were demoted, reasons were seldom publicized. With the exception of rumor, Soviet citizens learned nothing of the personalities, family life, or personal interests of their leaders. Finally, the circular flow of power remained an important influence on political promotion. Patronage, in which successful Party leaders promoted loyal clients with whom they had past connections, accounted for many personnel changes within the Party structure. This dynamic is changing dramatically now as conflicts are openly played out in public view, but the legacy of the Stalinist system of power still has a powerful impact.

Stalinism bred a culture of fear and paranoia. Even those too young to have experienced this atmosphere absorbed it from recollections of their parents. In the post-Stalinist period, the proverbial knock on the door at midnight no longer occurred unexpectedly, and those accused of unacceptable political behavior were first given warning by the authorities. But the aura of distrust has only begun to dissipate in the past five years. Until recently, citizens were cautious in revealing their true sentiments to all but the closest family or friends, and public demeanor did not reflect genuine sentiments. Citizens had a private language for use with trusted friends and a different language for use in public.

The ascendancy of Khrushchev to the top leadership position set the initial course as the new leadership attempted to deal with this Stalinist legacy. Khrushchev initiated a reassessment of the Stalinist period. This reassessment was largely frozen following Khrushchev's removal from office in 1964 but was revived in a

Attempts at De-Stalinization: From Stalin to Gorbachev / **2** more radical manner once Gorbachev came to power in 1985.

The Khrushchev Period (1956–1964): The Beginnings of De-Stalinization

Following Stalin's death, the immediate contenders for the leadership post included Laventri Beria, head of the NKVD (forerunner of the Committee for State Security, or KGB); Georgii Malenkov, Stalin's right-hand man, member of the Party Secretariat, and deputy head of the Council of Ministers; and Vlacheslav Molotov, an old Bolshevik who had served as Stalin's foreign affairs deputy and prime minister for some time in the 1930s and 1940s. All three, along with seven others (including Nikita Khrushchev, who seemed a less likely successor in 1953) were members of the Presidium, as the Politburo was known between 1953 and 1966. Shortly after Stalin's death, most of the remaining leaders agreed that the secret police should be brought under the political control of the state and Party. Soon Beria and his deputies in the NKVD were arrested and executed, presumably to prevent use of the secret police to win power. As Alec Nove writes, "The executions of these executioners proved to be the last *political* executions to date."[1] (Executions for criminal offenses and spying did, however, occur after this time. One also might argue that the execution of the Hungarian reform leader Imre Nagy in Hungary after the 1956 events, for example, was both political and Soviet inspired.)

In 1953, Malenkov appeared as the leading candidate, but he soon lost his post on the Party Secretariat. This left Khrushchev as the only Presidium member who also sat on the Secretariat. Malenkov's base of support was primarily in the state bureaucracy, which administered the massive economic machine established under Stalin's rule, while Khrushchev's support lay mainly in the Party structures. Unlike most other members of the Presidium, Khrushchev had spent his entire career in the Party apparatus and had considerable experience working in Ukraine. The Party had been drastically weakened as a political institution during the Stalinist period, but the state bureaucratic organs had grown with the increasingly complex economy. It was not immediately clear, therefore, that Khrushchev's stronger political base in the Party (and his position as first secretary in the Secretariat) would be of the same advantage to him as it had been to Stalin during the first succession conflict following Lenin's death.

Malenkov and Khrushchev had not only different constituencies but also diverse policy positions as well. Malenkov emerged as a champion of the consumer industries. During his ascendancy in 1953 and 1954, he strengthened these sectors both in the Soviet Union and in the Soviet-dominated countries of Eastern Europe. In contrast, Khrushchev not only expressed a particular interest in agriculture but also supported the continued emphasis on heavy industry and received crucial support from the military. Although Malenkov's position might have been favored among the population at large, the most powerful interests in the bureaucracy were more likely to be supportive of Khrushchev's continued commitment to heavy industrial development. Ironically, once Khrushchev's position as top leader was secured, he proceeded to strengthen the consumer sectors and make substantial improvements in social welfare (e.g., pensions, maternity leave, minimum wages, and abolition of tuition fees).

Although Party structures were weakened under Stalin, they retained a strong basis of legitimacy among the political elite, due to the key role the Party had played in the revolution and its central position in Leninist theory. Khrushchev made skillful use of his position within the Party apparatus and was able to build up support within the Party's Central Committee. On this basis, he consolidated his position as the leading figure in the Soviet Union. In 1956, he took a bold step in ensuring his ascendancy: at the Twentieth Party Congress, he made his now famous Secret Speech, which was addressed only to delegates at the Party Congress and later published abroad. (Only in 1988 was it finally published openly in the Soviet Union.) He attacked Stalin's "cult of the personality," meaning Stalin's personal usurpation of power and the irregular methods he had used in dealing with his opponents within the Party. Khrushchev criticized Stalin for undermining Party organs and suggested that Stalin's errors could be rectified only by returning to a Leninist path of firm reliance on Party authority. However, Khrushchev praised Stalin's economic strategy of the 1930s, including collectivization of agriculture. In this way, he affirmed the fundamental direction of past Soviet policy.

Khrushchev achieved several political purposes with his speech. First, he reassured the Party delegates that should he be leader, the arbitrary and arrogant abuse of power would cease. Although Khrushchev himself had not been an innocent bystander, he implicated Malenkov and his allies as instruments of Stalin's misguided policies. Khrushchev sought to turn the tide of Party opinion against them and, at the same time, reaffirm Party dominance over the state bureaucracy in which Malenkov had his political support. In 1957, Malenkov, Molotov, and others challenged Khrushchev's leadership through a vote of the Party Presidium. Khrushchev quickly and skillfully convened a special meeting of the Central Committee, to which the Presidium was theoretically responsible, to condemn the effort to depose him. His opponents were then dubbed the anti-Party group because of their alleged attempt to undermine established Party procedures for their own advantage. Following this defeat, Malenkov and his allies were demoted to insignificant positions.

Having consolidated his position, Khrushchev embarked on a policy program that was often innovative but sometimes contradictory and controversial. Western scholars disagree over whether fluctuations in policy were due to successful political opposition to Khrushchev's initiatives or whether his approach was an inherently erratic one. In any case, Khrushchev did succeed in placing a higher priority on agriculture and reorganized Soviet institutions, in part to cement his own political support and in part to give agricultural policy a higher profile.

In 1957, before the showdown with the anti-Party group, Khrushchev proposed replacing the powerful economic ministries, which were responsible for various branches of the economy (e.g., agriculture, metallurgy, and light industry) with *sovnarkhozy* (regional economic councils). Khrushchev's support in the ministries was relatively weak, and this reform was meant to strengthen Party organs (which were organized on a regional basis), where Khrushchev had his strongest political backing. Khrushchev's reorganization attempt was ultimately unsuccessful from an economic standpoint because regional autarky and poor coordination among the *sovnarkhozy* simply replaced the previous problems that had resulted from the central power of the branch economic ministries. Over the next several years, the *sovnarkhozy* had to be made progressively larger to improve coordination. Once Khrushchev was removed from the top post in 1964, his successors immediately reversed this reform, and the old economic ministries were restored.

In 1962, Khrushchev instituted yet another reorganization scheme, dividing the regional Party organs into two sections: one in charge of industry and the other in charge of agriculture. In this way, agricultural interests would have their own institutional base and, presumably, would be in a stronger position. However, this change was not a shrewd political choice. The old secretaries of the previously united regional Party organs lost their posts, and Khrushchev undermined his own base of support among the Party *apparatchiki*, many of whom sat on the Central Committee.

In addition, Khrushchev's part in the Sino-

Soviet split and the Cuban Missile Crisis did little to improve his image among the Party elite. The breakdown in friendly relations with Communist China, marked by the withdrawal of Soviet technical assistance from China in 1960, reflected long-standing tensions between the two countries, rooted in geopolitical competition and Chinese resentment of Soviet dominance within the socialist bloc. While Khrushchev was not himself responsible for these conflicts, the fact that they culminated in an open split during his rule undermined his reputation as an effective leader of the socialistic bloc. During the Cuban Missile Crisis of 1961, Khrushchev was forced to reverse his plan to station short-range nuclear missiles in Cuba, under threats of retaliation from the United States. Khrushchev's humiliating capitulation to U.S. strength again made him appear weak and imprudent to his colleagues in the Soviet leadership. In a striking move in 1964, the Central Committee voted to remove Khrushchev from his post as first secretary. Such an assertion of power by a major Party institution over the Party leader would have been unthinkable in the Stalinist period.

Once removed from power, Khrushchev disappeared from the political scene. Fallen leaders were executed in the Stalin period, but Khrushchev was simply stripped of all posts, not eliminated. He retired to his *dacha* (country cottage), where he lived until his death in 1971. In 1970, Khrushchev's memoirs were smuggled out of the Soviet Union and published in the West.[2] They will soon be published in the USSR.

The brief period of Khrushchev's dominance left an important mark on Soviet politics, even though some of his specific policy directions were reversed in 1965. During Khrushchev's rule, Stalinist methods were openly repudiated and some Leninist ideals revived. Khrushchev was in a sense a populist. He strongly favored increased, though controlled, popular participation. He allowed experts to participate in policy deliberations and to express diverse opinions in the media. The first years of the Khrushchev era are generally referred to as the Thaw because of the loosening of controls on literature. Khrushchev approved the publication of Aleksandr Solzhenitsyn's short novel *One Day in the Life of Ivan Denisovich*, which depicted life in a Stalinist labor camp; the piece appeared in the Soviet literary journal *Novyi mir* (New World) in 1962. Khrushchev's literary policy was always somewhat erratic, however, and took on a harder line after 1962.

The Brezhnev Era (1965–1982): The Period of Bureaucratic Conservatism

Upon Khrushchev's removal as first secretary of the Party, it soon became apparent that Khrushchev's former allies Aleksei Kosygin and Leonid Brezhnev would share power. Gradually, Brezhnev was able to assert his dominance as the "first among equals," but he was never able to gain the personal power enjoyed by Stalin. Since purges of top Party members had lost their legitimacy as an instrument of control, the new leadership had to find other methods of accommodating both the elite and the population at large.

The new leadership presumably learned several lessons from Khrushchev's experience. First, Khrushchev's ascendancy had reestablished the key position of the Party and made clear that support from the heavy industrial and military sectors was important for any aspiring leader. In 1964, one of the factors that had made Khrushchev vulnerable was the loss of active support from the military–industrial complex. Second, Khrushchev had legitimized agriculture as a major policy concern, which Brezhnev continued to promote, although with somewhat different methods than Khrushchev. Bureaucratic interests supporting assertive agricultural policy had developed by 1964. Third, a key factor in Khrushchev's downfall was that he had alienated too many elite groups. If pressed, the Central

Committee could override the general secretary (called the first secretary during the Khrushchev era); therefore, it was important that the general secretary anticipate potential opposition before it materialized. Twice during Khrushchev's leadership, the Central Committee had successfully asserted itself: first in 1957, in supporting Khrushchev against the anti-Party group of the Presidium (now renamed the Politburo), and again in 1964, in deposing him. However passive a role the Central Committee may seem to have played after 1965, its potential had been demonstrated. The new leadership was more cautious, anticipating the reaction of broader segments of Soviet society to its policies.

The Post-Stalinist Settlement

While it would be inappropriate to speak of a postwar settlement in the Soviet Union comparable to the pattern in Western Europe, we can speak of the emergence of a post-Stalinist settlement during the Brezhnev years. Vera Dunham has argued that in the late 1940s, Stalin himself forged a kind of "tacit concordat," or unspoken agreement, with what she calls the Soviet middle class, referring to "solid citizens in positions and style below the top officials and cultural elite, yet above the world of plain clerks and factory workers, of farm laborers and sales girls."[3] This group, many of whom were beneficiaries of Stalin's policies in the 1930s, exchanged political complacency for material gain and a comfortable private life. Dunham suggests that Stalin's power was rooted not in the intellectuals or common working people but in this new and growing social stratum. In the Brezhnev years, the concordat was extended to encompass broader elements of the population, including state and Party officials, the intelligentsia, and the less affluent sectors of society.

The late 1960s and early 1970s were a period of relative affluence, a quiet after the storms of Stalinism and de-Stalinization. Economic growth, while moderate compared to that of the

1930s, was used to a much greater extent to provide the population with a more comfortable life-style. As Dunham has suggested, the post-Stalinist leadership under Brezhnev seemed ready and able to extend the concordat to Soviet society at large.

The Tacit Social Contract. The political elite (i.e., the highest state and Party officials) has had a greater degree of autonomy in the Soviet Union than in Western Europe. The Party has always placed great emphasis on the unity of the leadership and has hesitated to expose divisions in its ranks for fear of mobilizing popular discontent. Thus, the first element of Brezhnev's social contract involved accommodating the political elite itself. Both Stalin and Khrushchev had subjected top officials to unpredictability and uncertainty about their positions in the government and about the government's policies (Stalin through the purges, and Khrushchev through repeated bureaucratic upheavals). In contrast, the Brezhnev leadership embarked on a policy of stability. He made few personnel changes; this policy gained for him the political loyalty of the elite. Some incumbents were demoted, but more important, Brezhnev allies were promoted as a result of the expansion of Party and state organs. Finally, death or retirement allowed additional promotions. In this way, Brezhnev was able to consolidate his own position, making use of the circular flow of power without alienating the Party and state elites.

Brezhnev's social contract with the elite involved a commitment to stability, regularity, and consultation. While Brezhnev was clearly the "first among equals" on the Politburo, it is unlikely that he could have made any major decision without consulting with other members, particularly the small, influential inner core, which included Nikolai Podgorny (until 1977), Aleksei Kosygin (until 1980), Mikhail Suslov (until his death in 1982), and Andrei Gromyko. Collective leadership had become a reality, even if Brezhnev's leading position was reinforced when he added the post of president (that is, chairman of the Presidium of the Supreme Soviet) in 1980 to his role as general secretary of the Party.

Another dimension of the social contract rested in the social and economic policies of the Brezhnev team. While there were few radical initiatives following 1965, the leadership did make an effort to respond to the rising expectations of a more educated citizenry. In the first place, the new leadership continued the increased emphasis on production of consumer goods. By the early 1970s, a considerable improvement had occurred in the Soviet diet, with the addition of more meat and dairy products. At the same time, durable consumer goods such as television sets, washing machines, and refrigerators became accessible to more Soviet families (see Table 2.1). An effort was made to increase housing construction substantially, although shortages remained. (Between 1965 and 1982, per capita useful living space increased from 9.7 to 13.2 square meters in urban areas.[4]) The proportion of the state budget devoted to consumer goods production increased, as did investment in agriculture. Further, the economic reform program instituted in 1965 (but largely abandoned by the early 1970s) sought to improve product quality.

Social policies were directed toward the least affluent in society. The Soviet regime continued to ensure security of employment and low inflation rates on necessities of life (e.g., housing, basic food items, transportation, education, and health care) while raising prices of luxury goods (e.g., furs, alcohol, and cars). Wage differentials between educated white-collar sectors, on the one hand, and the peasantry and working class, on the other, declined. The peasants who worked on collective farms gained pension coverage, a guaranteed wage level, and an internal passport, which gave them more geographic and social mobility. Although schools and social services in rural areas remained inferior and possibilities for social advancement more limited, the advantages of city over country were somewhat reduced.

For the intelligentsia, the regime offered in-

Table 2.1 Provision of Urban and Rural Population with Various Goods at the End of the Year (total items per 1,000 persons)

	1970	1975	1980	1985	1989
Clocks	1,193	1,319	1,523	1,580	1,647
Televisions	143	215	249	293	316
Cameras	77	77	91	102	102
Refrigerators and freezers	89	178	252	275	276
Bicycles and mopeds	145	156	144	165	176
Sewing machines	161	178	190	190	185
Washing machines	141	189	205	205	216
Tape recorders	21	46	73	110	150
Radio sets	199	230	250	289	285

Source: Tsentral'noe statisticheskoe upravlenie SSSR (Central Statistical Administration of the USSR), *Narodnoe khoziaistvo SSSR 1983: statisticheskii ezhegodnik* (The Economy of the USSR in 1983: Statistical Yearbook) (Moscow: Iz. Finansy i statistika, 1984), p. 442; *Narodnoe khoziaistvo SSSR 1989: statisticheskii ezhegodnik* (The Economy of the USSR in 1989: Statistical Yearbook) (Moscow: Iz. Finansy i statistika, 1989), p. 121.

Table 2.2 Influence of Social Origin on Respondent's Social Position at Commencement of Labor Activity (in percent)

Social Position of Respondent's Father	Social Position of Respondent				
	Worker	Intelligentsia	Specialist Employee	Collective Farmer	Total
Worker	72.7	15.4	9.4	1.5	100.0
Intelligentsia	43.5	45.0	8.8	2.7	100.0
Nonspecialist employee	56.8	22.1	16.0	5.1	100.0
Collective farmer	55.0	12.4	7.3	15.3	90.0*

*Figures as taken from the original source do not sum to 100 percent.
Source: N. A. Aitov, "The Dynamics of Social Mobility in the USSR," trans. in *Soviet Sociology* 14, nos. 1–3 (1985–86), p. 257. Based on a Soviet survey conducted in Magnitogorsk in 1976.

creased opportunities for political participation by involving experts in policy debates; increasing debate in scholarly journals; and frequently calling upon economists, legal scholars, and other experts to provide advice on issues of economic and social policy. The prestigious Academy of Sciences, which has numerous research institutes throughout the country, was given increased autonomy, making a recurrence of the Lysenko fiasco unlikely. While some members of the intelligentsia complained of inadequate material incentives (because of the regime's more egalitarian wage and social policies), incentives for working within the system were reinforced by increased recognition and access to information.

The Soviet regime continued to exercise strict control over dissidents (e.g., the crackdown on the Helsinki Watch Group, which monitored human rights violations, in the late 1970s). Further, contact with the West was discouraged. Travel to Western countries remained restricted mainly to scholars, state/Party functionaries, athletes, and artists. While tourist travel to the Soviet Union from the West became commonplace, Soviet citizens were discouraged from having sustained contact with Western visitors. In this way, the regime hoped to stem rising expectations that would be difficult to satisfy. At

the same time, the official media continued to disseminate information emphasizing unemployment, inflation, and crime in the West.

The tacit social contract of the Brezhnev era had a "carrot and stick" character. The repressive apparatus of the state continued to punish those who exceeded permissible bounds of dissent, but methods of control were more predictable and less violent than in the Stalinist period. More and more citizens had grown up under Soviet rule and were accustomed to life under the system, and older population groups could compare their present situation favorably with the past. Lacking a democratic tradition, the Soviet people had few alternatives with which to compare Soviet politics. The Brezhnev leadership was apparently quite successful in finding a formula for stability and possibly even legitimacy.

Incremental Reform. Once Khrushchev's economic reforms and reorganizations were reversed in 1965, basic economic and political institutions were changed only incrementally during the Brezhnev era. The ministerial structure that existed before 1957 was reinstated, the regional economic councils were abolished, and Party organs were again reunified at the regional level. In 1965, under Kosygin's guidance, a moderate economic reform was instituted to improve productivity and quality without compromising the basic authority of the central Party bodies. However, even this limited reform placed contradictory demands on enterprise managers. Entrenched interests opposed a more comprehensive and far-reaching approach. By the early 1970s, these problems resulted in the virtual dismantling of the Kosygin reform. Growth rates continued to decline gradually. Other moderate attempts to alter the economic structure were made, but with little effect on economic performance.

Policy change was cautious and gradual in other areas as well. Increased investment and ambitious programs of land reclamation and irrigation reflected a commitment to improve agricultural production, but the collective and state farm structure was not altered, and the rights of the peasantry to cultivate their private plots also were maintained. Improvements in pension programs and other social benefits for the collective farm workers helped lift the lowest socioeconomic strata. These and other reforms produced no major systemic change but were efforts to smooth out the rough spots in policy performance without antagonizing important elements of the Soviet political elite. Thus, despite the existence of central economic planning, which might have allowed a periodic and thorough reassessment and redirection of priorities, only moderate changes in policy were made during this period. Last year's plan provided the basis for this year's plan, with only minimal alterations or reform. The style of politics was bureaucratic and the content conservative.

Oligarchic Pluralism. The Brezhnev regime allowed experts and bureaucratic interest groups more opportunities for input into decision making. One U.S. scholar suggested that Soviet politics was moving in the direction of "institutional pluralism,"[5] which differed from pluralism as we know it in the West in that only certain types of interests received a hearing from policymakers, primarily those of large institutional bodies (e.g., economic ministries, prestigious scientific bodies, and regional organs). According to this view, Soviet politics was increasingly characterized by politics of the possible, carried out through bargaining, negotiation, and compromise. Leaders consulted with those who had the most at stake in a particular policy area.

Although Western scholars sometimes spoke of interest groups in Soviet politics during the Brezhnev era,[6] these groups were informal and were not visible entities. Their existence was inferred by observing opposing opinions in the Soviet media: several individuals (e.g., scholars, Party officials, and state bureaucrats) expressed a similar viewpoint and sought to persuade the political authorities. Individuals expressing common viewpoints could not join in autonomous lobbying organizations, such as the National Farmers' Association or Sierra Club. Nor could proponents of similar policies hold public meetings to work out political demands or strategies. Such activities were not permitted. Soviet theoreticians denied the existence of interest group conflict, although some did admit that different interests and viewpoints existed in Soviet society.

Some Western scholars suggested that the Soviet political process under Brezhnev was more corporatist than pluralist.[7] That is, officially sanctioned organizations provided a link between the state and the population, and it was only through these organizations that the interests and views of the various constituencies had an impact on policy-making. Because these were state- or Party-run organizations, ordinary citizens were very limited in their ability to exert autonomous political pressure. Passive communication of one's viewpoint, by not buying a certain product or by coming to work late or drunk, were alternative modes of political protest, since there were no channels of direct political protest.

Writing in the 1970s and 1980s, some Western scholars did anticipate a further broadening of permissible debate in the Soviet Union, as the issues facing the leadership became more complex and required greater input from experts. But Western scholars did not foresee the radical turn of events that actually occurred in the late 1980s. As we shall see in succeeding chapters, by 1987 the fundamental nature of the political process was being transformed. The failure of Western Sovietologists to anticipate these radical developments reflects the general unpredictability of human life. But it also resulted from the shackles placed not only on political life, but also on scholarly research during that era.

Principles of Soviet Government in the Brezhnev Period

Both students and scholars face a difficult task in understanding the Soviet political process and political institutions. Many of the mechanisms and structures that traditionally characterized the Soviet polity continue to influence the political process. At the same time, new structures are evolving before our eyes. The legacy of the past is strong, but the momentum toward new patterns is growing ever more forceful. While the political structures and processes of the Brezhnev period are, in an important sense, history, they still strongly affect the "new politics" of *perestroika*.

Typical of this ambiguity is the unclear status of the Soviet constitution itself. In 1977, under Brezhnev's leadership, a new constitution was adopted (replacing the 1936 Stalinist constitution). Until *perestroika*, the constitution was more of a symbolic than a legal document. There was no intention or mechanism to enforce its provisions. The actual powers of political institutions diverged greatly from descriptions in the constitution. A stated goal of *perestroika* has been to create a genuine and effective constitution, which can provide a true legal foundation for Soviet government. Since 1986, numerous

radical amendments to the 1977 constitution have been adopted. Laws that quite explicitly contradicted the 1977 constitution were sometimes passed and the constitution amended only later. These laws were deemed such important steps in the process of *perestroika* that they could not await the process of constitutional reform. Following the coup d'état in August 1991, important provisions of the existing constitution were suspended to allow formation of new institutional mechanisms that would radically shift power to the republic level, away from the center. Drafting and approval of new constitutions to reflect the new political realities was placed on the political agenda at the center and in the republics. Thus, like the political system itself, the constitution has been in flux.

Another feature makes Soviet political institutions confusing to Western observers. Traditionally, Soviet political institutions have had different functions and powers from their apparent counterparts in liberal democracies, and we have had much less opportunity to observe them in practice. Therefore, until recently, a certain amount of detective work or informed inference was involved in trying to understand the political process in the Soviet Union. Students of Soviet politics often have found themselves baffled by this lack of information and by the uniqueness of Soviet institutional arrangements.

As we review the major principles governing politics in the Brezhnev period, we should keep in mind that every one of the principles discussed here is now under challenge in the Soviet Union. Some of these principles (such as a single-party system, Party/state governance, administrative federalism, political-economic centralism, and democratic centralism) have already been disavowed; and others (such as the primacy of collective interests) are in the process of fundamental transformation. We examine these changes in detail in Chapter 4. Here we provide an overview of the principles governing politics before *perestroika*.

A Single-Party System. Until recently, there was only one political party in the Soviet Union. By the early 1920s, all alternative parties had been repressed, and none was allowed to re-emerge.

How could one speak of a political party if there was no political competition? In the Western context, the reality reflects the origin of the word *party*—namely, a part or division. In general, however, political parties not only organize political competition but also serve other functions. The monopolistic CPSU, like political parties elsewhere, sought to mobilize the population in support of certain goals and, in this way, provided a link between the political authorities and the population. It also articulated a distinct political ideology and tried to create a coherent belief system for its adherents. Like Western parties, the CPSU was an important mechanism (in fact, the only significant mechanism) for selecting political leaders, through membership recruitment and its own internal promotion structure.

Soviet authorities explained that only one party was necessary because Soviet society was deemed to be free of class contradictions and, therefore, the CPSU could represent all the working people of the Soviet Union effectively. This point of view is now questioned in the USSR: Surely parties can represent social forces other than classes, and it is debatable whether the Soviet Union has eliminated all class conflict. On the contrary, Milovan Djilas, a former leader of the Yugoslav Communist Party, later turned dissident, suggested in the mid-1950s that the professional revolutionaries making up the core of Bolshevik-type parties formed the foundation of power for a new ruling class.[8] Some contemporary Soviet commentators also seem to be gravitating toward this type of analysis.[9] Party leaders clearly have enjoyed economic and social privileges sometimes attributed to a ruling class.

Party/State Governance. One of the most confusing aspects of Soviet political life in the Brezhnev period was the existence of parallel Party and state institutions throughout the system. In Western polities, there are both party institutions (local party organizations, party conferences, executive committees, and so forth) and state institutions (the legislative, executive, and judiciary). This may seem reasonable in the Western context, since parties alternate in power and, thus, in control of the state structures. Since only one party (the CPSU) existed in the Soviet Union, the roles of Party and state organs were blurred. In practice, functions and personnel overlapped between state and Party organs.

As a rule of thumb, one could say that the Party provided the basic ideological guidelines and set the broad parameters of policy, while the state administrative organs were in charge of implementing the policies laid out by the Party. Thus, one could think of Party organs as policy-making organs and state organs as executive organs. As Western experience has demonstrated, however, executive organs often take on a de facto policy-making role because of their expertise, their day-to-day involvement in dealing with problems, and their organizational resources (including their size). This pattern applied in the Soviet Union as well, where state organs also had some policy-making functions and were an important source of information for the Party authorities as they formulated policy.

Soviet state institutions looked very much like Western parliamentary structures in terms of formal constitutional powers. The 1977 Soviet constitution provided for a parliament (called the Supreme Soviet), a cabinet (called the Council of Ministers), and a prime minister. As in West Germany, there was also a president who formally headed the Soviet state. There were even local councils (structurally similar to Western city councils or state legislatures) that existed to represent the population at the city, regional, and republic levels. This structural similarity to Western parliamentary institutions provided a useful guide in understanding the constitutional powers and organizational structure of these state institutions, but it was misleading in trying to grasp the real power of these bodies. True legislative power lay with the Party, not the Supreme Soviet, and there were parallel state and Party institutions at most levels that interacted in a complex manner.

This duality of institutions (the parallel state and Party structures) had its origins in the 1920s. Initially, the Soviet Union was to be a land of soviet power. The soviets were not a part of the Bolshevik Party but represented the broader mass of workers, soldiers, and peasants. These institutions were to be the basis for workers' power under the ideological leadership of the CPSU. But as the soviets were weakened during and after the civil war, they came to be dominated by local Bolshevik Party organs. Their functions as representative and legislative bodies gradually gave way to submission to Party dominance. The soviets and other state institutions were maintained, although they took on quite different functions than those originally foreseen by the early revolutionary leaders. Only now is significant power again being transferred to the political bodies representing the population as a whole.

Democratic Centralism. We have already summarized democratic centralism—discussing policy questions before a decision is made but enforcing strict discipline thereafter, and electing leaders through a hierarchical delegate system—in the context of early Party organization. It remained the organizational principle of Party operation over the years and was even extended to apply to state organs in a modified form. Over time, especially from the late 1920s to the mid-1950s, the centralizing dimension came to predominate over the democratic dimension. Elections were uncontested, and minority opinions, at least on controversial or sensitive issues, often were denied expression even before a decision was made. The range of policy debate on less sensitive domestic issues, however, expanded considerably following the death of Stalin.

Political-Economic Centralism. Under Brezhnev, almost all aspects of the economy were state owned and run (exceptions included the private peasant plots and the unofficial black market). Consequently, it was virtually impossible to draw a distinction between economic and political power in the Soviet Union. The leading state organs were ultimately responsible for supervising the operation of economic enterprises and associations; virtually all adults were employees of the state (or of collective farms, which also were subject to state directives). Political and economic institutions were organized in a centralized, hierarchical manner, with lower organs being responsible in one way or another to higher bodies in the chain.

Administrative Federalism. Under the 1977 constitution, the Soviet Union was formally a federal system. The most important federal units were the fifteen union republics. Within some republics, there were (and still are) additional federal units called autonomous republics, autonomous regions, and national areas. The federal units were founded on ethnic divisions. The Soviet Union has more than one hundred distinct ethnic groups. The largest group, the Russians, accounts for slightly more than one-half of the population. Each republic is dominated by one ethnic group. For example, the Russian Republic is dominated by the Russian population, and the Georgian Republic is dominated by the Georgian population. To qualify for union republic status, an ethnic group had to reside on an external border of the Soviet Union; other sizable ethnic groups that are located in the interior of the country were given status as autonomous republics, autonomous regions, or national areas.

According to Article 76 of the 1977 constitution, "a Union Republic is a sovereign Soviet socialist state that has united with other Soviet Republics." Thus, in theory, the union republics had freely ceded certain powers to the central government; by extension, they should be able to redefine those powers or even secede from the Union (Article 72). In practice, this was not possible, and no mechanism existed for the assertion of the union republics' sovereignty. Furthermore, secessionist and nationalist strivings were subject to strict political repression.

By the same token, in theory the constitution granted each union republic independent authority in all fields not granted to the central all-Union authorities (i.e., the authorities of the Soviet Union as a whole). But here again, practice deviated from proclamations in the constitution; the powers of the union republics were greatly limited and were largely of an administrative, rather than a policy-making, character. Although the union republics did adopt their own constitutions, economic plans, and budgets, and they could regulate certain elements of cultural life, these powers were exercised under the strict guidance of the highly centralized CPSU. The limited autonomy of the union republics was exemplified by the fact that their budgets were also part of the central budget of the Soviet Union. The precepts of democratic centralism restricted the ability of the republic authorities to undertake bold initiatives or to exercise some of the powers granted to them formally in the constitution, such as the right to secede from the union. The union republics were given little genuine authority to make policy; they generally implemented policies made at the center. Therefore, federalism in the Soviet Union was little more than a formality, since federalism, by definition, involves some actual division of decision-making authority among various levels of government. In this sense, one could perhaps speak of *administrative federalism*, the delegation of some administrative authority to the constituent federal units, which had an ambiguous status in exercising their constitutionally defined powers.

On the one hand, however restricted the power of the union republics and other federal units was, federalism did allow ethnic elites to experience upward political mobility within their own regions. The Party's first secretary of the republic was almost always of the dominant ethnic group in the region (although the second secretary was usually a Russian, or at least from a Slavic group ethnically similar to the Russians). Furthermore, in the late Brezhnev period, the indigenous elites in the union republics became a lobbying force for regional interests. For example, they pressed for greater investment funds for their republics or for greater representation of indigenous elites in state and Party posts. On the other hand, the division of the Soviet Union into federal units made it easier for the Russian-dominated elites to inhibit the formation of strong identifications among ethnically similar groups, such as the various Islamic peoples of Central Asia, where there are five union republics. Thus, identification as an Uzbek, a Kazakh, or a Kirgiz often was stronger than a common Islamic identity. Federalism was an important instrument for management of ethnic conflict in the Soviet Union. At the same time, it provided the institutional foundation for what one Western scholar has called a "new nationalism" among indigenous ethnic elites.[10] This new nationalism is now posing a major challenge to the nature of the federal structure itself, as we shall see in later chapters.

Collective Interests versus Individual Rights. Liberalism never gained a strong foothold in Russia, nor did there develop a strong ideological commitment to individual rights such as exists in many Western polities. The interests of society as a whole predominated. This notion is rooted in traditional Russian culture, as well as in Marxism, which emphasizes the social context of human life.

Traditionally in the Soviet Union, human rights were viewed primarily in socioeconomic terms rather than in terms of civil liberties (e.g., freedom of speech, assembly, or the press). The 1977 constitution guaranteed such social rights as the right to work; to rest and leisure; to health protection; to maintenance in old age, sickness, and disability; to housing; to education; and to cultural benefits. It also guaranteed citizens civil liberties such as freedom of speech, the press, and assembly (Article 50) and "the right to associate in public organizations that promote their political activity and initiative and satisfaction of their various interests" (Article 51). These and other rights guaranteed in Chapter 7 of the constitution were subject to the provision that "citizens exercise their rights and freedoms as inseparable from the performance of their duties and obligations" (Article 59) and to the condition that exercise of these rights will "not be to the detriment of the interests of society or the state, or infringe the rights of other citizens" (Article 39).

Most Western polities also place limits on the exercise of such individual political rights when they come into conflict with broader social or national interests, but in the Soviet Union, the range of actions that was considered threatening to state and social interests was broader than in most Western polities, and, therefore, the exercise of these civil liberties was more restricted. This different attitude toward individual rights also was reflected in the legal process. There has been less emphasis in the Soviet Union on the observation of procedural guarantees in determining legal culpability and more readiness on the part of the authorities to judge the substance of the case without adhering to strict procedural regulations. Since the death of Stalin, however, concerns of "socialist legality" had increased the application of regularized procedures in nonpolitical cases. Under *perestroika*, the notion of the rule of law and individual rights are undergoing radical reassessment.

The Decline of the Post-Stalinist Settlement

The Brezhnev team's implicit social contract was effective at maintaining political stability for some years, but it was not adequate for the late 1980s. By the late 1970s, a series of interconnected problems reached dramatic proportions, just as the aging Brezhnev team seemed to have lost even the minimal dynamism it once had. At the root of these problems was a faltering economy. Growth rates, which had been between 6 and 7 percent annually in the 1950s, dipped below 3 percent by the last half of the 1970s and fell even lower in the 1980s. Slower growth meant greater difficulty in satisfying consumer expectations. While Soviet growth perhaps was not unusual by Western standards, per capita income was considerably lower than in the West (see Table 2.3). Competition among various sectors of the economy (military, agricultural, industrial, and consumer) and among various geographic regions also increased.

The arms race placed great pressure on the Soviet economy. To maintain parity with the United States, the USSR had to devote a considerably larger proportion of its gross national product (GNP) to the military sector because the Soviet GNP was smaller than that of the United States. Western estimates for Soviet expenditures ranged from 10 to 20 percent of the GNP, compared to 7.2 percent for the United States in 1982.[11] In July 1990, Soviet foreign minister Eduard Shevardnadze stated that one-fourth of the Soviet budget went for military expenditures.[12] The real cost was even greater because the highest-quality materials and personnel were diverted to the Soviet military from other sectors of the economy.

Other factors also complicated economic policy by the late 1970s. Exploitation of natural resources was becoming more expensive, deterioration of the environment was increasing, and demographic patterns suggested serious future imbalances in the distribution of labor. In addition, the massive investment in agriculture was producing only minimal improvement, so grain had to be imported from abroad, and food shortages continued. As economic problems mounted, the legitimacy of the system declined. By the early 1980s, corruption pervaded all levels of the Party and state organs, generating cynicism and low morale in the population.

Item	Kilograms	Minutes of Work-Time				
		Washington	Munich	Paris	London	Moscow
Flour	1.0	5	9	6	6	28
Bread	7.0	112	189	126	175	119
Noodles	2.0	28	32	22	28	68
Beef	1.0	69	150	119	115	123
Pork	1.5	63	150	108	117	176
Minced beef	1.0	37	70	80	63	123
Sausages	1.0	33	75	75	51	160
Cod	1.0	61	45	118	72	47
Sugar	3.3	30	33	30	36	191
Butter	0.5	28	26	24	25	111
Margarine	2.0	46	34	36	64	222
Milk (liters)	12.0	72	84	96	108	264
Cheese	2.0	200	130	118	130	370
Eggs, cheapest (units)	18.0	14	22	23	29	99
Potatoes	9.0	63	36	36	27	63
Cabbage	3.0	27	21	27	30	36
Carrots	1.0	11	10	7	13	19
Tomatoes	1.0	23	28	25	32	62
Apples	1.0	10	15	15	23	92
Tea	.1	10	10	17	5	53
Beer	3.0	33	24	21	54	48
Gin/vodka (liters)	1.0	87	106	153	187	646
Cigarettes (units)	120	54	96	48	150	90

Slower expansion of the economy meant decreased chances for upward social mobility. Young people had to lower their aspirations, and many took jobs below their skill levels. High levels of alcoholism contributed to a decrease in life expectancy for Soviet men, and an increase in infant mortality signaled a crisis in the health care system. By the late 1970s, social discontent of various types had spawned an active dissident movement, which the regime began to attack with new vigor in 1979.

These social and economic problems converged with a major change in leadership in the early 1980s. The new appointments Brezhnev had made at the top level were primarily men of his own generation; thus, the average age of voting Politburo members increased over time, reaching sixty-nine in 1981. At lower levels of the Party, there was more turnover and, therefore, younger leadership (e.g., the average age of first secretaries of regional Party committees was fifty-seven in 1980), although in virtually

Table 2.3 (continued)

Item	Hours of Work-Time				
	Washington	Munich	Paris	London	Moscow
Weekly basket*	18.6	23.3	22.2	25.7	53.5
Monthly basket*	74.2	93.2	88.8	102.8	214.0
Monthly rent	51.0	24.0	39.0	28.0	12.0
Total of monthly basket and rent	125.2	117.2	127.8	130.8	226.0
TV, black and white	38	49	44	35	299
TV, color	65	143	106	132	701
	Months of Work-Time				
Small car	5	6	8	11	53
Large car	8	9	12	18	88

*Basket of consumer goods for four persons at Soviet level of consumption in March 1982.

Source: Keith Bush, "Retail Prices in Moscow and Four Western Cities in March 1982," *Radio Liberty Research Supplement*, 4 June 1982, p. 7.

every sector of political life, the governing elite was older during the Brezhnev years than during previous regimes.[13] While the "stability of cadres" may have been a viable way of maintaining the loyalty of the existing elite, it produced a sluggish response to the pressing problems of the later Brezhnev years. In fact, Soviet discussions of the Brezhnev period now refer to it as *zastoi*, the period of "stagnation."

Brezhnev's preoccupation with foreign policy questions reinforced the tendency toward immobilization on domestic issues beginning in the late 1970s. The stability of cadres also created a serious block to upward mobility for younger politicians. While some of the younger men and women might rise to posts at the regional level, it was much more difficult to achieve a leading position at the central level. The reluctance of the older generation to give up the reins of power to younger individuals was evidenced by the appointment of Iurii Andropov (following Brezhnev's death in November 1982) and, later, Konstantin Chernenko (following Andropov's death in February 1984) to the position of Party

general secretary. Andropov was sixty-eight and Chernenko seventy-two when appointed to the post. Once the older generation began to pass away in the early to mid-1980s (by 1986, eight of the fourteen members of the 1981 Politburo had died or retired at an advanced age), there was bound to be a rapid shift in the composition of the top elite.

It was in this context that Mikhail Gorbachev, at age fifty-three (a relatively young leader by Soviet standards), took over the post of Party general secretary in March 1985, following Chernenko's death. Gorbachev represented a new generation. Born in 1931, he did not join the Party until 1952 and thus did not embark on his political career until shortly before the death of Stalin. Like many of his peers, he was greatly influenced by Khrushchev's de-Stalinization. It was a model and an inspiration, but at the same time it represented a yet unfulfilled mandate.

Unlike their predecessors, the men and women of Gorbachev's generation did not benefit personally from the purges. They feel more secure about the Soviet Union's position as an

Soviet citizens used to tell jokes about Brezhnev, such as this one:

The foreign minister of the USSR, Andrei Gromyko, on returning to the USSR from a diplomatic visit to the United States, told General Secretary Brezhnev that in the United States, applicants for government jobs are required to take a test. "Here is an example of a question," he said. "Who is my father's son but not me?"

Brezhnev hesitated and replied, "I don't know."

Gromyko said, "Well, it's my brother."

The next day Brezhnev was talking with fellow Politburo member Nikolai Podgorny. He repeated Gromyko's story and asked Podgorny the same question: "Who is my father's son but not me?"

Podgorny hesitated and replied, "Your brother."

Brezhnev looked surprised and exclaimed, "No, it's Gromyko's brother!"

Or, like this:

On Red Square in Moscow, a man shouts: "Brezhnev is an idiot!"

The militia seizes the man and puts him under arrest. He is sentenced on two charges: He is given fifteen days for hooliganism, and fifteen years for revealing a state secret.

international power. They also are more used to the politics of bargaining and compromise, and they stress pragmatic solutions more than ideological formulas. The changes ushered in by Gorbachev and his allies were partly a response to the new demands emanating from Soviet society, but they also reflect the different experiences and attitudes of a new generation.

The Economic Dilemma. Gorbachev inherited a difficult economic situation when he took office in March 1985. We have already discussed the declining economic performance and its effect on the tacit social contract. While Soviet leaders may have felt that Stalinist economic methods had served the country fairly well as it moved from relative backwardness to its status as an industrial giant, some parts of the leadership viewed these methods as increasingly inadequate to meet the demands of a technologically advanced and interdependent economy. Simple quantitative gains were no longer enough. Innovation, quality, technological improvement, and superior efficiency were needed.

The economic question was politically charged. How could the incentive structure be changed to encourage higher productivity, efficiency, innovation, and quality? Would a radical decentralization of economic power or a competitive market structure be necessary? Would real decentralization encourage ethnic self-assertion at the local level, possibly destabilizing the Soviet system? If a competitive market were accepted, wouldn't essential elements of the Soviet social contract—the guarantee of employment and low inflation—be undermined? These were the dilemmas that Gorbachev faced as he embarked on *perestroika*. But to understand their complexities, we need to become more familiar with the planning system as it existed in the Brezhnev years. In the following discussion, we use the past tense to describe that economic system. But as we shall see in Chapter 5, some of the features of the economic system under Brezhnev continue to operate as this chapter is written.

The Planning System. Since the 1930s, the Soviet economic system has been highly centralized. Its centralized character was due not only to the predominance of state control and ownership but also to the nature of the economic planning system itself. In the traditional Soviet model, Gosplan, the State Planning Committee, was responsible for working out the one-year and five-year economic plans, as well as overseeing their broad implementation. The one-year plans were operational in that they involved the issuance of specific instructions as to what should be produced, by whom, and in what quantities. They had the force of law.

Gosplan relied on the large branch ministries that oversaw the various sectors of the economy (e.g., machine building, light industry, and grain products) and other state committees (e.g., the Committee on Prices) in carrying out this function. Below the economic ministries were the industrial associations, which integrated several enterprises involved in producing a similar product type and often had research and development sections to further technical innovation in the field. At the bottom of the hierarchy were the state enterprises themselves. The ministries and larger enterprises or associations in key branches of the economy (e.g., the energy sector, military-related areas, and the chemical industry) were powerful institutional actors in the Soviet system. Most workers were employed directly by the enterprise (and thus by the state). To assist in formulating the one- and five-year plans, the enterprises provided information regarding their productive capabilities through the hierarchy to Gosplan. On this basis, the final plan was drafted, and the instructions were transmitted back to the associations and enterprises.

In the agricultural sphere, the *sovkhoz* (state farm) was the equivalent of the industrial enterprise. Some agricultural workers, however, were employed by *kolkhozy* (collective farms), which, theoretically, were not owned by the state but were collectively run and owned (except for the land) by the peasants themselves. In practice, however, production on both state and collective farms was under the guidance of the central plan. Only the small, private plots were outside the planning system.

Planning was based primarily on a system of input/output techniques and material balances. The central organs determined output goals, suppliers and buyers, prices, and the balance between wages and consumer goods. In other words, the enterprise did not respond to market forces, such as changing demand or market-price levels, as do firms in the West. Rather, the enterprise was obliged to try to fulfill the goals set out by the central planning organs.

For a large economy such as that of the Soviet Union, planning was a very complicated task. If Factory X was to produce a specified number of agricultural vehicles (tractors, trucks, and so forth), it had to receive the appropriate inputs, such as tires, transmissions, and metal, from its designated suppliers. The tire factory, in turn, had to receive the necessary amounts of rubber and metal. If, for example, the tires delivered to the agricultural machinery factory were the wrong size, the tractors could not be produced and the state farms would not be able to meet their output goals. Any bottleneck in the process or any miscalculation by the planning organs caused a chain reaction that reverberated throughout the economy. Gosplan itself worked out the balance of production for more than two thousand products (only a small proportion of the numerous types of output). Further instructions were handled by the ministries and associations or through direct contacts between suppliers and buyers. The entire process was a giant puzzle in which a change in one set of directions necessitated recalculation of numerous others.

To make the problem even more difficult, planning in the Soviet Union has traditionally been *taut*. To ensure that each enterprise worked to maximum capacity, the authorities allowed little slack in the plan. But when central planners obligated enterprises to produce at, or even beyond, realistic capacity, bottlenecks were all the more likely, as some enterprises failed to meet the plan and could not supply their customers. The result was a sellers' market. Pervasive shortages of desired goods compelled buyers (both the average consumer and the enterprise in need of raw materials) to accept inferior goods or get nothing at all. Furthermore, enterprises hesitated to exceed their plans, even if they had the capability to do so, since this would almost certainly result in higher quotas for the next plan period. Soviet authorities feared that abandoning taut planning would bring even larger gaps in production. In practice, enterprises often tried to hide capacity and to manufacture parts needed to produce goods demanded by the plan in order to reduce their dependence on unreliable suppliers. This in turn made it even more difficult for top planning bodies to retain an overview of productive capacities.

Legal, Semilegal, and Illegal Markets. Prices have traditionally fulfilled an entirely different function in the Soviet system than in the West. In the Soviet centralized planning model, prices did not convey messages about supply and demand as they do in a regulated market economy. Rather, they were primarily instruments to measure enterprise performance and regulate exchange of commodities in the economy. The enterprises produced according to the plan, not according to the manager's reading of demand. In the West, products in high demand and short supply will command high prices, luring other producers into the field, but in the Soviet Union, most prices were centrally established and subject to almost no short-term fluctuations, though they were reexamined periodically by the Committee on Prices and readjusted to meet changing circumstances. Authorities justified this approach on the ground that production decisions should be based on socially established goals, not on the anarchy of market fluctuations.

For the enterprise manager, prices provided a measure of how efficiently the factory was fulfilling its plan. Prices were used for accounting purposes. If the enterprise was producing as it should, costs and expenditures should balance or show a profit. If the books showed a profit due to efficient management, only a certain amount accrued to the enterprise bonus funds; the rest was returned to the state, but the manager was assured that he or she would be rewarded for the good job done by special bonuses, public praise,

or even career advancement. Under the Soviet Union's one-person management system, the manager was not responsible to collective or representative bodies (such as workers' councils or boards of directors) in carrying out his or her duties, but to the Party and the plan.

Market principles were permitted to operate in a modified form in a few areas of the Soviet economy, even before Gorbachev's attempted reforms. The consumer could pick and choose from available goods. In these cases, prices affected the consumer's choice. Consumer preferences, however, often were not fulfilled. Although planners sometimes encouraged enterprises to pay more attention to public demands, the light industrial enterprises producing consumer goods often were at the end of the supply line and thus often lacked the materials they needed. In the centralized model, the labor market also was subject to some principles of supply and demand. Wage levels were generally set at the center, but since Soviet workers could usually choose their own employer, enterprises sometimes juggled job classifications or central planners adapted wage levels in certain occupations to achieve the desired distribution. For example, wage levels in Siberia were higher than those in Moscow. Finally, market principles operated in free peasant markets, where produce from private peasant plots was sold legally and prices fluctuated to reflect supply and demand.

In other cases, market principles functioned in a semilegal or illegal manner. Because enterprises often could not get the materials they needed to fulfill the plan, the *tolkachi* (unofficial agents) sought sources of supply outside the plan. The result was an unofficial market, which was neither sanctioned nor suppressed by the authorities, who recognized that without this semilegal trade, bottlenecks would become overwhelming. Similarly, *shabashniki* (unofficial work brigades) were hired to complete rural construction projects more quickly and efficiently (and at much higher pay) than state enterprises. The authorities allowed the *shabashniki* to operate in the gray area between legality and illegality because they served a useful economic function. On a smaller scale, the store clerk sometimes put aside a rarely available chandelier for a special customer, expecting a similar favor in return. This type of quid pro quo effectively raised the price of the valued commodity not in monetary terms, but through a barter principle that reflected the true value of scarce goods and services. These activities were illegal but often tolerated, since they served as an outlet for consumer frustrations.

Other illegal trade, which the authorities did try to control, occurred on the underground black market—that is, surreptitiously through informal contacts out of public view. Items traded on the black market included Western commodities, goods stolen from the state at the workplace, and items produced in illegal underground factories operated for private profit. Prices on the black market escaped central control, but here the authorities were less willing to look the other way. Although blue jeans and other Western commodities bought from tourists commanded a high price on the black market, exchange in Western goods was especially discouraged because it affected the balance of trade and reinforced a fascination with the West. Since the official production system could not satisfy consumer expectations, the leadership was hardpressed to eliminate such illegal activities.

Deficiencies in Planning. Prior to Gorbachev's reforms, several attempts were made to alter the criteria for evaluating enterprises so as to place more emphasis on quality of output, productivity of labor, technical innovation, and satisfaction of the buyer's specific needs (i.e., in supplying the right size and specifications of tires to the tractor factory or the proper mix of shoe sizes and styles to the retail outlet). In practice, however, it proved extremely difficult to work out a set of criteria that achieved all of these objectives at the same time. Therefore, success in fulfilling the plan was still primarily judged

by fairly crude quantitative measures. The anecdotal case of the factory that produced oversized screws to meet its weight quota was not far from the truth. Small screws might be needed, but it was cheaper and easier for the screw enterprise to meet its output goal (measured in tons) by producing a much smaller number of larger screws. Although a sewing machine factory, for example, theoretically could refuse to accept the huge screws, if no other supplier were readily available, that enterprise often took them to keep in stock for later use. This catch-as-catch-can environment undermined efforts by planners to evaluate enterprises on the basis of the quantity of goods actually accepted by the customer.

This was only one of many problems in trying to operate a centralized planning system. Enterprises often hoarded raw materials, hid their reserves, and bought or sold on the unofficial market to obtain the materials they needed. By hoarding, they prepared themselves for a rainy day. Even if the sewing machine enterprise could not possibly use the huge screws, it might be able to barter them unofficially for something useful at a future date. By hiding productive reserves, the enterprise protected itself from the unrealistic quotas that are endemic to taut planning. This tendency to underestimate productive capacity in turn encouraged planners to overestimate enterprise capabilities, since they realized that hidden reserves did exist. And computer technology offered no panacea to planners. If central planners were misfed data from lower levels, no amount of computer sophistication could produce a realistic plan.

Levels of productivity were lower in the Soviet Union than in Western economies at comparable levels of economic development. By the end of the Brezhnev period, all resources, including labor, were increasingly in short supply, and yet the system was characterized by pervasive waste. Workers were hard to fire and thus were difficult to discipline and drive to higher levels of output. Natural resources often were underutilized. Free use of land was usually granted to enterprises, and charges for use of water and some mineral deposits were implemented near the end of the Brezhnev period only on a limited scale. Mining enterprises often were oriented toward a single goal. For example, a coal-mining enterprise used any method to extract coal at a low cost but discarded valuable minerals that could, at some expense, be retrieved for profitable use elsewhere. This type of waste was ever more costly as easily accessible deposits were being depleted. Future growth depended on more efficient use of existing capabilities, since new sources of labor, capital, and cheap raw materials were largely exhausted.

By the mid-1980s, the Soviet leadership confronted a maze of interconnected socioeconomic issues. Poor economic performance aggravated social problems and spurred consumer discontent; this in turn lowered citizen motivation and spawned resistance to state policy. In the face of these complex problems, would the Gorbachev team be able to forge a new social contract that could ensure continued stability and regime legitimacy? Could this be done without a full-scale market reform? Would the new regime be more responsive to popular interests than the old one was? By 1985, the Soviet system faced another major transition. While it might be delayed, delay might make the problems even more difficult to resolve, since the Soviet economy might continue to deteriorate even further. The Polish experience in the 1970s and 1980s demonstrated that economic reform is unlikely to succeed in the face of social upheaval or economic crisis, for an economy already in crisis has few reserves to fall back on as the inevitable short-term costs of economic reform are felt. As in Poland, the result might well be unpopular price increases, a lack of popular faith in the reform program, and resultant strikes and popular resistance. How would the new Soviet leaders respond? In subsequent chapters, we seek to answer these questions as we examine the evolution of Soviet politics and society since 1985.

Notes

1. Alec Nove, *Stalinism and After* (London: George Allen & Unwin, 1975), p. 123.

2. The memoirs have been published in the West in three volumes: N. Khrushchev, *Khrushchev Remembers* (Boston: Little, Brown, 1970); *Khrushchev Remembers: the Last Testament* (New York: Bantam, 1976); and *Khrushchev Remembers: The Glasnost Tapes* (Boston: Little, Brown, 1990).

3. Vera Dunham, *In Stalin's Time: Middleclass Values in Soviet Fiction* (Cambridge: Cambridge University Press, 1976), p. 5.

4. Gregory D. Andrusz, *Housing and Urban Development in the USSR* (London: Macmillan, in association with the Centre for Russian and East European Studies, University of Birmingham, 1982), pp. 286–287.

5. Jerry Hough, *The Soviet Union and Social Science Theory* (Cambridge, Mass.: Harvard University Press, 1977), chapter 1.

6. H. Gordon Skilling and Franklyn Griffiths, eds., *Interest Groups in Soviet Politics* (Princeton, N.J.: Princeton University Press, 1971).

7. Valerie Bunce and John M. Echols III, "Soviet Politics in the Brezhnev Era: 'Pluralism' or 'Corporatism'?" in *Soviet Politics in the Brezhnev Era*, ed. Donald Kelley (New York: Praeger, 1980).

8. M. Djilas, *The New Class*, rev. ed. (New York: Praeger, 1974), p. 39.

9. See, for example, Sergei Andreyev, "Causes and Effects," *Nedelia* (25 April–1 May 1988), pp. 10–11, trans. (condensed) in *Current Digest of the Soviet Press* 40, no. 25 (1988), pp. 13–17.

10. Teresa Rakowska-Harmstone, "The Dialectics

of Nationalism in the USSR," *Problems of Communism* (May–June 1974), pp. 300–321.

11. Cited in David Lane, *Soviet Economy and Society* (Oxford: Basil Blackwell, 1985), p. 56.

12. Excerpts from Shevardnadze's Speech at the Communist Party Congress, *New York Times*, 4 July 1990, p. 6.

13. Jerry Hough, *Soviet Leadership in Transition* (Washington: Brookings Institution, 1980), p. 61.

C H A P T E R

3

Gorbachev
and *Perestroika:*
From *Glasnost'* to Crisis

When Mikhail Gorbachev took office as general secretary of the CPSU in March 1985, few observers expected that he would embark on a full-scale program of political and economic reform. Although Western commentators had been predicting an imminent crisis in the Soviet system for years, the Soviet leaders had continued to muddle through with few fundamental changes. The selection of Iurii Andropov, and then Konstantin Chernenko, as successors to Brezhnev reflected the conservative orientation of the Party elite. While Andropov had mildly reformist tendencies, these took the form of an emphasis on social discipline and attacks on corruption and unearned income. As the former head of the KGB (the Soviet internal security agency), Andropov represented the predominant values of the Soviet system and, because of his access to KGB information, also probably had a clearer view than many other leaders of the true scope of corruption and decay in the system. Chernenko was, if anything, even more representative of the governing Party/state apparatus. He had been Brezhnev's right-hand man, in charge of organizational and personnel matters in the later years of Brezhnev's rule.

In his first few months in office, Gorbachev appeared to be following the basic directions laid out by his predecessors, particularly Andropov. He continued to stress social discipline and emphasized the importance of economic acceleration, a traditional Soviet concern. Gorbachev was a product of the Party's recruitment system: he had spent much of his career as first Party secretary in an agricultural region in southern Russia (Stavropol). The major features that distinguished Gorbachev from other candidates for the top Party post were his mildly reformist efforts in the agricultural sector in Stavropol, his somewhat younger age, and his unusually energetic style of leadership. Thus, in the summer of 1986, when the first edition of this book went to press, we posed the question "Do the changes being instituted by the new generation of leaders represent a genuinely new approach?" At that time, the answer was still maybe; by now, the answer is clearly yes. Since 1986, with fits and starts, Gorbachev's reform program took on an increasingly radical character and unleashed social forces that threatened to undermine not only Gorbachev's personal position but also the very underpinnings of national unity and political stability. The threat to the old power structures in turn elicited a defensive reaction on the part of the old elites. In early 1991 their interests were heavily represented in government structures and the attempt to remove Gorbachev in a coup d'état on August 19, 1991 placed in jeopardy a continuation of the reform process itself. Following the failed coup d'état, Gorbachev joined with reformist forces, led by his former rival Boris Yel'tsin, to pursue a breathtaking pace of change; shifting power to the republics, recognizing Baltic independence, and dismantling the CPSU's powerful apparatus.

Gorbachev's own goals have remained a subject of dispute. On the one hand, Gorbachev has continued to affirm his commitment to socialist values. In presenting his views to Party members in May 1990 as he stood for election as a delegate to the Twenty-eighth Party Congress, Gorbachev stated, "I would like to reaffirm to the Communists of this election district that I am committed to the socialist idea. For me, this is the guiding idea in my activity. It defines my position as a Communist."[1] At the same time, Gorbachev's view of socialism and communism came to deviate greatly from traditional Soviet conceptions. By mid-1990 he was willing to challenge such previously sacrosanct tenets as single-party rule, Soviet dominance in Eastern Europe, and exclusive state ownership of property. Nonetheless, Gorbachev continued to affirm his belief in socialist principles, even after the failed coup d'état in August 1991. But at that time he apparently came to recognize that the CPSU was no longer a viable agent for realizing these principles and thus recommended its dissolution. Increasingly Gorbachev's public point of reference has become West European social democracy.

The Soviet leader has repeatedly altered his position, in most instances (except in late 1990 and early 1991) accepting a broader scope of political pluralism and popular input. At the same time, Gorbachev often has articulated a compromise position between that of Party conservatives and that of more radical reformers. Only when popular or economic pressure has grown sufficiently to pose an imminent crisis

has Gorbachev altered his position. The limits of Gorbachev's flexibility have repeatedly been stretched, so that when Gorbachev did finally disavow his connection with the CPSU in late August 1991, some observers were only mildly surprised and others asked why he had waited until three days after the coup's failure to do so. At that time, Gorbachev not only abandoned his long-standing commitment to the CPSU, but also accepted a smaller union (of a yet undefined nature) in the face of rising demands for national independence. When faced with the choice, Gorbachev proved unwilling to sacrifice important reform objectives to preserve the unity of the Soviet Union itself.

Some Western and Soviet observers believe that Gorbachev has had a radical vision all along, that his ultimate goal was always a variant of Western social democracy combined with capitalist economic principles. Adherents of this view argue that Gorbachev often paid lip service to traditional Soviet socialist values in order to placate powerful conservative critics in the leadership (and perhaps conservative sentiments among the population). In this view the defeat of the coup d'état in August 1991 represented a long-awaited opportunity for Gorbachev to push forward the reform program. Other observers believe that in 1985 Gorbachev began with a vaguely defined reform vision and has acted as a politician par excellence in molding his views to meet changing circumstances. From this perspective, his shifting positions are seen to reflect changes in the constellation of forces in the elite and society at large, and thus may deviate as the balance of power shifts. Finally, other analysts have suggested that Gorbachev all along had in mind a reform program ultimately intended to preserve, rather than to undermine, the power of the political elite. These analysts would argue that Gorbachev finally abandoned those interests after the coup attempt only because he recognized the inevitability of their defeat. We may never have a definitive interpretation of Gorbachev's motives as he embarked upon *pere-stroika*.

Gorbachev and Political Leadership

Each major leader has ushered in a unique era in Soviet politics. But as societies become more complex, the ability of any single individual to shape the politics of his or her time in power becomes more limited, for the leader is constrained by more powerful social forces: larger, interdependent institutional structures; a more highly educated population; and the limited capability of any individual to master the knowledge and expertise necessary to maintain the required overview. Nonetheless, by any estimate, Mikhail Gorbachev has had an extraordinary impact on the course of Soviet politics, and indeed on the course of European history. Nonetheless, one should not overlook the fundamental social processes that have made the "Gorbachev phenomenon" possible.[2] Too often conversations, both inside the Soviet Union and in the West, have focused excessively on *his* intentions, fate, and capabilities. With the failure of the coup d'état, a similar preoccupation with Boris Yel'tsin emerged. Ironically, Gorbachev's remarkable reform program may have set in place a more regularized, democratic system of leadership selection, which itself will limit the ability of any individual to dominate the political scene. Perhaps the best measure for the success of Gorbachev's (or Yel'tsin's) reform program is the extent to which the reform process can proceed without them.

Like all previous Soviet leaders, following his selection as Party head in March 1985, Gorbachev had to consolidate his own position as leader by making a number of changes in personnel in top state/Party posts. By the time of the Twenty-seventh Party Congress of the CPSU in February and March 1986, Gorbachev had succeeded in making a remarkable number of new appointments, including a new prime minister, more than thirty heads of ministries and state committees, four full members of the Politburo, two new members of the Party Secretariat, four heads of union republic Party organizations, and almost a third of the *oblast'* (regional) Party chiefs. At the Party congress itself, a massive turnover of Central Committee membership occurred; 119 (almost 39 percent) of the 307 voting members had newly achieved that position. Five of the eleven members of the Party Secretariat were newly appointed at the end of the congress, and the Politburo itself acquired one new member with full voting status and two with nonvoting candidate status.

In his early months in office, Gorbachev accompanied these personnel shifts with sharp attacks on bureaucratic ineptitude and corruption. By February 1986, Gorbachev was even indirectly criticizing former Party leader Leonid Brezhnev for running a stagnant bureaucratic government. He soon began to oversee a restructuring of state and Party organs themselves, in an effort to reduce bureaucratic inertia and increase responsiveness to social needs.

The new leaders filling the top state and Party institutions were generally younger than the leaders of the Brezhnev period. For example, the average age of full Politburo members declined from sixty-nine in 1981 to sixty-four in 1986, and further to fifty-four in July 1990. Members of the Gorbachev generation were not only younger than the leaders of the Brezhnev era; they also shared formative experiences that shaped their habits and expectations in a way quite different from the experiences of their predecessors, who rose under the umbrella of the Stalinist purges of the 1930s. They had more regular career patterns (less disrupted by World War II) and were usually able to pursue a university education full-time upon completion of secondary school, unlike their predecessors, who often attended night school or went to work before continuing their education. While many were trained as engineers, as agronomists, or in other technical fields, some, like Gorbachev, had less technical specializations, such as law. (Gorbachev has studied agronomy in addition to law. Lenin, incidentally, also was trained in law.) The new generation of top leaders was increasingly specialized in career background, having worked mainly in one region, functional area, or branch of the economy, whereas the Brezhnev team consisted of generalists with diverse career experiences before reaching the top.

As Timothy Colton has pointed out, all of this meant that the traditional machine politics, which allowed a general secretary to firm up his position by installing his clients in subordinate posts, became less effective than previously.[3] While many of Brezhnev's top political appointees had previous career connections with him (drawn from a kind of "old boys' network"), fewer of those who rose on Gorbachev's coattails had a previous career link to the new leader. Criteria for promotion have, over time, given more importance to congruence of policy views, inclusion of those with policy expertise, and efforts to reflect diverse interests in society.

As Tables 3.1 and 3.2 suggest, turnover among top Party leaders continued throughout Gorbachev's term as general secretary. By July 1990, the membership of the Politburo was almost entirely different from that in 1986 or even in February 1990, before radical changes in the structure of the Politburo membership were instituted. By that time, some of Gorbachev's 1986 appointees to the Politburo had become Gorbachev's strongest political rivals. For example, by 1988 Yegor Ligachev had emerged as the leading conservative (now commonly referred to as the Right) in the CPSU leadership, criticizing many of Gorbachev's initiatives as a threat to traditional Soviet values of Party leadership and socialist development. At the Twenty-eighth Party Congress in July 1990, Ligachev stood as a candidate for deputy head of the CPSU against Gorbachev's nominee, Vladimir

Ivashko. Ligachev lost. At the other end of the spectrum, another Gorbachev appointee, Boris Yel'tsin, emerged in 1989 as the most popular leader in Russia, representing the radical reformist wing of the Party. This reformist group favored more rapid democratization, an attack on the Party's privileges and power monopoly, and a more rapid and thorough marketization of the economy. Oddly enough, in the contemporary Soviet context, this tendency is usually referred to as the Left, presumably since it favors radical change, more autonomy of social forces from the state, and a more thoroughgoing process of democratization. Of course, in the Western European context, this label would hardly make sense, since leftist parties there are more inclined to criticize free-market economics in favor of more social control over the economy. In May 1990, the radical Yel'tsin was chosen by the newly elected representative body in the Russian Republic to be chairman of that republic's supreme soviet. He resigned his Party membership in July 1990. In June 1991, he was elected president of the Russian Republic by direct popular vote, the first popularly elected leader in Russian history. With a 74.7 percent turnout, some 57.3 percent voted for Yel'tsin. The second runner (out of five candidates) was former prime minister of the USSR, Nikolai Ryzhkov, with 16.9 percent of the vote.[4]

Yel'tsin's status and power skyrocketed in late August 1991, when he stepped forward to provide leadership for resistance to the coup d'état that attempted to oust Gorbachev from the post of president. He was hailed both inside and outside the country as the savior of both Russia and the broader democratization process. This event also marked, at least temporarily, an era of new cooperation between Gorbachev and Yel'tsin. On September 3, 1991 Yel'tsin said: "the President has changed. . . . And now I trust him. I trust him entirely, or almost entirely, much more than three weeks ago when he was still capable of maneuvering and meandering. . . . If he continues with the democratic move-

Table 3.1   Politburo of the CPSU—February 10, 1990 (full members)

	Year of Birth	Ethnicity	Other Posts Held	Appointed to Politburo (full membership)
Gorbachev, M. S.	1931	Russian	Secretariat CPSU (General Secretary) Chairman of the USSR Supreme Soviet	October 1980
Ivashko, V. A.	1932	Ukrainian	First Secretary of Ukrainian Communist Party	December 1989
Kriuchkov, V. A.	1924	Russian	Head, KGB	September 1989
Ligachev, E. K.	1920	Russian	Secretariat CPSU	April 1985
Masliukov, Iu. D.	1937	Russian	Chair, State Planning Committee (Gosplan)	September 1989
Medvedev, V. A.	1929	Russian	Secretariat CPSU	September 1988
Ryzhkov, N. I.	1929	Russian	Head, USSR Council of Ministers	April 1985
Shevardnadze, E. A.	1928	Georgian	USSR Foreign Minister	July 1985
Sliunkov, N. N.	1929	Belorussian	Secretariat CPSU	June 1987
Vorotnikov, V. I.	1926	Russian	Chair, Presidium of Russian Republic Supreme Soviet; Deputy Chair, USSR Supreme Soviet	December 1983
Yakovlev, A. N.	1923	Russian	Secretariat CPSU	June 1987

Source: Data compiled by author.

ment and Russia, if he recognizes the independence of all other republics, yes, then his political life will be extended."[5]

From mid-1988 to the present, Gorbachev also proposed (and usually got approval for) numerous changes in state and Party leadership structures. Most of these innovations have made the state organs more independent of the traditional Party apparatus, thus reinforcing a general shift in power from old Party structures to revitalized state organs. Measures taken after the failed coup included suspension of Party activities and a radical shift of power to state structures at the republic level. These changes are discussed in more detail in Chapter 4.

Membership in top state positions also changed throughout Gorbachev's term in office, with a slew of new appointees joining the Council of Ministers from mid-1989 to 1990. Then in late 1990, some of these leading officials were removed and more conservative individuals were appointed, for example, Gennadii Yanayev as vice president, Valentin Pavlov as prime minister, and Boris Pugo as minister of the interior. These figures were among those who later led the coup d'état to remove Gorbachev, the man initially responsible for their appointment. Following the failed coup, Gorbachev judged that, with two exceptions, all of his appointees had proven unreliable, so he recommended removal of the entire government. New leaders were then selected to run the greatly weakened central

Table 3.2 The CPSU Politburo—July 15, 1990

	Year of Birth	Ethnicity	Other Posts Held on July 15, 1990	Major Occupation/ Educational Background
EX OFFICIO MEMBERS (GENERAL SECRETARY, DEPUTY GENERAL SECRETARY, AND HEADS OF UNION REPUBLIC PARTIES)				
Gorbachev, M. S.	1931	Russian	General Secretary of CPSU; President of the USSR	Party functionary/ law, agronomy
Ivashko, V. A.	1932	Ukrainian	Deputy General Secretary of the CPSU	Party functionary/ economist
Burokevicius, M. M.	1927	Lithuanian	Head, Lithuanian Communist Party	Party functionary/ historian
Gumbaridze, G. G.[a]	1945	Georgian	Head, Georgian Communist Party;* People's Deputy of the USSR; Chair, Presidium of Georgian Supreme Soviet*	Party functionary/ government official
Gurenko, S. I.	1936	Ukrainian	Head, Ukrainian Communist Party; People's Deputy of the USSR	Party functionary, government official/ engineer, manager
Karimov, I. A.	1938	Uzbek	Head, Uzbek Communist Party; President of the Uzbek Republic; People's Deputy of the USSR	Government official/ mechanical engineer, economist
Luchinskii, P. K.[b]	1940	Moldavian	Head, Moldavian Communist Party;* People's Deputy of the USSR	Party functionary
Makhkamov, K.	1932	Tadzhik	Head, Tadzhik Communist Party; Chair of Tadzhik Supreme Soviet; People's Deputy of USSR	Government official/ mining specialist

Table 3.2 *(Continued)*

	Year of Birth	Ethnicity	Other Posts Held on July 15, 1990	Major Occupation/ Educational Background
EX OFFICIO MEMBERS (GENERAL SECRETARY, DEPUTY GENERAL SECRETARY, AND HEADS OF UNION REPUBLIC PARTIES)				
Masaliev, A. M.[c]	1933	Kirgiz	Head, Kirgiz Communist Party;* Chair of Kirgiz Supreme Soviet;* People's Deputy of the USSR	Party functionary/ Engineer
Movsisian, V. M.[d]	1933	Armenian	Head, Armenian Communist Party*	Party functionary/ Veterinarian, Agricultural specialist
Mutalibov, A. N. O.	1938	Azeri	Head, Azeri Communist Party; President of Republic of Azerbaidzhan	Government official/ Mechanical engineer, Manager
Nazarbayev, N. A.	1940	Kazakh	Head, Kazakh Communist Party; President of Kazakh Republic; People's Deputy of the USSR	Party functionary/ Technician
Niyazov, S. A.	1940	Turkmen	Head, Turkmen Communist Party; Chair of Turkmen Supreme Soviet; People's Deputy of the USSR	Party functionary/ Physical engineer
Polozkov, I. K.	1935	Russian	Head, Russian Communist Party*	Party functionary/ Agricultural economist
Rubiks, A. P.	1935	Latvian	Head, Latvian Communist Party; People's Deputy of the USSR	Party functionary/ Engineer
Sillari, E. A.[e]	1944	Estonian	Head, Estonian Communist Party (independent branch)	Party functionary/ Engineer
Sokolov, E. E.[f]	1926	Belorussian	Head, Belorussian Communist Party;* People's Deputy of USSR	Party functionary/ Agronomist

Table 3.2   (*Continued*)

	Year of Birth	Ethnicity	Other Posts Held on July 15, 1990	Major Occupation/ Educational Background
OTHERS[8]				
Dzasokhov, A. S.	1934	Ossetian	CPSU Secretariat; USSR People's Deputy	Official in international relations, Party functionary/ Mining specialist
Frolov, I. T.	1929	Russian	Editor-in-Chief of *Pravda*; People's Deputy of the USSR	Editor/Philosopher
Prokofiev, Iu. A.	1939	Russian	Head, Moscow City Party organization	Economist
Semenova, G. N.	1937	Russian	CPSU Secretariat; Editor-in-Chief of *Krest'ianka Peasant Woman*; People's Deputy of the USSR	Editor, journalist
Shenin, O. S.	1937	Russian	CPSU Secretariat; USSR People's Deputy	Party functionary/ Civil engineer
Yanayev, G. I.[h]	1937	Russian	CPSU Secretariat;* Chair, All-Union Central Council of Trade Unions;* USSR People's Deputy	Party functionary/ Agricultural specialist
Stroyev, E. S.	1937	Russian	CPSU Secretariat; USSR People's Deputy	Party functionary/ Agronomist

*These individuals were removed or resigned from the post indicated between July 15, 1990, and the failed coup attempt (August 19–21, 1991).

[a]Removed in January 1991, because he was no longer head of the Georgian party organization. He was not replaced on the Politburo.

[b]Luchinskii was added to the CPSU Secretariat in 1991 and remained on the Politburo even when he was no longer head of the Moldavian Communist Party organization. G. I. Eremei, his successor in that post, was added to the Politburo (April 1991).

[c]Replaced by D. B. Amanbaev (April 1991).

[d]Replaced by S. K. Pogosian (January 1991).

[e]An additional Estonian, L. E. Annus, representing the Estonian Party based on the CPSU platform, was added in January 1991.

[f]Replaced by A. A. Malofeev (January 1991).

[8]M. S. Surkov was added in April 1991, representing the All-Union Army Party Committee, and P. K. Luchinskii was kept on as part of the "other" category when he was replaced as Moldavian Party head.

[h]Elected vice president of the USSR by the CPD in December; removed from the CPSU Politburo and Secretariat in January 1991.

state structures. These were generally individuals who had proven themselves loyal to the president and to the new constitutional order during the abortive coup.

In 1989 and the early months of 1990, new, younger leaders were also taking on leadership posts in some major Soviet cities as a result of competitive elections for local soviets. These individuals, largely untainted by former connections with the ruling CPSU apparatus, are highly popular and may form the basis for the future generation of Soviet leaders. They would be likely candidates to succeed Gorbachev and his allies in top leadership posts in the 1990s. Although most of these individuals have been Party members, several resigned from the CPSU in July 1990. Among these younger leaders are Gavriil Popov, a radical economist selected mayor of Moscow by the newly elected Moscow soviet in the spring of 1990; his deputy mayor Sergei Stankevich, a historian; and the mayor of Leningrad, Anatolii Sobchak, a lawyer and outspoken reformer.

At various times since 1985, Westerners have speculated that Gorbachev's own position as top leader might be in jeopardy, either from opposing forces in the elite or due to his declining popularity among the population at large. For example, preceding the important Twenty-eighth Party Congress, speculation was rife that fellow Politburo member Yegor Ligachev, representing conservatives in the Party, might stand against Gorbachev for election to the top Party post. At the plenum in late April 1991, heavy criticism from Central Committee members led Gorbachev himself to raise the question of his own resignation; the suggestion was decisively rejected by the Politburo and the plenum. At each stage Gorbachev has been able to adjust his position to placate a sufficient portion of the elite. At the same time, his popularity among the general population has declined dramatically. Gorbachev's more radical rival, Boris Yel'tsin, clearly has maintained a higher popularity rating than Gorbachev. After the failed coup d'état in August 1991, power seemed to shift radically to Yel'tsin, and some observers declared Gorbachev's political career over. At this writing, these predictions have not materialized. For as the Soviet Union seemed on the verge of disintegration, no other member of the elite was able to present himself as a viable alternative national leader. It quickly became evident that Yel'tsin's role as president of Russia might well bring him into conflict with the interests of other national groups—he could not simultaneously be the "savior" of the Russian people and also protect the interests of Russia's neighboring republics. At this writing, however, Gorbachev's future role as president as well as the durability of the union he hopes to lead remain unclear.

The Gorbachev Era: A Periodization

In this section, we chart changes in the Gorbachev era by dividing it roughly into periods marked by important shifts in the reform program. We do not have the benefit of hindsight, which allows historians to delineate the key turning points in social and political development, but we attempt to lay out a preliminary road map for understanding the progression of change in the Soviet system since 1985.

Consolidation of Support: March 1985 to Early 1986

In its initial phase, *perestroika* was largely an economic program. When Gorbachev assumed his new post, he recognized that the Soviet economy was not performing well and that its improvement depended on streamlining the top-heavy centralized planning system, improving incentives for workers and enterprises, and upgrading the technological base of Soviet industry. Although Gorbachev supported economic decentralization and increased enterprise autonomy, he did not advocate a shift from state ownership as the basic property form. In addition, his attitude toward flexible prices and market principles was unclear.

The restructuring of the economy was to provide the foundation for economic acceleration, which would in turn allow an improved standard of living. Slow economic growth and poor quality production had eroded the tacit social contract of the Brezhnev period. Gorbachev recognized that continued social harmony depended on a better quality of life for the average citizen. This would require not only increased production of a wide variety of high-quality consumer goods but also a rise in agricultural output (to improve the Soviet diet), better and more housing, higher-quality health care, and expanded public services (e.g., day care, laundries, restaurants, and public transport). Without such improvements, worker motivation would remain low and social ills, such as alcoholism, black market activities, petty theft, and absenteeism, would grow.

In the early months, the Gorbachev government affirmed its support for the ambitious Food Program announced in 1982 and enunciated a comprehensive program for developing consumer goods production and the service sphere. Despite the optimistic goals set out in these documents, however, methods proposed to realize these targets were modest and marked no real deviation from past policy.

The commitment to simultaneously raising the standard of living and achieving economic acceleration through technological upgrading may have been misguided in this early phase. Because economic growth has been such a strong priority of Soviet policy over the decades, Gorbachev may have felt compelled to make growth (or acceleration) a regime priority to ensure support for his program among the political elite. Investment funds were limited, however, and were inadequate both for major improvements in the consumer sector and for technological innovation in the industrial sector. Furthermore, any real structural reform in the economy would produce temporary dislocations that would most likely reduce, rather than increase, the short-term rate of economic growth.

By emphasizing both economic growth and an improved standard of living, Gorbachev raised people's expectations, but without having a viable reform program capable of fulfilling those hopes. The new Soviet leadership confronted a vicious circle: economic improvement demanded cooperation from the people, which would be hard to win until the reform program showed results. As long as persistent shortages continued to be the only "reward" for effort in the workplace, Soviet citizens were unlikely to exert themselves to make a new economic model succeed.

To gain public support and spur better quality work, Gorbachev continued Andropov's campaign to root out corruption and eliminate unearned incomes. Gorbachev repeatedly criticized *leveling*, the policy of reducing income differentials pursued by the Brezhnev leadership. He emphasized that hard work merited high reward. Thus, income differentials should increase to provide an incentive to productive citizens. In attacking pervasive corruption, Gorbachev also hoped to reestablish a link between honest effort and reward. Corruption and illegal activities had made it difficult to inculcate a work ethic and had undermined popular belief in the fairness of the system. The new leadership needed to demonstrate that corruption would be tolerated neither among the elite nor at the base of society. Extensive publicity was given to the punishment of high officials for illegal acts. Several ministers and regional Party leaders were removed from office after public chastisement for mismanagement, graft, or nepotism.

The average Soviet worker also was reprimanded for absenteeism, late arrival at work, drunkenness, and petty theft. In May 1985, the Central Committee endorsed aggressive measures to fight alcoholism. At the Party Congress in February and March 1986, consumption of alcoholic beverages was prohibited, and it was reportedly difficult for delegates to find a drink. Alcohol abuse was blamed for poor work discipline, industrial accidents, a rising divorce rate, and a decline in male life expectancy from 66 years in the mid-1960s to an estimated 61.9 years by the mid-1980s.[6] The antialcohol campaign was, however, largely unsuccessful. It stimulated the widespread production of moonshine, spurred resentment against the government, and eliminated an important source of government revenues derived from taxes on alcoholic beverages. Rather than reducing illegal economic activity and black market production, the antialcohol campaign reinforced these tendencies. In this way, it undermined other key components of Gorbachev's reform package. These problems led the government largely to abandon the campaign.

Despite Gorbachev's ambitious goals, other early policy changes only tinkered with the existing system (for example, experiments with increased enterprise autonomy in certain industries and the reorganization of bureaucratic agencies). Even these limited measures faced considerable resistance from conservative elements in the Party apparatus and in the state economic structures.

On the political front, Gorbachev's program had not yet crystallized. We previously discussed the massive personnel changes he oversaw. In an important symbolic gesture, Gorbachev signaled his intention to revive Khrushchev's interrupted agenda of de-Stalinization. He scheduled the opening of the Twenty-seventh Party Congress for February 25, 1986, thirty years to the day after the opening of the Twentieth Party Congress, at which Khrushchev presented his historic Secret Speech. At the same time, Gorbachev also distanced himself from some of Khrushchev's more utopian goals. When Khrushchev's 1961 Party program was revised under Gorbachev's guidance at the Party congress in February and March 1986, the new document no longer foresaw the withering away of the state, economic parity with the United States, or a transition to communism in the near future (although communism was maintained as a long-term goal). The new document reflected a more pragmatic, commonsense approach.

In commenting on the document, Gorbachev pointed "first of all, to the continuing of the basic theoretical and political aims of the CPSU." He made repeated references to Lenin's views in explaining the revisions. In the same speech, Gorbachev pinpointed his understanding of the key notion in the new program: "Using acceleration of the country's social and economic development to achieve a qualitatively new state of Soviet society . . . the Party proceeds from the decisive role of the economy in the development of society."[7] These statements suggested that political development was to take a backseat to economic and social change. While the Party document referred to advances in Soviet democracy and increased public involvement in administration and decision making, these goals had secondary status. This emphasis on socioeconomic change as the key to progress was fully in accord with past Soviet orthodoxy. The program also did not challenge fundamental economic structures or alter the Party's traditional focus on scientific and technological advancement as the motor of social progress.

By the middle of 1986, Gorbachev had not revealed his priorities, nor had he enunciated a well-thought-out package to realize the multiple goals he supported in the economic sphere. He did, however, increasingly acknowledge that economic reform could not occur without some more fundamental changes in Soviet society itself. This in turn led to the next phase of *perestroika*.

The Eruption of Glasnost': *Spring 1986 to Mid-1987*

If economics was at the forefront of *perestroika* in the first phase, by early 1987 the process had taken on a more distinctively political tone. The first step in this transition was Gorbachev's enunciation of and commitment to glasnost'. Often mistaken for a Western conception of free speech, glasnost' actually means "openness" or "publicity." It was in late 1986 to early 1987 that glasnost' took on importance in the Soviet reform process. Controls on the media were eased, eliciting a barrage of public discussion and criticism covering most aspects of Soviet history, culture, and policy. Over time, the limits on public debate receded even further. By 1989, data on Soviet policy failures, environmental degradation, health hazards, accidents, levels of poverty, drug use, prostitution, and crime became everyday fare in the Soviet press. By 1990, even the top political leadership was subject to open public criticism and Lenin himself was under attack.

Why did Gorbachev endorse glasnost'? Again we confront the difficult question of Gorbachev's motives. In the short term, glasnost' offered Gorbachev strategic advantages. To pursue more radical economic reform, he needed a broader base of political support for his reform program. While he had some allies among those he had appointed to Party and state posts, they were not powerful enough to counter the resistance posed by the entrenched Party/state apparatus. To whom could Gorbachev look?

The group to benefit most from glasnost' was the intelligentsia, that more highly educated stratum whose livelihood and satisfaction derive from self-expression. Writers, journalists, artists, and social scientists, whose business it is to write and express themselves publicly, were immediately able to reap the benefits of the new openness. Furthermore, they often tried to mobilize public opinion in support of perestroika's broader program. In June 1986, on the eve of the Soviet Union's Writers' Congress, Gorbachev met informally with a group of prominent Soviet writers and appealed to them for support. Prominent reform-minded social scientists such as Tatiana Zaslavskaia (a sociologist) and Abel Aganbegian (an economist) also were brought on board. They were encouraged to publicly state their criticisms of the old economic structures and in this way to help mobilize public opinion behind Gorbachev's efforts.

Once initiated, however, glasnost' was not a tool that Gorbachev could easily control. A whole new public culture was in the making. The media were no longer simply a mouthpiece for the leadership; they took on an independent character of their own and soon presented diverse and conflicting viewpoints. At the same time, the official cultural organizations (for example, the Union of Cinematographers and parts of the theater industry) elected new leaders who were often (but not always) champions of artistic freedom and glasnost'. Cultural figures often were willing to challenge publicly the old shibboleths of Soviet ideology.

Glasnost' mobilized the intelligentsia, as well as a portion of public opinion, in support of perestroika. It also made the Soviet media more attractive to the average citizen. Suddenly there was some real news in Izvestiia (which means "news" in Russian). Other publications, which took even bolder stands, became even more popular. Through glasnost', Gorbachev sought to regain credibility for the leadership and the media, and in this way to cement support for his program. By early 1987, lines formed at Soviet news kiosks early in the morning, as eager Soviet citizens competed to buy the limited copies of some of the more provocative publications. (These included Ogonek, a weekly magazine, and the weekly newspapers Argumenty i fakty and Moskovskie novosti, the latter of which is published in English as Moscow News). As Gail Lapidus put it, Gorbachev hoped to substitute "voice" for "exit," drawing the Soviet population back into the political dialogue and reducing the appeal of both emigration and dissent.[8]

In late April 1986, a major accident occurred at the Chernobyl nuclear power plant some fifty miles north of Kiev, the capital of the Ukrainian Republic. In the first days, Soviet authorities did not reveal the occurrence or scope of the accident. Elevated radiation levels were first made public in Sweden. Gradually, the Soviets released more information about the tragedy, which spread a wave of radiation over the western portion of the Soviet Union and much of Europe. After several days, residents were evacuated from the surrounding regions, but later evidence suggested that these actions were too late and too little. The accident will have as yet unknown consequences for the health of the local population.

The Chernobyl accident helped activate a broad-ranging and active grassroots movement targeted not only at nuclear power plants but also at other polluting installations. It also helped push glasnost' forward by activating the public's demand for accurate and timely information and by reinforcing public skepticism of official reassurances. In April 1990, one deputy to the Supreme Soviet asserted that the Chernobyl accident had brought about an irreversible change in the people's mental and psychological state.[9] The occurrence was a human tragedy, but it also imposed an economic burden on the new Gorbachev regime, a burden that was the result of decades of mismanagement.

In endorsing glasnost', Gorbachev, purposefully or not, helped trigger social conflict that he would soon be unable to control. By early 1987, it was clear that those opposing some of Gorbachev's key initiatives would be allowed expression. But the lingering question of Gorbachev's motives remained. According to one interpretation, Gorbachev was using glasnost' mainly as a tool to achieve other ends—for example, to muster public support for his attacks on the entrenched bureaucratic apparatus. Adherents of this view emphasized that controls on the press could be just as quickly enforced as they were lifted. Other observers viewed Gorbachev's initiatives more sympathetically. They

saw him as gradually pursuing a radical vision in which glasnost' was but a first step, which in turn would generate support for more broad-ranging political and economic change.

We may never be able to determine Gorbachev's initial motives in easing controls on public discussion, for soon glasnost' activated social sentiments and movements that were no longer susceptible to easy control from above. By the end of 1990, one heard voices from the Soviet Union lamenting an excess of glasnost'. The Soviet citizen was hearing too much that was negative about his or her society and saw too little hope for solutions. Illusions of the past had been destroyed, but no new vision was strong enough to replace them.

The Conservative Backlash and the Response: Mid-1987 to Fall 1988

Despite Gorbachev's success in placing his supporters in key posts in the state and Party structures, there was much opposition to his reform program both within the Party/state apparatus and among the population at large. With glasnost', the prevailing value system was placed in question. Previous Soviet leaders, especially Stalin and Brezhnev, were subject to increasingly sharp public criticism, and traditional claims about the superiority of the Soviet system were belied by the rash of unfavorable information published about Soviet society. Furthermore, people felt unsure about their own positions: would cutbacks in bureaucratic structures mean losing one's position? Having experienced the upheavals of the Stalinist and Khrushchev periods, some individuals were anxious in the face of the vigorous public attacks on corruption and lax work habits.

Party officials, beneficiaries of the Brezhnev era, feared demotion and saw the values they had espoused (and perhaps believed in) placed in question. Their fears were likely reinforced in

January 1987, when, at a key speech before a Central Committee plenum, Gorbachev identified *demokratizatsiia* as an essential component of *perestroika*. He also proposed the selection of Party officials in competitive (intra-Party) elections.[10] Furthermore, at the June 1987 plenum of the Communist Party Central Committee, Gorbachev gained acceptance of an economic reform package that foresaw an increasing role for enterprise autonomy and a decreasing role for both central (ministerial) economic authorities and the Party apparatus. In this context, it is not surprising that resistance to *perestroika* surfaced once *glasnost'* revealed the weaknesses in the Soviet system.

At first, the conservative backlash appeared to moderate Gorbachev's own tempo of change. There was speculation in the summer of 1987 that Gorbachev was losing control when he failed to appear in public for fifty-two days. (He was apparently on vacation and also writing his book *Perestroika: New Thinking for Our Country and the World.*) When he resurfaced, Gorbachev was soon confronted by a minor political crisis when Boris Yel'tsin, a Gorbachev appointee to candidate membership on the Politburo (and simultaneously head of the Moscow Party organization), issued an unprecedented attack on Party privilege at a Central Committee meeting. Yel'tsin's comments elicited a strong reaction from Party conservatives. In November 1987, Yel'tsin was removed as Moscow Party head and subsequently from his position on the Politburo. Gorbachev failed to support Yel'tsin's more radical position, but when the affair became public, Yel'tsin's cause gained broad support. He was seen as a victim of old Party methods. Only later was he allowed to explain his side of the story publicly. On November 2, 1987, as noted before, Gorbachev's speech on the seventieth anniversary of the October 1917 revolution was deemed by reformist elements of the intelligentsia to be tepid and timid in its assessment of Stalinism. Thus, it appeared that Gorbachev himself was retreating in the face of conservative opposition.

On March 13, 1988, the next skirmish began. A Leningrad chemistry teacher, Nina Andreyeva, submitted a letter to a conservative weekly, *Sovetskaia Rossiia*. Andreyeva probably did not write the letter herself. Conservative professors of Marxism-Leninism in Leningrad, discontented with the more radical turn of the reforms, may have been the ghostwriters, hoping to give the letter more popular legitimacy if it appeared to come from an "average" citizen. Entitled "I Cannot Forgo My Principles," the piece provided a defense of Stalinism, with overtones of anti-Semitism and xenophobia.[11]

Party conservatives (perhaps including Yegor Ligachev) used the letter's publication as an opportunity to propagate their views. The letter was reprinted in other media around the country. When there was no immediate response from Gorbachev and the reform leadership, apprehension and fear grew that the letter had official support and marked a change of course. Finally, on April 5, 1988, a refutation appeared in the official Party newspaper *Pravda*, reaffirming the Party's reformist path. From that point, the tide seemed to turn again in favor of reform. At the special Party conference held in June 1988, Gorbachev enunciated a broad-ranging program of *demokratizatsiia*. The political dimension of *perestroika* was now taking command.

Perestroika *of the Political System: Summer 1988 to January 1990*

From June 28 to July 1, 1988, a specially convened Nineteenth Party Conference was held to further the process of *perestroika*. In practice, however, the conference saw Gorbachev retake the initiative and push forward a broad-ranging package of political reform, which was confirmed in December 1988 through constitutional amendments passed by the formal state legislative authority, the Supreme Soviet. These changes saw the creation of a whole new structure of state representative organs, which we discuss in detail in Chapter 4. A real representative body was established, to be chosen largely on the basis of contested, competitive elections.

The first elections for the body occurred in March 1989, and the first meeting of the new representative body (the Congress of People's Deputies, or CPD) opened on May 25, 1989. A smaller working parliament (the Supreme Soviet) was selected from it and convened on June 9, 1989. These innovations marked the beginning of broad changes in virtually all Soviet political institutions. Subsequent aspects of the reform included formation of a Committee on Constitutional Review; establishment of the new post of president of the USSR; and the adoption of new, more liberal legislation and regulations dealing with, for example, the press, criminal justice, citizen appeals of administrative decisions, the electoral system, and public organizations (including political parties).

In the face of widespread ethnic unrest and local political activism (discussed in Chapter 5), the continued existence of Soviet federalism also was put in question. New laws on the local economy and local self-management and on the division of powers between central and republic-level organs were adopted over the next two years. This legislation legitimized and attempted to institutionalize processes of political decentralization that were occurring de facto in the face of popular pressure. Local and republic authorities in many parts of the country were demanding (and in some cases trying to seize) control over economic planning functions, ownership of natural resources, and increased autonomy in establishing linguistic and cultural policy. The Soviet Union, under Gorbachev's guidance, was embarking on an experiment in *demokratizatsiia*. *Perestroika* now took on a political face, which, according to many commentators, made the process irreversible. As with *glasnost'*, Gorbachev initiated *demokratizatsiia* but has been largely unable to control its effects or progression.

Under Gorbachev's guidance, the CPSU itself embarked on a process of transformation. In late September 1988, Gorbachev was able to consolidate his position further when the Central Committee plenum approved additional changes in the membership of the Politburo. In April of 1989, at another Central Committee plenum, 122 members of the Central Committee and Central Inspection Commission resigned. Many of these were the so-called dead souls, holdovers who had originally had seats in the body by virtue of positions they had held in other political bodies (for example, as first secretaries of regional Party organizations). They had subsequently been removed from these posts but had retained their positions in the Central Committee, since the membership of that body is normally changed only at the regular Party congress held every five years. With Gorbachev's support, it was decided to hold the next regular Party congress in 1990, one year before its regularly scheduled time. This would presumably allow Gorbachev to put in place a more reform-minded Central Committee and gain stronger Party support for his agenda.

At Party meetings, Gorbachev urged the Party to reduce its involvement in the day-to-day functioning of government and to rely primarily on ideological leadership and persuasion. As noted, in early 1987 he proposed competitive elections for lower Party offices. This policy would undermine the hold of Party officialdom on the political recruitment process; it was not endorsed by the Central Committee at that time. In November 1988, the central Party apparatus was restructured, reducing the number of paid employees and eliminating the central Party structures that paralleled the top state organs.

By late 1989, pressure was mounting for the CPSU to give up its constitutional monopoly on political power. One of the most vocal advocates of this viewpoint was the late Andrei Sakharov, prominent physicist and former Soviet dissident. Sakharov had been exiled to the city of Gor'kii (now given its previous name, Nizhnii

Novgorod) from January 1980 until Gorbachev personally informed him of his release on December 15, 1986. Sakharov had been elected a member of the CPD (as a representative of the prestigious Academy of Sciences) and had become a leading spokesperson for more radical voices in the new Soviet parliament. Sakharov did not live to see his democratic vision of Soviet society realized. (He suffered an untimely death on December 14, 1989, and was deeply mourned by broad segments of the Soviet population.) Nonetheless, it was a striking testimony to the change that had already occurred in Soviet politics to see the head of the CPSU, Mr. Gorbachev, publicly debating Mr. Sakharov on the floor of the CPD. In 1984, one could have only imagined such a scene in a fantastic work of political fiction. By 1989, the drama was played out in real life before the Soviet citizenry.

Other signs of the increasingly tenuous position of the CPSU included the withdrawal of the Lithuanian branch of the Party from the CPSU in December 1989. In forming an independent political party (leaving a smaller "loyalist" party behind), the Lithuanian communists drove the first wedge in the top-down unity of the CPSU. Other republic party organizations were to follow this path—the Estonian in March 1990 and the Latvian in April 1990. In January 1990, Gorbachev had not yet accepted the notion that the CPSU should allow other parties, but in reality they were already in existence within the communist movement itself and also growing spontaneously in the fertile soil of *glasnost'*.

At the same time, the economic reform was halting and generally unsuccessful. The Law on the State Enterprise, which took force in January 1987, contained the major elements of Gorbachev's conception for decentralizing the state-run economy. In practice, however, implementation of the law was sporadic and inhibited by the strong power of the central economic organs. It was law on paper only, not in practice. The economic situation in the country was deteriorating, a process that has intensified right up to

the writing of this chapter. A new Law on Cooperatives, adopted in May 1988, did allow the establishment of small nonstate enterprises, which it was hoped would help to fill in gaps primarily in the consumer and service sector. Although the number of cooperatives increased over time, the prices they charged often were considered exorbitant by the average Soviet consumer, engendering resentment among the population at large. Conservative local officials often placed obstacles in the paths of the new cooperatives, making it difficult for them to function. Many cooperatives also were subject to extortion from a growing Soviet "mafia."

During this time, Gorbachev began talking about long-term leasing of land to farmers and thus about the revival of some sort of family farming. The NEP of the 1920s offered an increasingly appealing model to reform-minded economists. Proposals to diversify ownership types in the countryside materialized in legislation on land and property in early 1990. The question still remained whether Soviet farmers would take the initiative, given the country's history of failed reforms and policy reversals. The personal costs of failure might be high, while the status quo offered the peasant predictability and minimal security. Local officials in some areas were not sympathetic to the trend toward privatization in agriculture. By March 1991, however, some form of private land ownership had been endorsed by the parliaments of the Baltic republics, the Russian Republic, Ukraine, Armenia, and Moldavia.

By early 1990, none of the efforts to revive state structures or to develop a legalized nonstate sector had produced marked benefits for the Soviet consumer and worker. Although wages did rise minimally, shortages of goods intensified. Basic commodities such as sugar and soap were rationed in many areas of the country, and the gap between buying power and available goods continued to grow. As the official economy failed to perform adequately, the target of Andropov's and Gorbachev's early reforms, corruption and semilegal markets, became even more important mechanisms for the distribution of goods.

Social tensions also were rising. During the summer of 1989, more than ten thousand coal miners in the Siberian Kuzbass region went on strike. They were joined by miners from the Donbass region of Ukraine and Vorkuta in Siberia. Their grievances went beyond traditional workplace concerns to include demands for worker self-management in the mines, formation of independent trade unions, an improvement in consumer goods and food supplies, replacement of local Party officials, the closure of cooperative enterprises, and the repeal of Article 6 of the Soviet constitution (the constitutional foundation for CPSU dominance). (One wonders whether the lack of soap might have been the final straw!) Gorbachev initially praised the miners for taking the initiative to improve their own situation, and the government made broad-ranging promises to the miners to bring an end to the strike. These promises were largely unfulfilled by the summer of 1990, bringing a further rash of short strikes, this time with a more radical tenor. Over time, the authorities became less enamored of the workers' independent strikes, as the interruption in coal production threatened, in combination with other factors (such as a growing antinuclear movement), to create energy shortages.

Social groups sprang up surrounding other issues, especially in protest of environmental deterioration. Under popular pressure, dozens of productive enterprises were closed because of excessive pollution. This in turn caused shortfalls in the production of some goods (e.g., paper, pharmaceuticals, and energy) and reinforced the shortage conditions in the economy.

During the summer and fall of 1988, the Soviet Union's diverse ethnic population began to make itself felt. Popular movements for national self-determination emerged most quickly and strongly in the three small Baltic republics of Estonia, Latvia, and Lithuania but were soon to follow in other regions as well. At first Gor-

Source: *Argumenty i fakty*, no. 32 (August 1990), p. 5.

bachev applauded these fledgling organizations, seeing in them popular support of his struggle against entrenched bureaucratic interests. Over time, however, it became clear that the Baltic popular fronts ultimately wanted real state independence for each of the Baltic republics, a goal that Gorbachev could not countenance.

On November 16, 1988, the Estonian Supreme Soviet issued a declaration of sovereignty, reinforcing it with an amendment to its republic constitution that limited the applicability of all-Union legislative acts in Estonia. Gorbachev immediately proclaimed these provisions unconstitutional and was supported in his position by the USSR Supreme Soviet. Other than use of brute force (which Gorbachev rejected at that time), there was no way to enforce these proclamations. Likewise, no legitimate mechanisms existed to adjudicate such disputes between the center and the periphery. Similar disagreements followed between the central authorities and the republic authorities in Latvia and Lithuania.

Each of the three republics also declared its own indigenous language the official state language and restored the old national flags. On August 8, 1989, the Estonian Supreme Soviet adopted residency requirements for voting, in effect disenfranchising those who had recently moved to the republic and challenging the notion of a common Soviet citizenship. The measure represented a surrogate for establishment of actual Estonian state citizenship, which was a logical extension of the republic's commitment to independence. The action then elicited strikes among non-Estonian workers (mostly Russians) in the republic. The law was declared unconstitutional by the central Supreme Soviet, and its application was suspended by the Estonian government.

Support for national sovereignty in the Baltic republics was reinforced by the results of local and republic elections held from December 1989 through March 1990. Candidates of the popular front organizations won decisive victories, setting these republics on a clear collision course with Moscow. In the Baltics, communist power, even of the independent communist bodies that had split from the CPSU, was on the wane. The process culminated in Lithuania's declaration of independence, which occurred on March 11, 1990. This action elicited a major national crisis, discussed in Chapter 5.

At the same time, ethnic tensions were rising elsewhere in the Soviet Union. The two republics of Armenia and Azerbaidzhan became embroiled in a sometimes violent conflict over the status of a small region in the Azerbaidzhan Republic called Nagorno-Karabakh. In 1989, 77 percent of the population of 189,000 was of Armenian ethnic origin, although the region is surrounded by regions inhabited predominantly by Azeris (the indigenous population group in Azerbaidzhan). Following a decision made in February 1988 by the local soviet in Nagorno-Karabakh, on June 15, 1988 the Supreme Soviet of the Armenian Republic supported demands that the region be joined to the Armenian Republic. The Azerbaidzhan government objected, and the Armenian demand was rejected by the central Soviet authorities.

An earthquake in Armenia in December 1988 claimed an estimated twenty-five thousand lives. This even further accentuated the crisis, as it imposed major economic hardship, made the care of refugees from Nagorno-Karabakh more difficult, and increased the Armenians' sense of threat. In the face of sometimes bloody confrontations between Armenians and Azeris, Nagorno-Karabakh was temporarily placed under special rule from Moscow from January 1989 until the end of November 1989. This measure did not defuse tensions, however, and when the region returned to its previous status (with some greater role for Armenian input and leadership), tensions again mounted.

Subsequent conflicts between other Soviet nationalities (for example, between the Georgians and the Abkhaz population; the Moldavians and the Gagauz, a Turkic-speaking minority; and the Uzbeks and the Kirgiz in Central Asia) suggested that ethnic rivalries could not be solved simply by decentralization of power. Resentment against Russian dominance has combined with conflicts (often predating Soviet rule) between neighboring ethnic groups to produce a complicated and volatile situation, especially in the southern regions of the country.

Meanwhile, national self-assertion was rearing its head in the Soviet Union's allied states in Eastern Europe. (These developments are discussed in detail in Part VIII). Under the influence of Gorbachev's reforms, restrictions on public debate and organization were eased even further in Hungary and Poland, so that by the end of 1989, the monopoly of communist power had been destroyed in these countries. In late 1989, Gorbachev apparently made clear to the other Eastern European leaders that he would not allow Soviet troops to support suppression of indigenous democratic movements. In rapid succession, the communist regimes in the German Democratic Republic (GDR), Czechoslovakia, Romania, and Bulgaria confronted broad-based popular opposition in the form of massive demonstrations and rallies. By January 1990, a noncommunist government headed Poland; the Hungarian and Polish communist parties had dissolved and reconstituted themselves as social democratic parties; the Socialist Unity Party in the GDR had seen a complete turnover in leadership and was seeking noncommunist forces as coalition partners (in March 1990, the party would be voted out of office, leading to a rapid process of national unification with West Germany); the Communist Party in Czechoslovakia had lost its hold on power; and the Communist government led by Nicolae Ceauşescu in Romania had fallen.

The rapidity of these developments stunned observers in both East and West. Combined with Soviet concessions in arms reductions, they created an even stronger groundswell of popular support for Gorbachev's reform efforts among the Western public. Particularly in sanctioning the dismantling of the Berlin Wall, Gorbachev provided tangible evidence of his commitment to a more open, democratic approach. Broadly supported by the Soviet population, Gorbachev's Eastern European policy bolstered domestic demands for self-determination and free emigration rights in the Soviet Union itself. (To be sure, it also raised alarm in some sectors and elicited fear of the possible threat posed by German unification.) In the face of the Lithuanian challenge, Gorbachev had to draw a clear line between what would be permitted to the sovereign peoples of Eastern Europe and what would be allowed for the formally "sovereign" republics of the Soviet federation. Whereas previously Gorbachev's *perestroika* was at the vanguard of

political reform in the Soviet bloc, by the beginning of 1990, the USSR was already lagging behind several of its Eastern European allies in the process of democratization and economic transformation. This was just one of the many contradictions facing Gorbachev as he entered the new decade.

By the beginning of 1990, the political and economic crisis in the USSR had reached proportions that were unprecedented in recent Soviet history. In unleashing *glasnost'* and *demokratizatsiia*, Gorbachev had hoped to provide a political foundation for his program of economic restructuring and in this way further his own agenda. In the process, however, he had lifted the lid on a tangle of interconnected social and economic tensions. Gorbachev argued to Party conservatives that the present crisis was a product of decades of misguided policies and that it was impossible to return to the status quo ante; therefore, the process of radical reform had to be pushed even further if the crisis was to be overcome.

Toward Multiparty Pluralism or a Return to Authoritarianism? February 1990 to August 1991

Gorbachev had made a habit of changing his mind. In December 1989, he had rejected the notion of rescinding the CPSU's monopoly on political power; in February 1990 he staked his personal position on achieving that goal. At its meeting in that month, the Central Committee, after heated debate and strong persuasion by Gorbachev, endorsed an amendment to the Soviet constitution removing the clause (Article 6) that confirmed single-party rule. As in the past, Gorbachev sensed that a radical gesture was required to abate popular discontent and distrust. Gorbachev won some time. The change was formally adopted by the CPD in March 1990, and by the end of the Twenty-eighth Party Congress in July 1990, the CPSU was already facing the prospect of a major rupture. Radical reformists such as Boris Yel'tsin, Gavriil Popov, and Anatolii Sobchak quit the CPSU; other disgruntled Party members announced their intention to quit and form an alternative party. While Gorbachev criticized these actions, they seemed fully consonant with the direction set in February 1990, and shortly thereafter the CPSU leader himself issued a decree sanctioning the creation of independent press organs, seemingly reinforcing the general direction of change set by the radicals.

Local elections throughout the USSR in late 1989 and early 1990 (both for republic and lower-level organs) strengthened the position of radical forces in many areas as well. Moscow, Leningrad (now St. Petersburg), Sverdlovsk (now Yekaterinburg), Kiev, Minsk, and other cities were put in the hands of newly elected soviets, which in turn chose reform-minded mayors who were strongly supportive of further democratization, economic decentralization, and market reform. On May 29, 1990, the newly elected Supreme Soviet of the largest federal unit in the Soviet Union, the Russian Republic, elected Yel'tsin as its head. He articulated a program of republic sovereignty, market reform, and a rapid shift from Party to popular rule. In most of the union republics, nationalist forces gained support, putting pressure on the center to cede economic and political authority to the regions. The future political unity of the country was put in jeopardy.

Despite Gorbachev's efforts to push *demokratizatsiia* in the Party, the CPSU lagged behind. A newly formed Russian branch of the CPSU elected a conservative (Ivan Polozkov) as its leader on June 23, 1990 (he resigned the post in the summer of 1991), and many reform-minded communists in Russia wondered whether they could, in good conscience, remain in the Party. In the early months of 1990, the pace of resignations from the Party increased dramatically. At the Twenty-eighth Party Congress, Gorbachev headed off conservative resis-

tance, but the congress did not push reform further. Large parts of the Soviet public began to view the Party as irrelevant and had little interest in the congress. The real political action was occurring elsewhere, in the local government bodies or in non-Party public organizations.

For the time being, Gorbachev remained head of the CPSU, but he supported a shift in power from Party to state organs. He lobbied for and was elected to fill the new office of president of the USSR in March 1990, establishing a center of status and authority separate from the CPSU. Speculation was rife in the early months of 1990 that Gorbachev might bail out of the top Party post and concentrate his efforts on his new position as president. His failure to do so by mid-1991 apparently reflected his concern that this might cause a dangerous polarization between a more conservative CPSU and the more radical elements in the new state structures and in new groupings splintering off from the CPSU. Furthermore, the Party still commanded considerable power in many areas, particularly in the less urbanized parts of Russia.

The summer of 1990 also saw an intensification of the economic crisis (shortages increased, affecting real staples such as bread as well as luxury "staples" such as cigarettes). Shelves in state-run grocery stores were nearly bare. In the face of this crisis, a shift in the focus of economic reform occurred. Gorbachev and his economic advisers articulated stronger support for radical market measures, including the breakup of monopolistic state enterprises, accelerated steps toward convertibility of the ruble, and support for a variety of ownership forms (including non–state-owned enterprises) in both the industrial and agricultural sectors. Passage of new laws on land, property, and the state enterprise in early 1990 laid the legal groundwork for the economic transition. The leaders seemed uncertain, however, about the proper policy on pricing, as strong resistance to proposed price increases on bread led to their withdrawal.

In July 1990, the head of the Russian Repub-

Shortages and Their Effects

The Cigarette Riots

Annual Soviet consumption of cigarettes is estimated at 480 billion, or approximately 2,800 cigarettes per adult Soviet citizen. In the summer of 1990, a shortage of cigarettes resulted in riots in many large Soviet cities, an explosion of black market prices, the introduction of ration cards, and the expenditure, by central and local governments, of scarce hard currency for the purchase of cigarettes abroad. The popular response to the cigarette shortage was more explosive than public reaction to shortages of other, seemingly more essential goods.

Ironically, 1990 saw record crops of tobacco in the Soviet Union, but harvesting and transport were interrupted by ethnic strife in Transcaucasia. In addition, most cigarette factories in the Russian Republic were closed due to equipment failure or lack of filters, rolling paper, or hard currency to purchase cellulose acetate, an essential filter ingredient not produced in the Soviet Union. Imports from Bulgaria were down due to domestic problems there and disputes with the Soviet Union over payments. Finally, an agreement with the two largest U.S. producers, RJR Nabisco and Philip Morris Co., promised to bring in 34 billion cigarettes in the next year. Nonetheless, the smokers, suffering acute nicotine withdrawal, were indignant and sometimes aggressive.

Sources: Adapted from "Smokers' Revolt Succeeds in Moscow," *New York Times*, 23 August 1990, p. A3; and "In Moscow, Cigarette Addicts Will Get Just Half Pack a Day," *New York Times*, 29 August 1990, p. A2.

The Birth Control Crisis

Birth control devices are chronically in short supply in the Soviet Union. Soviet production of condoms is woefully insufficient to meet demand, and their quality is low. The Pill is virtually unavailable. One consequence is a large number of unwanted pregnancies. According to Soviet statistics, nine out of ten first pregnancies are aborted, and the average woman has three to four abortions during her lifetime. An estimated 85 percent of Soviet women have at least one abortion. Seven of ten abortions are performed without anesthetic, often under unsanitary conditions, which may result in infections or permanent infertility. According to *Moscow News*, six hundred to seven hundred women die each year in the Russian Republic alone as a result of abortions.

Abortion on demand has been state policy since the Khrushchev era. Stalin had previously outlawed abortions to help raise the birthrate. Despite slow population growth in the European portion of the USSR, Soviet authorities have not restricted legal access to abortion, but neither have they placed a priority on increasing supplies of birth control devices.

Source: Adapted from "Abortion in the Soviet Union" *World Press Review*, August 1989, p. 55.

---

lic, Boris Yel'tsin, proposed a five-hundred-day plan for a rapid transition to a market economy (commonly called the Shatalin plan, after the radical economist Stanislav Shatalin, who was closely associated with its development). In late summer 1990, cooperation between Gorbachev and Yel'tsin in pursuing the plan seemed increasingly likely, and Gorbachev seemed to be edging even closer to the "democratic" pro-reform elements in society.

On September 24, 1990, the Supreme Soviet reinforced Gorbachev's formal authority by granting him the power to issue decrees to stabilize the deteriorating economic situation, and in October 1990, that body committed itself to a historic transition from central planning to a decentralized market economy. Despite these commitments, some worried that the additional powers granted the president might be used to quell local initiatives. At the same time, it became strikingly evident that the president's decrees were largely ineffectual, since they often met with continued resistance from conservatives in the state/Party bureaucracy or were declared illegitimate by the governments of the theoretically sovereign union republics and the newly declared "sovereign" regions, districts, and cities. There appeared to be an inverse correlation between the scope of power granted to the president and the government's ability to win voluntary compliance with the president's decisions. This paralysis of state authority intensified the crisis atmosphere in the country and warned of increasing political polarization.

It was in this context that a sea change began in October 1990, although its progression and significance became clear only at the end of that year and its effects did not culminate until the August coup. Rather than charging forth with the radical Shatalin plan (and thus cementing his association with the more strongly reformist sector of the elite and population), Gorbachev equivocated and came forward with his own economic program. The plan was a hybrid of the Shatalin plan and the more conservative approach supported by Prime Minister Nikolai Ryzhkov and most of the state bureaucracy. This approach was endorsed by the Supreme Soviet but sharply criticized by Yel'tsin and, over time, most of the leading economists who had championed the marketization process. Yel'tsin committed the government of the Russian Republic to proceed on its own with the more rapid and radical Shatalin blueprint. Added to all of Gorbachev's other difficulties was the question of

whether he could gain cooperation from this largest union republic and how many other republics would follow Yel'tsin's lead and unilaterally pursue their own agendas.

Between October 1990 and August 1991, minimal progress was made by the central government in effecting the transition to a market economy, and economic relations in the country took on an increasingly chaotic character. Indeed, it appeared that, following the enunciation of his own compromise economic plan in October 1990, Gorbachev began gradually to retreat from his commitment to rapid economic change and continued *demokratizatsiia*. As both the economic crisis and the crisis of national unity grew, in November 1990 Gorbachev proposed yet another reorganization of state organs, again augmenting the powers of the president. He also came forth with his draft of a new union treaty (revised again in March 1991), intended to draw back the restive republics, which had all declared themselves sovereign or independent by December 1990 (see Table 3.3). Principled and unambiguous rejection of the proposed treaty by several republic governments followed. Gorbachev stated with increasing clarity that he would not oversee even a partial breakup of the Soviet Union. The president also was under growing pressure from elements in the military, security forces, and Party apparatus to reexert control in the country. Some significant portion of the population also believed that something should be done to restore order.

In late 1990, the situation in the Soviet Union was highly unstable and the future unknown. Earlier that year, then Politburo member Aleksandr Yakovlev had depicted *perestroika* as an effort "to break the 1000-year old Russian paradigm of non-freedom." Other comments suggested the difficulty of the endeavor. One elected deputy called the USSR "a society in which one burning match can blow up an entire system."[12] Gorbachev himself cautioned that a civil war was possible. Yegor Yakovlev, the editor of the popular weekly *Moscow News*, warned in late Oc-

Table 3.3   Popular Votes on the Federation and National Independence

| | Vote on the All-Union Referendum[1] (March 17, 1991) | | Alternative Plebiscites on Independence | |
	Turnout[2]	Percent Voting for Preservation of the Union	Turnout[2]	Percent Voting for Independence
Russia	75.4%	71.3%		
Ukraine	83.5	70.2	Vote planned for Dec. 1991	
Belorussia	83.3	82.7		
Azerbaidzhan	75.1	93.3		
Kazakhstan	88.2	94.1		
Kirgiz (Kyrgystan)[3]	92.9	94.6		
Tadzhikistan	94.4	96.2		
Turkmenistan[4]	97.7	97.9	n.a.	over 94
Uzbekistan	95.4	93.7		
Lithuania[5]	Official Boycott		84.5%	90.5%
Estonia[6]	Official Boycott		82.9	77.8
Latvia[7]	Official Boycott		87.6	73.7
Georgia[8]	Official Boycott		90.5	98.9
Moldavia (Moldova)[9]	Official Boycott			
Armenia[10]	Official Boycott		95.5	over 99

[1]The referendum question was posed as follows: "Do you consider it necessary to preserve the Union of Soviet Socialist Republics as a renewed federation of equal, sovereign republics in which human rights and the freedom of people of all nationalities will be fully guaranteed?"

[2]Percent of eligible voters taking part.

[3]The Kirgiz Supreme Soviet changed the name of the republic from the Kirgiz Soviet Socialist Republic to the Socialist Republic of Kyrgystan on October 26, 1990.

[4]Independence vote held on October 26, 1991.

[5]Independence vote held on February 9, 1991.

[6]Independence vote held on March 3, 1991.

[7]Independence vote held on March 3, 1991.

[8]Independence vote held on March 31, 1991. Some Western analysts have concluded that pressure was exerted on Georgian voters to support independence by threatening to deny Georgian state citizenship to the population of regions in which the majority voted against independence. See Elizabeth Fuller, "Georgia Declares Independence," *Report on the USSR* 3, no. 16 (19 April 1991), pp. 11–12.

[9]On May 23, 1991, the Moldavian Supreme Soviet changed the name of the republic from the Moldavian Soviet Socialist Republic to the Republic of Moldova.

[10]Independence vote held on September 21, 1991, with the intention to follow the legally established procedure for secession.

Sources: Referendum results are from "Ob itogakh referenduma SSSR sostoiavshegosia 17 marta 1991 goda," *Pravda*, 27 March 1991, p. 2; independence votes are from various issues of *Report on the USSR* (Radio Liberty/Radio Free Europe) and the Soviet media.

tober 1990 that "people's patience has run out and so has time. The present administration can't stop our country's tumble into ruin."[13]

In late December 1990, Gorbachev's close associate Eduard Shevardnadze sounded the alarm when he resigned from his post as Soviet foreign minister in protest against increased tendencies toward authoritarian rule. His words rang true when, in January 1991, Soviet troops moved into Vilnius, the Lithuanian capital, on the pretext of pursuing draft dodgers. On January 12, 1991, Soviet forces took over the television center in Vilnius following a bloody confrontation with supporters of the popularly elected proindependence government. Thirteen Lithuanians and one Soviet soldier died. While Gorbachev claimed he had neither approved nor had previous knowledge of the military action, he justified strong measures as necessary to defend minority rights in Lithuania and ensure maintenance of order. Furthermore, he did not condemn Party forces in Lithuania (forming a self-proclaimed National Salvation Committee), which supported the military assault and sought to take over state control from the elected Lithuanian government.

These events, and similar ones following shortly thereafter in the Latvian capital, led observers to speculate about the causes of the growing reliance on military force. Had Gorbachev succumbed to overwhelming pressure from conservative military and political elements? Had he himself become convinced of the need for strong-armed tactics to keep the Soviet Union intact? Or was this a minor deviation on a continuing course of economic and political reform? Even if the latter was Gorbachev's intent and belief, could the democratic experiment be made compatible with state repression directed at the democratically elected Baltic governments?

The Lithuanian events were accompanied by other worrisome changes. The leadership's explanation for the crackdown in Vilnius seemed hauntingly similar to past Soviet rhetoric, and controls on media reports increased. In February 1991, the army and police presence increased on the streets of Soviet cities, and the KGB was authorized to examine and confiscate books and documents of business enterprises. While these measures were justified as necessary to maintain civil order and dampen the rising wave of crime, reformers saw them as instruments to control potential political opposition and protest. These developments polarized Soviet society even further. In early 1991, it seemed that the center (formerly represented by Gorbachev) was dropping out of the political spectrum and that it might be increasingly difficult for the more radical reformist elements to regain the initiative. Even Gorbachev's own considerable political finesse might not be adequate for him to reclaim his role as a legitimate reformer, capable of forging moderate political compromises.

By late April 1991, however, there were some signs that the tide might again be shifting in favor of the reform elements and Gorbachev himself seemed to be making yet another tactical adjustment in course. Even though the reform-minded democratic forces were fragmented and disorganized, Yel'tsin, championing the cause of republic sovereignty and further democratization, provided a focal point for opposition to the conservative retrenchment that took hold in late 1990 and early 1991. Events in March and April 1991 reflected the deep contradictions in Soviet society and the disruptive conflicts at the level of state authority. On March 25, the Cabinet of Ministers issued a resolution prohibiting a demonstration planned in Moscow for March 28 to support Yel'tsin's continued role as head of the Russian Republic. Over one hundred thousand demonstrators came out nonetheless, but a violent confrontation with the fifty thousand militia called out was avoided as both sides exercised restraint. The incident put the capital city on the brink of civil strife and seemed to heighten awareness of the high stakes involved should the war of nerves erupt into violence. The relatively peaceful denouement to the Moscow events seemed to mark yet another turning point and served as a harbinger of new efforts at reconciliation and compromise. By June it appeared that the further consolidation of control by the military/security/Party apparatus had been halted, at least temporarily.

A nationwide referendum, held on March 17, 1991, provided another public focal point of conflict. The referendum question asked Soviet citizens to affirm their support for preservation of the USSR "as a renewed federation of equal sovereign republics, in which human rights and the freedom of people of all nationalities will be fully guaranteed." Gorbachev hoped that the ambiguous wording of the proposition would assure support and that the vote would lend legitimacy to his project for restructuring the federation. In fact, the plan elicited considerable conflict. Six republics (the Baltics, Georgia, Armenia, and Moldavia) boycotted the referendum, but in the remaining republics 76.4 percent of those participating voted for the proposition. The meaning of the vote was not entirely clear. Some voters were expressing their attitude toward Gorbachev himself; others were affirming their support for sovereignty, human rights, and national equality; others saw a positive vote as an expression of support for a continued union of some type; many were probably confused and voted as they had always been instructed to vote, in favor of whatever was proposed to them. The strongest votes in favor of the referendum occurred in the Central Asian republics and in Azerbaidzhan (with over 93 percent of those voting affirming the proposition in each of these republics), but even in Russia and Ukraine the vote in favor was over 70 percent.

Several republics added additional questions to the ballot or altered the wording of the proposition slightly to accommodate local concerns. Ukrainians were also asked to affirm their support for their republic's declaration of sovereignty and in Western Ukraine they were polled on the desirability of Ukrainian independence. In Russia, the vote supported Yel'tsin's proposal to create the post of president of the republic to be elected by popular vote. (That election occurred subsequently on June 12, 1991, winning Yel'tsin the post.) Four of the boycotting republics (the Baltics and Georgia) held advisory referenda on independence around the time of the all-Union referendum, and these referenda all passed by a wide margin (see Table 3.3). Armenia held such a vote in September 1991.

The immediate political impact of the referendum was unclear, because, while it had passed, the nonparticipation of several republics placed its legitimacy in question. However, on April 23, 1991, a significant breakthrough occurred in the context of the so-called nine-plus-one talks, involving the heads of the nine republics that had passed the referendum and Gorbachev, representing the central government. This agreement foresaw the conclusion of a revised union treaty, adoption of a new constitution within the following six months, and new elections for the presidency and central state organs to be held in 1992. Further negotiations followed, producing a draft treaty that recognized the sovereignty of the union republics, guaranteed noninterference in their internal affairs by the center, and enabled the republics to embark on their own programs for transition to a market economy. The center was to act mainly as a coordinator of activities, and a whole series of adjustments in the economic sphere was to strengthen the hand of the republic governments. The anticrisis agreement that resulted from the talks appeared to provide a possible foundation of cooperation not only between the rivals Yel'tsin and Gorbachev, but also for the core of republics that had affirmed their commitment to some kind of union in the March referendum.[14]

At the same time, some movement occurred in the economic sphere in January 1991. In the face of monetary and economic collapse, the government undertook a monetary reform to reduce the supply of excess currency in the economy. Fifty- and one-hundred-ruble notes were removed from circulation (providing some limited compensation to individuals holding the bills). In April 1991 the long-awaited and much-dreaded price increases were finally implemented, reaching an average of 170 percent on a range of consumer goods.[15] Workers were compensated with a sixty-ruble monthly supplement, hardly adequate to make up the difference. Unfortunately, consumer hoarding had preceded the price increases, so once the measure was implemented, shop stores were empty, adding insult to injury. Demonstrations and strikes occurred in various regions of the country in protest. In the face of popular dissent, the government was finally forced to rescind for many everyday goods the additional 5 percent sales tax (hostilely referred to as the presidential tax). The exchange rate for the ruble was adjusted further to the ruble's disadvantage in April 1991, making tourists with hard currency rich and attractive targets for speculators and street entrepreneurs, but hopefully also moving the ruble one step closer to convertibility.

These events suggested that in mid-1991 Gorbachev might again be adjusting his course, this time moving back closer to the mainstream of reformist goals. Consultations with market-minded economists (such as Grigorii Yavlinsky) were reported in the press, cooperation between Gorbachev and Yel'tsin seemed possible again, and Gorbachev's own speeches emphasized the need for continued economic and political change. In the economic sphere the limited measures to correct the monetary imbalance were not indicative of an effective overall reform strategy, but they did suggest a willingness on the part of the government to take unpopular steps to try to correct an increasingly untenable situation. Gorbachev's zig-zag course appeared to be responding to the precarious balance of forces that threatened to rock the Soviet polity from the side of incipient dictatorship (referred to as Pinochetism, after the former Chilean dictator) to the brink of breathtaking reform initiatives. In the summer of 1991 despair reigned, as further economic decline seemed inevitable

Table 3.4   Soviet Fears, October 1990 (in percent)

Is there any danger of a coup by the right-wing or conservative forces?	
Yes	33%
No	21
Hard to say	46
Is there any danger of a coup by the left-wing or radical forces?	
Yes	17%
No	27
Hard to say	56
Do you fear that a food shortage may strike the Soviet Union in the coming months?	
Yes	62%
No	26
Not sure	12
*What's the quickest way to correct the situation in the Soviet Union?**	
More powers for the Soviet president	9
The Ryzhkov-Abalkin economic program	3
The Shatalin-Yavlinsky economic program	15
New forces ready to use a "strong hand" and restore order	16
A federal government the public may trust	8
The republics taking over all power	25
Other remedies	2
Nothing can remedy the situation today	9
Hard to say	16

*People could pick several answers for this last question. That is why the total exceeds 100 percent.

Source: Public opinion poll of 1,356 persons in twenty-one population centers of eleven regions in the USSR, conducted by the All-Union Centre for the Study of Public Opinion. *Moscow News*, no. 46 (25 November–2 December 1990), p. 4.

and Soviet citizens feared hunger, dictatorship, and civil strife (see Table 3.4). And yet there were still some hopeful signs—political conflict was expressed openly, the old system seemed incapable of reviving itself, and some kind of

Gorbachev and *Perestroika: From Glasnost'* to Crisis / **3** reconciliation between the republics and center seemed possible.

The Coup D'État and Another Russian Revolution

On August 20, 1991, the new union treaty was to be signed by five republics (Russia, Belorussia, Kazakhstan, Tadzhikistan, and Uzbekistan), with four others likely to follow in the fall (Turkmenia, Kyrgystan, Azerbaidzhan, and maybe Ukraine). Those that had boycotted the March referendum had decided, at least for the time being, not to participate. This was the apparent trigger for an attempted coup d'état by conservative members of Gorbachev's own government, who apparently viewed the agreement as a death sentence for the Soviet Union and their own power. Several top officials, including the Soviet vice president, the prime minister, and the heads of the KGB, the Interior Ministry, and the Defense Department, colluded and presented Gorbachev with an ultimatum at his *dacha* in the Crimea. Gorbachev refused to declare the state of emergency demanded by the coup plotters; he was held captive and in isolation, as the would-be leaders declared the formation of a special State Committee on the State of Emergency, claiming Gorbachev was ill and that his post was now in the hands of the vice president, Gennadii Yanayev. The leaders of the coup announced that "the policy of reforms, launched at Mikhail Gorbachev's initiative . . . has entered for several reasons a blind alley. . . . We intend to restore law and order straight away, declare a war without mercy to the criminal world, eradicate shameful phenomena discrediting our society."[16]

Both the Soviet and world public were shocked by the events. For three days the fate of the coup attempt was unclear. It soon became evident, however, that the coup leadership was acting indecisively and with some restraint. They failed to detain Boris Yel'tsin, the popular president of Russia, and they also did not cut off communication with the outside world (although they did impose internal controls on the media). By the end of the second day, tens of thousands of Muscovites congregated around the Russian parliament building, supporting Yel'tsin's demands that state power immediately be returned to Gorbachev's hands. Similar rallies occurred in Leningrad. The Russian parliament, under Yel'tsin's leadership, became the symbol and focal point for reformers and democrats, as they barracaded the building against military attack. Several units from the military and KGB refused to obey orders of the coup leaders and some defected to the side of the Russian leadership. Despite skirmishes and the death of three young men defending the parliament building on the night of August 20, the coup finally collapsed on August 21. Gorbachev returned to Moscow the next morning to resume his post. A revolution had occurred as thousands of Russians and people from other national groups mobilized to defend and extend the fragile and muddled achievements of *perestroika* and *glasnost'*.

Disoriented from his isolation, Gorbachev only grasped the momentous change that the failed coup had wrought after three days. Pressed by the victorious Yel'tsin and his supporters, Gorbachev resigned his post as Party leader and recommended that Party organs implicated in the coup disband. He seemed deeply dismayed and shocked by the disloyalty of those he himself had appointed, and he acknowledged his mistakes, even if he did not fully explain his reasons for making the appointments. The momentum for radical economic and political reform was dramatically accelerated; the back of the conservative opposition had been broken, although there were still fears of a repeat performance, particularly if economic problems continued to mount.

In the aftermath of the failed coup, the authority of the central government disintegrated. Gorbachev ordered the government to resign, since it had proven itself unreliable; criminal charges were brought against numerous officials. One by one most of the republics that had not yet declared their independence did so; the draft union treaty slated for signature on August 20 was already an anachronism. The prospect of national disintegration and political chaos now threatened to join the very real economic collapse that already was occurring. While the Baltic republics successfully pressed forward with their claim to state independence, several of the other republic leaders recognized that some sort of cooperation would be required to overcome the political and economic crisis. At an extraordinary meeting of the CPD beginning September 2, 1991, the head of the Kazakh republic, Narsultan Nazarbaev, presented a hastily contructed proposal for interim leadership. Hashed out by Gorbachev and the leaders of ten republics (excluding the Baltics and Moldova, but with Georgia participating as an observer), the proposal involved suspension of key portions of the constitution to allow formation of transitional institutions to work out a proposed new inter-republic treaty, a new constitution, and forms of economic cooperation. The plan radically shifted most power (excluding matters such as defense and security) to the republics and specified that each could determine its own role in any future union. (The transitional institutional structures are described in Chapter 4.) Gorbachev, using his typical skills of parliamentary manuever, railroaded a revised version of the plan through a resistant CPD. He finally won approval, a victory that perhaps indicated that there was still a role to be played by the embattled and betrayed Gorbachev. Following the meeting of the CPD, the new State Council immediately recognized the independence of the Baltic states.

While the coup and its aftermath had solved none of the dramatic political and economic problems, it created an entirely new context for their resolution. Gorbachev seemed determined to cooperate with Yel'tsin and the more radical "democrats" in the republics in forging a smaller and weaker union, and in pushing forward economic reform. A precarious road lay ahead and by mid-November when this chapter went to press, the future seemed as unclear as ever. History was proceeding at an unprecedented and nearly unmanageable pace. The only certainty seemed that now it was truly impossible to turn back. Should authoritarianism rear its head again, it would be different from the decades of Communist Party dominance. At the same time, the forces favoring democratic and market reform seemed to be in the driver's seat, at least in Russia. Shifting power to the republics might, however, lead to considerable backtracking on the reform agenda in some of the republics where a less firm base for an autonomous civil society existed. Already in mid-September this uneven movement toward democratization and market reform was evident. Semi-authoritarian power structures might well prevail in some republics (e.g., in the Central Asia republics, Georgia, and Azerbaidzhan), reminiscent of the old, but with a new nationalist ideological cloak. The struggle for democracy and market reform was now beginning in earnest.

The Contested Principles of Reform

When the first edition of this book was published in 1987, it contained a list of "principles of Soviet government," very similar to the discussion contained in Chapter 27 of this edition. It is difficult, and would perhaps even be misleading, to provide the same type of catalog for the Soviet Union as it enters the 1990s. The political transformations occurring there have involved not only changes in institutional structures (which we examine in the next chapter) but also the reformulation of the basic ideological principles that justified past structures of power. More importantly, however, the meaning of these new formulations is evolving through a process of political struggle.

Before *perestroika*, the Party articulated the authoritative definition of key political concepts

Gorbachev and *Perestroika:* From *Glasnost'* to Crisis / **3** (such as socialism, communism, democratic centralism, socialist legality, and vanguard party). Those wishing to contest those definitions had to do so subtly, using esoteric language, or illegally, in dissident writings or publications abroad. By the end of the 1980s, the CPSU no longer had that type of control over the educational and political indoctrination system. In the context of *glasnost'*, new ideas, including those endorsed by Gorbachev himself, became the subject of wide-ranging and sometimes heated debate in the press and in society at large. By early 1990, the meaning of both old and new ideological principles was contested; their validity, meaning, and application were issues of political dispute. By late 1991 a real crisis of values was at hand and many Soviet citizens weren't sure what to believe in.

The Party's Disputed Ideology

The demise of the CPSU in the fall of 1991 was preceded by the erosion of many of the Party's traditional ideological precepts. In a policy statement adopted at the Twenty-eighth Party Congress in July 1990, the Party expressed its support for "humane and democratic socialism" and made only scant reference to communism as a goal. It affirmed principles previously rejected, such as separation of powers, a multiparty system, diverse forms of property ownership, a regulated market economy, and the emergence of a civil society (a society in which "all social groups and communities have rights guaranteed by law and the real chance to express and stand up for their interests").[17] These commitments marked a radical change from past ideological principles.

Likewise in 1990, within the CPSU itself, discussion raged over the validity of traditional concepts such as vanguard party and democratic centralism. A radical (minority) wing of the Party adopted its own democratic platform in January 1990, preceding the Twenty-eighth Party Congress.[18] (Other, smaller splinter groups in the Party also prepared independent platforms.) In that document, the group disavowed the concepts of democratic centralism and vanguard party. Instead, it advocated transformation of the CPSU into a parliamentary party of the Western variety, ready to compete on an equal footing with other political parties for power. The program advocated a repeal of the antifactionalism rule adopted in 1920, the acceptance of horizontal links between local party organizations, a transfer of power to the soviets, and "the replacement of the principle of democratic centralism by basic democratic principles (elective offices, *glasnost'*, succession in office, and the subordination of the minority to the majority), with statutory guarantees provided for the protection of the minority's rights."

The Democratic Platform united only an estimated 5 to 10 percent of the delegates to the Party congress in July 1990. At the end of the congress, leading members of the group, unhappy with the conservative tenor of the meeting, made known their intention to quit the CPSU and form their own party in October 1990. Many were delegates to a new party founded in November 1990 and calling itself the Republican Party of Russia.

As some radical members of the CPSU advocated rejection of key ideological tenets of past Party rule, Gorbachev and the Party congress continued to defend the vanguard notion and antifactionalism. In May 1990, Gorbachev explained that "the CPSU Central Committee and I myself are firmly committed to a vanguard-type Party."[19] But at the Party congress, he explained the vanguard concept in somewhat nontraditional terms:

> We consider that this vanguard role cannot be imposed on the community, that it can only be won by an active struggle for the interests of the working people, by actual performance and by the Party's entire political and moral image. The CPSU will pursue its policy and work to retain the mandate of the ruling party within the bounds of the democratic process, involving elections for legislative institutions at the national

and local level. In this sense it will operate as a parliamentary party.[20]

At the same time, Gorbachev declared himself in favor of free debate, diverse platforms, and dissent within the Party, but he warned that "there is a threshold which, if crossed, would cripple the Party. And that is to form factions with their own special discipline."[21] By July 1991, however, Gorbachev endorsed a new draft Party program that involved further alteration of traditional Leninist values.[22]

In contrast to Gorbachev's views, other elements in the Party favored maintenance of the more traditional notions of democratic centralism and the vanguard party. As these examples illustrate, by 1990 even within the CPSU itself there was little agreement regarding the basic principles that should govern both internal Party life and Soviet politics overall. These internal clashes were symptomatic of the Party's loss of ideological leadership in society as a whole.

Even more dramatic than the changes *within* CPSU ideology was the change in the status of that ideology in Soviet political life. The CPSU no longer had a monopoly on correct doctrine. Diverse ideologies were propagated publicly, including those rooted in neo-Marxist, nationalist, liberal, religiously based, and democratic socialist principles. Gorbachev himself emphasized that correct policy can emerge only through the interaction of diverse viewpoints. The notion of socialist pluralism also gained official approval. In early 1991 both Gorbachev and official Party proclamations continued to place future Soviet development within the socialist framework, but the meaning of the word *socialism* was publicly and broadly contested. For some, Western social democracy clearly qualifies as socialism; for others, socialism must be firmly rooted in some notion of working-class dominance; still others see socialism as incompatible with a regulated market economy and privatization of economic life.

New ideological concepts also have emerged.

We have mentioned some of these earlier, such as *glasnost'* and *demokratizatsiia*. Closer examination of these and other ideas will provide guideposts for understanding the evolving parameters of political conflict in this transition period.

Glasnost'

As initially conceived, *glasnost'* had a social purpose: it was to further the process of reform and create a more legitimate and credible arena of public discourse. Consequently, even through mid-1990, censorship remained in some areas, and the state/Party apparatus still maintained a close watch over the media, which were still largely responsible, at least in principle, to a variety of official state and Party organs. The assumption that *glasnost'* should serve *perestroika* was evident in Gorbachev's periodic meetings with the editors of the leading publications.

In October 1989, Gorbachev reprimanded the editor of a highly popular weekly, *Argumenty i fakty*, for publishing results of an unsystematic opinion poll ranking the popularity of deputies to the new CPD. The poll did not include Gorbachev but put radical reformers (including Boris Yel'tsin and Andrei Sakharov) at the top of the list. Gorbachev deemed the publication disrespectful and insulting to the deputies. The editor of the weekly, Vladislav Starkov, was asked to resign, but the newspaper's editorial collective and a portion of the public rallied behind him. He refused to resign but did publish a poll favorable to Gorbachev in the next issue. Nonetheless, the ability of even the top Party leadership to restrict unwanted publications was waning.

Over time, under the auspices of *glasnost'*, parts of the intelligentsia demanded an extension of the range of self-expression and justified their claims in terms largely consistent with the Western liberal tradition. They emphasized that free expression must be conceived as a basic right

Source: *Izvestiia*, 12 October 1990, p. 1.

Soviet Advertisement for *Izvestiia*
Top: Thank God we don't live in America!
Dialogue: "I want to subscribe to *Izvestiia*."
"That is 95 dollars, sir."
Bottom: A subscription to *Izvestiia* can be paid for in rubles! In the United States, a yearly subscription to *Izvestiia* costs 95 dollars. By the black market exchange rate, a yearly subscription to *Izvestiia* costs an American 1,900 rubles. [At the newly established official exchange rate for tourists, 95 dollars was worth about 2,200 rubles in April 1991.] And here in the USSR it costs only 22 rubles 56 kopecks—and read for the whole year!

rather than as an instrument to achieve other goals. A new Press Law, which went into effect in August 1990,[23] reflected a partial evolution toward some notion of free speech. Citizens were guaranteed the right to establish independent publications, prior censorship was forbidden, and newspapers could bring suits to seek the release of secret information. However, publications still had to register with the state and identify their sponsor. Furthermore, Party publishing houses still had control over most aspects of the physical process of publishing, as well as over distribution of most paper, which has been chronically in short supply. In early 1991, intensified control over the electronic media was evident when the popular critical documentary television show "Vzgliad" (Viewpoint) was canceled, and the main evening news show "Vremiia" (Time) reverted to presenting a clearly one-sided version of the day's events.

Despite the remaining obstacles, by 1990 a wide range of independent and influential newspapers circulated freely in various parts of the country. They represented a new political force and were both a product of *glasnost'* and, in most cases, advocates of its continued extension. In spring 1991, the Russian Republic established its own television channel, offering the viewers an alternative to the central electronic media. The transition from the ideology of *glasnost'* to the reality of a Western notion of free speech became embedded in a political struggle against the remnants of the Party's indoctrination machine.

In the spring of 1990, the newly elected reformist governments in Moscow and Leningrad (now St. Petersburg) claimed control over television broadcasting in their cities, hoping to loose the Party's hold on the electronic media. A central decree issued on July 15, 1990, declared television broadcasting to be independent of all political public organizations, including the CPSU.[24] In the summer of 1990, the Moscow city soviet also supported the establishment of two independent newspapers in the city after the

Moscow Party organization refused to cede control of its daily, *Moskovskaia pravda*. Similar encounters occurred elsewhere throughout the country.

During the three-day coup d'état in August 1991, the coup leadership reexerted control over the internal media, leaving only isolated outposts of free communication inside the country. Ironically, news reports to the outside world were largely uncontrolled, and thus foreign broadcast services such as BBC (British Broadcasting Services) and Radio Liberty were able to retransmit information from Western Europe back into the USSR. Loyal aids of the captive Gorbachev were even able to rig up a shortwave receiver to pick up BBC broadcasts for the Soviet president. Once the coup was defeated, the independent media blossomed even more fully than before. *Pravda* (the newspaper of the CPSU) was temporarily closed, to reopen as a self-proclaimed independent newspaper; and the evening news show (*Vremiia*) was given a new name (*TV Inform*) and new popular announcers, as it attempted to free itself from its stodgy, official image. Confiscation of Party property promised to release the grip of the old political forces on the mass media. Yet in some of the republics in the weeks after the coup, reports of new forms of media control began to surface. Perhaps the battle over *glasnost'* and free speech was not over after all, but was shifting its venue to the level of the newly independent or sovereign republics.

A Law-Based State

The official commitment to the rule of law also marks a break from past interpretations of Marxist-Leninist ideology, but here again the meaning of the new principle is being shaped by political struggle. The policy statement issuing from the Twenty-eighth Party Congress affirmed CPSU support for a "law-based state . . . in which democratically adopted laws and the equality of all citizens before the laws have undisputed preeminence."[25] According to the document, this notion rules out "the dictatorship of any class, political party, grouping, or the managerial bureaucracy," a view in sharp contrast to previous doctrine, which saw law serving the working class and its vanguard party, the CPSU. Soviet officials also have affirmed their commitment to the protection of human rights as defined by the United Nations. Official policy now supports the enhancement of judicial independence and elimination of "telephone justice," a term referring to the telephone calls from Party officials to judges instructing them how to rule in a case. The enactment of numerous new laws and the adoption of wide-ranging constitutional amendments also reflect an effort to provide a legal foundation for *perestroika* and ensure a greater correspondence between law and reality.

Beneath these widely acclaimed principles lies ambiguity about the real meaning of the term *law-based state*. Is law simply to be used to further the leadership's own political and economic objectives (for example, by passage of new laws consistent with his reform objectives and use of anticorruption charges to eliminate unsympathetic personnel)? Or are the new legal mechanisms intended to produce an independent legal system, free of political interference, which might, in any given instance, work for or against particular policy goals?

William Butler, a Western expert on Soviet law, raises a further question. Does the term *law-based state* simply imply that the state is bound by its own laws, whatever their content, and without a higher authority to ensure compliance?[26] (This notion conforms closely to the Russian word *zakon*, which refers to statutory, positive law enacted by the highest parliamentary authority, whatever its particular substance.) Or does it suggest a polity grounded in some type of natural law, reflecting a basic conception of "right" or "rights"? (This notion is expressed more closely by the Russian word *pravo*.) If the term refers to *zakon* rather than *pravo*, it mandates legality in the strict sense, but it could be consistent with the enactment of laws that, from a Western perspective, violate certain fundamental rights. Some interpret the emergency and decree powers granted to the new presidency, both initially in March and April 1990 and reinforced later, as potentially allowing just such violations.[27] A proposed law defending the "honor and dignity" of the president raised similar concerns, but amendments added before passage by the Supreme Soviet in May 1990 assuaged most worries. The law does not apply to political criticism and criminalizes only insults to the president expressed "in an indecent way."[28]

A law passed on December 23, 1990, established an independent body, the Committee for Constitutional Review, to oversee the compliance of acts of bodies and officials with the constitution. This innovation marked a first step toward realization of a limited application of judicial review, even if the new committee's powers are mainly advisory and consultative. Indeed, in September 1990, the committee declared a presidential decree unconstitutional. (The decree shifted control of demonstrations and public meetings to the central Council of Ministers from the Moscow city soviet.) While the committee's ruling was not binding on the president and would ultimately have been enforceable only by a two-thirds vote of the CPD, the decision made clear that even the president should be subject to the rule of law.[29] The new union treaty that was to be signed on August 20, 1991, foresaw the creation of a Constitutional Court. Following the coup d'état attempt, the fate of this proposal is unclear, since the continued existence of the authority of centrally adopted laws was placed in question.

Other conflicts over the application of the rule of law have arisen, most notably in the widely discussed controversy centering on Telman Gdlyan and Nikolai Ivanov, special public prosecutors responsible for pursuing especially important cases. (In March 1989, Gdlyan and Ivanov were both elected to the CPD and thus gained legal immunity from prosecution for criminal offenses.) In investigating charges of corruption against high Party officials in Uzbekistan, Gdlyan and Ivanov allegedly violated proper investigative procedures by forcing false confessions, terrorizing suspects, issuing threats to gain cooperation, and taking relatives of the accused into custody. In response to these accusations, Gdlyan denied use of illegitimate methods and defended his energetic efforts to prosecute the perpetrators of "lawlessness" and "mass terror" in Uzbekistan. He suggested that central Party officials were implicated in the corruption and were cooperating in a cover-up to protect the guilty parties.[30]

In April 1990, after an extensive investigation, a special commission of the CPD concluded that many of the accusations against Gdlyan and Ivanov were justified.[31] Responding to the commission's report, the Supreme Soviet did not remove the immunity of the two investigators, so no criminal charges could be brought against them, but it did approve their removal from their posts at the prosecutor's office. The resolution also included strong criticism of the leadership of the prosecutor's office, which had failed to pursue criminal charges against corrupt officials and had not adequately overseen the special investigatory group.[32]

Public sentiment over the case was intense and generally supported Gdlyan and Ivanov, despite the commission's findings. This is somewhat surprising, since one of the cochairs of the commission was himself a prominent former dissident, Roy Medvedev. Western observers have interpreted the popular support for Gdlyan and Ivanov as an indication of the low level of commitment to legal culture among the Soviet population. Medvedev explained the popular reaction somewhat differently:

Since Brezhnev accepted gifts that could well be considered bribes, gifts worth tens and hundreds of thousands, if . . . others took these bribes, the people have become convinced that the entire rul-

ing clique acted the same way. . . . The people have become convinced that there were many bribetakers in the country's leadership, and therefore they believe Gdlyan and Ivanov. I understand this. People take their side because they see them as defenders of the people's interests.[33]

Here was a conflict about the propriety of violating proper legal procedures in the interest of achieving a "higher" goal (in this case, successful prosecution of allegedly corrupt officials). Such violations may represent an inverted form of the Party's traditional manipulation of law to serve its "higher" goals. Could the new "revolutionary justice" of the *glasnost'* era be easily perverted to justify almost any action?

The coup attempt and its fate in August 1991 suggested, however, that perhaps the commitment to *rule of law* has made significant inroads both among parts of the elite and the population. First, the coup plotters themselves apparently felt compelled to give their action a legal facade. While their usurpation of power was clearly unconstitutional, they tried to make it appear legitimate by declaring the Soviet vice president Gennadii Yanayev to be the new leader. The coup plotters also showed some restraint in their use of force to suppress opposition: opposition leaders were not arrested; demonstrations and rallies were, in practice, allowed to proceed; and military assaults on outposts of resistance (most notably the Russian parliament) did not occur. Was this restraint an indication that even the coup plotters (or at least lower military and security officers) had internalized some respect for the laws of the land? Or was it simply a function of disorganization and poor planning?

On the other hand, those actively opposing the coup showed a clearer commitment to the *law-based state*. Despite Gorbachev's personal unpopularity and the rivalry between Gorbachev and Yel'tsin, the latter and his supporters rallied to defend the constitutional order. Their struggle was not waged in order to save Gorbachev personally, but rather to save the achievements of the reform and the supremacy of the constitutionally established legal structure. This is perhaps the most extraordinary aspect of the August events—a crucial segment of the Russian population (as well as many non-Russians) were ready to risk their lives to preserve the imperfect and wobbly structures of the new constitutional order. This was a sharp contrast to the utopian and abstract goals of previous revolutionary upheavals. The *way* decisions were made was taking on as much importance as their *substance*. And this, of course, is one crucial component of the liberal notion of the law-based state. On the other hand, some warned of a possible "witch-hunt" against former communists in the aftermath of the coup, and others suggested that the suspension of some constitutional provisions by the CPD after the failed coup (in response to heavy parliamentary manuevering by Gorbachev) was a "state coup." The *Nezavisimaia gazeta* (Independent Newspaper, Moscow) wrote: "The country finds itself hostage to a 'round table' of presidents. . . . there are neither spectators nor a referee. And if there was a referee, it would be meaningless—the game is played without rules."[34] To be sure, some rules were laid down and the transitional institutions were approved by the CPD. But again, questions arose about the depth of commitment to the "law-based state." And what conception of law was it anyway?

Demokratizatsiia

As noted previously, we should not assume that the Soviet notion of *demokratizatsiia* is synonymous with Western conceptions of democratization, even if the Western experience does provide a clear reference point for reform discussions in the Soviet Union. (There are, of course, disagreements about the meaning of democracy in the West as well.) The concept of democracy also plays a role in Leninist theory (see Chapter 1), and in appropriating the term for his reform

agenda, Gorbachev has been able to place himself in that tradition.

Lenin argued that true democracy is possible only when economic exploitation has been eliminated. Thus, according to Lenin, it is impossible to achieve complete democracy within capitalism. Soviet interpretations of Lenin traditionally have understood democracy as a vehicle for the realization of the interests of a social class (the working class) rather than for the expression of individual interests or interests of other groups. Growing out of this view is the traditional CPSU practice of Party representation based on workplace constituencies. Even deputies to the Supreme Soviet often did not live in the districts they represented, but rather were employed by an enterprise in the region. Central control also ensured that formal representative bodies (the soviets) included a significant proportion of workers and other demographic groups.[35] Finally, in Leninist theory, groups are conceived to have objective interests that they may or may not themselves recognize. Thus, a vanguard party is needed to present and struggle for those interests.

This traditional Marxist-Leninist approach to democracy deviates from the mainstream Western liberal view (although it does, in some cases, have some resonance with certain variants of socialist ideology and, in other cases, bear some resemblance to corporatist structures in some Western European countries). In Western polities, the expansion of democratic rights was historically linked to the rise of capitalism. Some liberal theorists would even see the two as inextricably connected, in that capitalism makes possible the economic independence of the citizen and provides an economic foundation for political competition. In this view, some of the negative features of capitalism can be mitigated by state regulation, thus facilitating equal access to power for all social groups.

Furthermore, despite some corporatist tendencies in certain Western European countries, liberal theory has generally seen the individual, rather than social classes, as the basis for political representation. Thus, territorial rather than workplace constituencies have predominated. Likewise, in most Western polities, there is no built-in expectation that elected bodies should include a certain proportion of workers, women, or other demographic groups. As long as election procedures are fair and accessible to all citizens, voters may choose their representatives from whatever social class or group they prefer.

Finally, in liberal democratic theory, the notion of objective interest is weak. An individual is generally considered to be the best judge of his or her own interests. Consistent with this view, political parties are less concerned with shaping a correct political consciousness than with reflecting the self-understood interests of their constituents.

Where does the *demokratizatsiia* of *perestroika* fit into this picture? Was it primarily rhetoric to legitimize Gorbachev's attack on the power of entrenched Party/state bureaucrats— a rhetoric, in fact, also appropriated by new political forces in the USSR? Did *demokratizatsiia* represent a genuine attempt to revive and realize Leninist norms? Or does it involve the adoption of a different conception of democracy, more consistent with Western liberal theory? Soviet commentators themselves disagree about the proper interpretation of *demokratizatsiia*. There are vocal advocates of different interpretations in the USSR and abroad.

In general, the practice of Soviet democracy seems to be evolving in a direction more consonant with liberal democratic notions than with Leninist theory. At the same time, this evolution is halting and dissenting voices continue to be heard. For example, a coalition of workers organized as the United Front of Workers (UFW) of Russia has demanded that deputies to local soviets be elected from production units (factories) rather than territorial districts. They also have protested the low proportion of deputies of

working-class background in the new parliamentary organs and have supported quotas to ensure their presence in the soviets.[36] The UFW also opposes market reforms in the economy. Some critics see such reforms as pushing the Soviet Union toward capitalism and thus undermining the prospects for Soviet democracy by increasing social inequality. Such viewpoints seem grounded in a Leninist vision of democracy. Until now these views have not prevailed, nor have they received support in the leadership's reform program. Although Gorbachev himself lays claim to the Leninist heritage, his view of *demokratizatsiia* seems to have moved a step closer to the liberal democratic tradition.[37]

Particularly as the central government is weakened and power shifts to the republic level, the commitment to a liberal conception of democratization may vary greatly between regions in the USSR. Those republics that have had closer historic links to the West (the Baltics, perhaps Russia and Ukraine) may evolve more quickly in this direction than those areas (Central Asia, Transcaucasia) with less firm indigenous roots for liberalism. Political struggle will continue to determine which conceptions will prevail. The defeat of the coup d'état in late August 1991 was hailed both inside and outside Russia as a victory for the "democrats" and for "democratization." Nonetheless, the longer struggle over the realization and proper meaning of the term is just beginning.

National Sovereignty: A New Federation or National Independence?

In 1989, a new issue forced itself onto the Soviet reform agenda—the place of the union republics and other national subunits within the Soviet Union. By late 1990, declarations of sovereignty and independence were proliferating. Some called the process a "parade of sovereignties" and one Soviet article referred to a "separatism mania: "A huge country only yesterday has been turned into a mosaic of independent principalities. The Republics keep turning away from the Center, the regions from the Republics, the cities and districts from the regions. We have been overwhelmed by a separatism mania."[38] The meaning of this phenomenon is, however, far from self-evident.

In 1990 and early 1991 both Gorbachev and advocates of Lithuanian independence affirmed the principle of national sovereignty, but they conceived of the term in vastly different ways. For Gorbachev and the CPSU leadership, sovereignty meant a devolution of key functions to the union republic governments, within the context of a voluntary federation. This would involve the supremacy of central (all-Union) laws in agreed-upon areas, a single Soviet citizenship, a unified currency, and continued central authority in areas related to foreign relations, energy, and national defense. Gorbachev expressed this radical new conception of the federation when he stated that "what we need is a real union of sovereign states."[39] At the same time, the policy statement issuing from the Twenty-eighth Party Congress affirmed that "the Party proceeds from the recognition of the right of nations to self-determination, including secession, but does not confuse the right to withdrawal from the USSR with the expediency of such a withdrawal. . . . [I]t is important to preserve the integrity of the renewed Union as a dynamic multinational state."[40]

A radically different view of sovereignty was evident in the position of the leaders of the Lithuanian Republic. For them, national sovereignty could not be realized short of full independence from the USSR (expressed in the declaration of independence issued March 11, 1990). The governments of other union republics put forth yet other definitions of sovereignty during 1989 and 1990 (see Table 3.5). By the end of 1990, all fifteen union republics had declared themselves sovereign or independent. Following the failed

coup d'état in August 1991, most republics that had not yet done so declared independence (Table 3.5), and the trend began to spread to levels below the republic level. The motivations for this rash of declarations were complex and their meaning unclear. In the first instance they are based on the premise that the constituent units of the USSR, the republics, are the rightful source of political authority. Any union must rest on voluntary adhesion by each republic, rather than on coercion from the center. This notion is grounded not only in modern conceptions of national self-determination, but also in Leninist theory itself and the explicit language in the 1977 Soviet constitution.

Clearly, for some republics (the Baltics) the goal from the very beginning was true national independence. Lithuania, Latvia, and Estonia achieved this goal in September 1991, when both foreign governments and the weakened Soviet state recognized Baltic independence. Factors leading other republics to declare independence in August and September 1991 were complex. Some, such as Moldova and Georgia, probably prefer independence, while others probably accept the necessity of a newly constituted confederation of sovereign states. Why, then, did even these republics declare sovereignty, and then full independence? They may have feared increased Russian domination in the union, as Yel'tsin's star rose and other leaders from the Russian republic were rapidly co-opted into the top posts at the center. This fear was reinforced when Yel'tsin suggested, shortly after the coup, that border adjustments might be necessary if neighboring republics became independent. In other cases, elites at the republic level may have been trying to protect themselves from radical measures (such as dismantling of the CPSU) emanating from the center that might threaten to undermine their own bases of power. Other republics might not want to be left off the bandwagon, fearing that their bargaining power would be weakened in future negotiations if they

Table 3.5 Declarations of Sovereignty and Independence of the Republics[a]

Non-participants in the March 1991 Referendum (chronologically, by date of declaration of independence)

	Declarations of Sovereignty	Declarations of Independence
Lithuania[b]	May 18, 1989	March 11, 1990
Estonia[b]	November 16, 1988	March 30, 1990[c] August 20, 1991
Latvia[b]		May 4, 1990[c] August 21, 1991
Armenia		August 23, 1990[d] September 23, 1991[e]
Georgia	November 1989[f]	April 9, 1991
Moldova	June 23, 1990	August 27, 1991

Participants in the March 1991 Referendum (by dates of declarations of independence, then sovereignty)

	Declarations of Sovereignty	Declarations of Independence
Ukraine	July 16, 1990	August 24, 1991[g]
Belorussia	July 27, 1990	August 25, 1991
Azerbaidzhan	October 4, 1989	August 30, 1991
Uzbekistan	June 20, 1990	September 1, 1991
Kyrgystan	December 11, 1990	September 1, 1991
Tadzhikistan	August 24, 1990	September 9, 1991
Turkmenistan	August 23, 1990	October 27, 1991
Russia	June 8, 1990	
Kazakhstan	October 25, 1990	

[a]The declarations and reassertions of independence differed from the various declarations of sovereignty in that they, in essence, did not recognize continued Soviet rule in any form. The republics declaring sovereignty generally stated that they remained part of the Soviet federation but that the laws promulgated by the given republic's supreme soviet would take precedence over those of the USSR.

[b]The Baltic states of Estonia, Latvia, and Lithuania formally reasserted their independence, emphasizing that they had never joined the USSR. The Soviet government recognized the independence of the three Baltic states on September 6, 1991.

[c]The first declaration indicated the beginning of a transition for restoring independence, while the second declaration indicated that the transition was deemed complete.

[d]Declared its intention to leave the USSR through the constitutional process, subject to the results of the referendum on September 21, 1991.

[e]Affirming the results of the referendum held on September 21, 1991.

[f]Declaration of sovereignty achieved through the adoption of a series of laws.

[g]Subject to a referendum on December 1, 1991.

Sources: Compiled by the author from *Report on the USSR* (Radio Liberty/Radio Free Europe); *New York Times.*

didn't play their "independence card," forcing Moscow to woo them back. In some ways the "independence mania" of these post-coup weeks seemed to be a radicalized rerun of the "sovereignty mania" that had occurred a year before.

The central authorities all along had given lip service to the notion of sovereignty, but they had rejected all claims that republics could secede at will or declare their laws superior to central legislation. In early 1991, it seemed unlikely that the widely diverging concepts of sovereignty (particularly those advocated by the center and the Baltic governments) would be capable of reconciliation. The difficulty was exemplified by the inability to agree on a procedure for a republic to secede legitimately from the Union. Should secession of a republic be subject to final approval by the CPD, as the Law on Secession, adopted in April 1990, required?[41] Should the nationwide referendum (held in March 1991) on maintenance of the existing boundaries be binding on individual republics? Or should it be strictly in the domain of the republic itself to decide, as the Lithuanian leaders maintained? The political crisis engendered by the failed coup seemed to sweep away the fine theoretical distinctions in the debate, as the authority of the central government virtually collapsed. Now the question was not whether republics *could* be sovereign, independent or the like, but rather whether some regularized process could be set in motion to allow the various republics to realize their aspirations without throwing the entire region into anarchy. The question no longer involved abstract disputations on "sovereignty," but attempts to fashion a political process that could allow the republics to realize their sovereignty, given the tangled economic, ethnic, and political web that bound the former Soviet republics to one another. Given a real opportunity to choose, some of the republics might well back off from their more radical declarations.

Other ambiguities complicated discussions about sovereignty and independence. How should minorities within each republic be treated? Who would protect their rights? At a more fundamental level, should the collective rights of the titular nationality in each republic predominate over the rights of individual citizens, particularly minority groups? These questions of principle were topics of direct political conflict from 1989 through 1991. For example, just as the Georgians were considering independence for their republic, conflicts erupted over the rights of South Ossetians and Abkhazians, minorities within the Georgian Republic, who claimed that their right to self-determination was being denied by Georgian authorities. In October 1990, a Turkic-speaking minority in Moldavia, the Gagauz, declared its own secession from the Moldavian Republic. The Moldavian parliament, which had already demanded sovereignty for Moldavia within the USSR, declared the Gagauz action unconstitutional. Violent confrontation was narrowly averted when some Moldavian "volunteers" sought to put down the Gagauz secession.

In late 1989 and 1990 in Estonia, some members of the Russian minority protested against planned restrictions on the use of the Russian language in official documents and residency requirements that would deny some the right to vote for public office. Ironically, Moscow espoused the primacy of individual rights, and the Baltic governments appeared as defenders of collective (national) rights. Gorbachev affirmed this position at the Twenty-eighth Party Congress: "For all this, human rights must retain priority over the interests of national sovereignty and autonomy. . . . This must be engrained in the constitutional fabric of the Union and each of the republics."[42] This position was, of course, politically expedient for Gorbachev, since it implied a role for the central government in mediating conflicts between individual rights and national sovereignty. The dispute over sovereignty and independence turned many traditional positions upside down, at least for the moment, but at the same time raised fundamental questions about individual and collective rights.

The principles we have discussed in this section (*glasnost'*, *demokratizatsiia*, a law-based state, and sovereignty/independence) remain disputed concepts in the USSR. The outcome of these conflicts will not be decided by CPSU doctrine and power (as in the past), but through political struggle in the newspapers, streets, factories, and government halls of Dushanbe, Riga, Kiev, Kishinev, and Moscow.

Notes

1. *Pravda*, 14 May 1990, p. 1, trans. in *Current Digest of the Soviet Press* (hereafter *CDSP*) 42, no. 19 (1990), p. 1.

2. See Moshe Lewin, *The Gorbachev Phenomenon: A Historical Interpretation* (Berkeley: University of California Press, 1988).

3. Timothy Colton, *The Dilemma of Reform in the Soviet System* (New York: Council on Foreign Relations, 1984), pp. 43–45.

4. Reported in *Pravda*, 20 June 1991, p. 1.

5. Quoted in *New York Times*, 4 September 1991, p. A15.

6. See David E. Powell, "The Emerging Health Crisis in the Soviet Union," *Current History* 84, no. 504 (October 1985), pp. 325–326.

7. "Report by M. S. Gorbachev, General Secretary of the CPSU Central Committee," *Pravda*, 16 October 1985, pp. 1–2, trans. in *CDSP* 37, no. 42 (13 November 1985), pp. 3, 4.

8. Gail Lapidus, "State and Society," in *Politics, Society, and Nationality Inside Gorbachev's Russia*, ed. Seweryn Bialer (Boulder, Colo.: Westview Press, 1989), pp. 127–129.

9. Deputy V. P. Krishevich, *Izvestiia*, 26 April 1990, p. 3, trans. in *CDSP* 42, no. 18 (1990), p. 5.

10. *Pravda*, 28 January 1987, pp. 2–3.

11. For an English translation of the letter, see David Lane, *Soviet Society Under Perestroika* (Boston: Unwin Hyman, 1990), pp. 108–117.

12. *Izvestiia*, 16 March 1990, trans. in *CDSP* 42, no. 14 (1990), pp. 17–18.

13. *Moscow News*, 28 October–4 November 1990, p. 7.

14. See "Vstrecha 'deviatki' na dache: oni podpisali ne tol'ko zaiavlenie dlia publiki . . ." and "Chto reshili na prirode?", *Kommersant*, no. 17 (22–29 April 1991), pp. 1, 3.

15. For analysis of the increases, see "Vse stalo dorozhe na 170%," *Kommersant*, no. 17 (22–29 April 1991), p. 19.

16. "State of Emergency Committee's Statement: A Mortal Danger Has Come," *New York Times*, 20 August 1991, p. A13. Speculation about Gorbachev's possible involvement in planning the coup circulated in both the USSR and the West following the putsch attempt. At the time of this writing, however, no evidence has appeared to support such allegations.

17. "Towards a Humane, Democratic Socialism (Policy Statement of the 28th Congress of the CPSU)," in *Documents and Materials: 28th Congress of the Communist Party of the Soviet Union* (Moscow: Novosti, 1990), p. 86.

18. Published in *Pravda*, 3 March 1990.

19. *Pravda*, 18 May 1990, p. 1, trans. in *CDSP* 42, no. 19 (1990), p. 2.

20. "Continuing Along the Road of Perestroika: Political Report of the CPSU Central Committee to the 28th CPSU Congress and the Party's Tasks," a speech delivered by Mikhail Gorbachev on 2 July 1990, in *Documents and Materials: 28th Congress of the Communist Party of the Soviet Union* (Moscow: Novosti, 1990), p. 42.

21. Ibid., p. 50.

22. "O proekte novoi programmy KPSS," *Izvestiia*, 26 July 1991, pp. 1–2.

23. *Izvestiia*, 20 June 1990, p. 3.

24. *Izvestiia*, 16 July 1990, p. 1.

25. "Towards a Humane, Democratic Socialism," p. 87.

26. William E. Butler, "The Rule of Law and the

Legal System," in *Developments in Soviet Politics*, ed. Stephen White, Alex Pravda, and Zvi Gitelman (London: Macmillan, 1990), p. 105.

27. See the relevant legislation in *Pravda*, 16 March 1990, pp. 1, 3; *Izvestiia*, 9 April 1990, pp. 1–2.

28. For the law, see *Izvestiia*, 23 May 1990, p. 4. For a discussion of it, see Celestine Bohlen, "Insulting Gorbachev Now Illegal, But It All Depends on the Tone," *New York Times*, 22 May 1990, p. A10.

29. See *Izvestiia*, 15 September 1990.

30. *Izvestiia*, 25 December 1989, trans. in *CDSP* 42, no. 10 (1990), pp. 11–12.

31. Francis X. Cline, "Furor Grows among Soviets over a Corruption Scandal," *New York Times*, 18 April 1990, p. A10.

32. *Izvestiia*, 19 April 1990, p. 1, trans. in *CDSP* 42, no. 18 (1990), p. 19.

33. *Izvestiia*, 28 September 1989, p. 6, trans. in *CDSP* 41, no. 40 (1989), p. 12.

34. "Scenes of Soviet Autumn," *New York Times*, 10 September 1991, p. 1.

35. Some attempt at demographic proportionality has traditionally been applied to the structure of deputies elected (in noncompetitive elections) to the soviets, but the traditionally more powerful Party bodies have been demographically unrepresentative. For example, in the late Brezhnev years, workers made up about 15 percent of Central Committee members; women were only about 4 percent. Thus, the principle has had largely symbolic significance in Soviet practice.

36. Elizabeth Teague, "Perestroika and the Soviet Worker," *Government and Opposition* 25, no. 2 (1990), pp. 208–209.

37. John Gooding provides a well-documented, balanced discussion of this in "Gorbachev and Democracy," *Soviet Studies* 42, no. 2 (April 1990), pp. 195–231.

38. Nikolai Petrov and Leonid Smirnyagin, *Moscow News*, no. 43 (4–11 November 1990), p. 7.

39. "Continuing Along the Road," p. 25.

40. "Towards a Humane, Democratic Socialism," pp. 88–89.

41. *Pravda*, 7 April 1990, p. 2.

42. "Continuing Along the Road," p. 26.

C   H   A   P   T   E   R

4

Political
Institutions

The study of Soviet institutions used to be the study of bureaucracy. Now it is the study of revolution, and the revolution is not over. We are witnessing a painful process of institution building in a region with extremely limited democratic traditions, immense economic problems, and a complex web of long-suppressed ethnic conflicts. The results thus far have been momentous—the defeat of the dominant political force (the CPSU), the construction and reconstruction of new governing structures, and the dismantling of an empire. The entire process has occurred at breakneck speed. As you read this chapter you will undoubtedly be astonished by the rapidity of institutional change discussed, the sheer number of organizational charts presented, and the layering of the old with the new at every phase of the analysis. The process is hard to describe and even harder to really understand. When studying political institutions in the USSR in the late 1980s and 1990s, one cannot conceive of them as rigid structures, but rather as part of an evolving political environment. The fluid political processes that underlie the institutional changes are never fully captured in the structures themselves, but have helped, at each phase, to bring the next transition.

The state institutions, which used to be mere arms of the Communist Party, have seen a revival of power and numerous restructurings.

Thus far, the most dramatic changes occurred in the spring of 1989 and in September 1991. The 1989 changes heralded the birth of a civil society struggling to free itself of control from above. New quasi-democratic parliamentary bodies replaced the old rubber-stamp organs of previous decades. Now deputies spoke out freely and this gave courage to society at large to begin the process of political self-determination. With the failed coup d'état of August 1991, another turning point occurred. The final blow was struck to Communist Party control as well as to central domination of the republics. The now-old "new" structures once again had to be refashioned to capture the radical decentralization of power, but at the same time to provide a framework for averting total economic collapse. These new transitional structures will undoubtedly soon be superseded by others. In this chapter we discuss each of these transition points and the intermediary steps between, trying to show the roots of the new in the old, but also the revolutionary significance of the transformations.

The State: Administrative and Soviet Structures

A crucial dimension of political reform since the Nineteenth Party Conference in 1988 has been a shift in power from the CPSU to newly constituted state structures. Efforts to restructure the state organs have focused on a revitalization and *demokratizatsiia* of the soviets (the legislative bodies). At the same time, Gorbachev called for a reduction in the size and power of the central executive organs (the ministries). This has involved attempts to devolve economic decision making to the enterprises and finally to the market. For purposes of clarity, we first examine the new soviets and then the changing executive structures.

The Soviets

Since the revolutions of 1917, the soviets, or councils, have existed at all levels of the state structure to represent the population. These have been the formal legislative organs of the Soviet polity. In the early 1920s, however, these organs lost most of their autonomy to CPSU dominance, and they became largely legitimatory, symbolic institutions. Only in 1989 did a process of revitalization begin to transform the soviets into true instruments of public representation.

Beginning in the 1930s, the soviets were directly elected at each level by universal suffrage. Unlike the system in the Party organs, selection did not involve a delegate system, with lower bodies electing representatives to higher bodies. In addition, the soviets allegedly represented all of the working people, not just Party members. In fact, a substantial portion of deputies elected to the soviets were not Party members.

Despite the apparent "democratic" nature of the soviets, until reforms were instituted in 1989, these organs were fundamentally flawed as instruments of democratic control. First, with the exception of some experiments in 1987, elections were not competitive; only one candidate was presented to the electorate. Therefore, the nomination process was crucial. Various public organizations (e.g., the trade unions, work collectives, and Komsomol) made suggestions, but the Party actually had control over the selection process. Thus, any non-Party candidates who were nominated for office were deemed to be loyal and trustworthy to the Party.

Second, citizens were obligated to vote, so the usual turnout rates were reported at over 99 percent. In the same way, results showed more than 99 percent of the voters approving the name on the ballot, although citizens could cross off the name of the single candidate by entering a special voting booth. Since voters otherwise simply dropped their ballots in the box without entering the booth, a voter was advertising his or her dissent by exercising the right to reject the proposed candidate. Nonetheless, in a small number of cases, a majority of the electorate in a district did reject the candidate offered. When this happened, a new candidate was placed before the electorate.

Because elections were controlled, the Party could ensure that the soviets, to some extent, were demographically representative of the population at large. In this sense, they *appeared* to be more representative than Party bodies such as the Central Committee. For example, in 1984 workers constituted 35.2 percent of the deputies of the Supreme Soviet, whereas only 4 percent of Central Committee members elected in 1981 were from that group. In the same year, collective farmers constituted 16.1 percent of the Supreme Soviet deputies but less than 1 percent of the voting members of the Central Committee. Thus, a significant proportion of the population had occasion, at some point and at some level of the system, to participate in activities of the elected soviets. One effect of such participation may have been to inculcate an acceptance of the normalcy of compliance with and conformity to existing political structures. The soviets also provided formal democratic legitimation for Soviet politics, as the Party claimed that all citizens had the opportunity to participate in the selection of their representatives.

A third flaw related to the manner in which the soviets carried out their legislative functions. Until late 1988, their decisions were apparently always unanimous. The deliberative function of meetings was negligible, except in some cases at the local level. Policy was initiated from other quarters, usually the Politburo. Based on information provided by the Party apparatus or ministerial organs, the Politburo often placed an issue on the policy agenda and oversaw the formulation of draft legislation or executive decrees and resolutions. Most legislative enactments were initially approved by the Presidium of the Supreme Soviet, later to be rubber-stamped by the full legislative body. Legislative commissions of the Supreme Soviet frequently involved deputies in discussion of draft legislation and sometimes generated proposed revisions of drafts, but their acceptance ultimately depended on the approval of top state and Party leaders.

The most active and influential members of the legislative commissions were officials who held important posts elsewhere in the system, not the deputies of peasant or working-class background. At the local level, the soviets had some impact on policies related to local recreational facilities, day care, and housing, although even in this area, the executive organs of the local soviets (the soviet executive committee and its various departments and committees) were more important than the elected soviets themselves. Furthermore, local state organs faced huge obstacles in realizing their plans, due to budgetary and planning constraints rooted in the central economic planning system.

The reforms proposed by Gorbachev and subsequently adopted by constitutional amendment in 1988 did, therefore, bring radical transformations in the structures and functions of soviet organs (see Tables 4.1 and 4.2). First, elections were made competitive. The inaugural elections to the new CPD on March 11, 1989, saw more than one candidate running in all but 384 of the 1,500 constituencies.[1] In many cases, more than two candidates were on the ballot and runoff elections were required if none received a majority of the vote. Each candidate was encouraged to issue a programmatic statement to assist

voters in making a choice. Local elections held throughout the Soviet Union in the spring of 1990 were even more broadly contested. On February 24, 1990, elections in the Lithuanian Republic involved de facto competition between various political parties, but the names of the parties were not included on the ballot. In October 1990, the first explicitly multiparty elections occurred in the Georgian Republic. A coalition of groups called the Round Table won the majority of seats, putting CPSU deputies in a minority. Through direct popular votes on June 12, 1991, Boris Yel'tsin was elected president of the Russian Republic and reform leaders Anatolii Sobchak and Gavriil Popov both were confirmed in their positions as mayors of Leningrad and Moscow, respectively.

To be sure, in 1989 and 1990 there were irregularities in the electoral process in some instances. In some constituencies, the Party apparatus was still able to exert considerable influence over the nomination process. Furthermore, a weary population, wary of promises and sometimes confused by the profusion of unfamiliar candidates, turned out in declining numbers in the local elections of 1990. Overall voter turnout in the March 1989 elections was over 89 percent; in the 1990 elections it declined, for example, in the Russian Republic to below 70 percent but rose again to over 70 percent in the June 1991 vote. Despite these problems, the new electoral procedures, at least initially, vastly increased both the legitimacy and the vitality of the soviet structures.

Ironically, competitive elections, at least initially, increased the proportion of CPSU members in the new legislative bodies at the center (87 percent of deputies elected to the new CPD in 1989 were CPSU members or candidate members, as compared to 71.5 percent of deputies elected to the previous Supreme Soviet). The new electoral system also produced a legislative body less reflective of the demographic composition of the population than previously. For example, in 1989 only 23.7 percent of elected

Table 4.1 Professional Composition of the Supreme Soviet, 1984 and 1989, and the Congress of People's Deputies (CPD), 1989 (in percent)

	Supreme Soviet 1984	CPD 1989	Supreme Soviet 1989
Top political leadership	1.5%	0.7%	0.2%
Top and middle-level managerial personnel	40.0	39.8	32.8
Lower-level managerial personnel	6.6	25.3	35.3
Workers, collective farmers, and nonprofessional office employees	45.9	22.1	18.3
Intelligentsia	6.0	10.2	12.5
Military	3.7	4.0	1.8
KGB	1.1	0.4	0.2
Pensioners	n.a.	1.6	0.9
Priests	0.0	0.3	0.0

Note: Percentages for the military and KGB were calculated by Mann, Monyak, and Teague and added to official Soviet data; for this reason, the columns do not total 100 percent. The figure for pensioners in 1984 was not given in the source, although there certainly were pensioners in the Supreme Soviet at that time.

Source: Dawn Mann, Robert Monyak, and Elizabeth Teague, Center for International and Strategic Studies and Radio Free Europe/Radio Liberty, *The Supreme Soviet: A Biographical Dictionary* (Washington: Radio Free Europe, 1989), p. 31.

deputies were workers or collective farmers, as compared to 51.3 percent for the prereform Supreme Soviet. Representation of women also declined from 32.8 percent to 15 percent in 1989.[2]

Although the CPSU could no longer engineer the composition of the soviets, the Party apparatus retained influence over the nomination process in many regions.[3] Furthermore, the greater public prominence of Party members and educated citizens facilitated their success. The Georgian elections of October 1990 were, however, a harbinger of the future. CPSU candidates won only 30 percent of the seats in Georgia. Throughout the USSR, non-Party figures have gained new public recognition. Indicative of the trend is the fact that the three leaders who won posts in the June 12, 1991 election in Russia (Yel'tsin, Sobchak, Popov) had quit the Communist Party in 1990. Decisions taken in late August 1991 to suspend CPSU activities and to confiscate Party property will force any successor "communist" party (should such a party be permitted) to compete on a relatively equal basis with other political forces. Given public sentiment, this will almost surely mean a dramatic decline in its representation in elected offices.

An additional innovation characterized the national elections of 1989. The new representative body, the CPD, included 750 deputies elected from a wide variety of official public organizations, such as the CPSU, the official trade unions, the Writers' Union, the Academy of Sciences, and the Komsomol. Selection of deputies from these bodies was subject to easier manipulation by the entrenched Party elite,[4] but in some cases these elections became highly controversial. A notable case involved the widely respected physicist and former dissident Andrei Sakharov, who initially failed to win one of the seats allocated to the prestigious Academy of Sciences. Sakharov was subsequently nomi-

Table 4.2 Composition by Nationality of Various Political Bodies

Ethnic Group	% of Soviet Population (1989)	% of Party Members Who Belong to Ethnic Group (1989)	% of Congress of People's Deputies (1989)	% of Supreme Soviet (1989)	% of Council of Union	% of Council of Nationalities
Russians[a]	51.0%	58.6%	45.6%	38.0%	55.0%	21.0%
Ukrainians[a]	15.5	16.1	11.5	11.1	16.6	5.1
Uzbeks[a]	5.8	2.5	3.9	3.3	3.3	3.3
Belorussians[a]	3.5	3.9	4.2	3.7	3.7	3.7
Kazakhs[a]	2.9	2.1	2.4	2.4	2.6	2.2
Azerbaidzhanis[a]	2.4	1.9	2.7	3.7	1.8	5.5
Armenians[a]	1.6	1.5	2.7	3.0	1.1	4.8
Tadzhiks[a]	1.5	0.5	2.0	2.8	1.5	4.1
Georgians[a]	1.4	1.7	3.2	3.7	1.8	5.5
Moldavians[a]	1.2	0.6	1.9	1.8	1.1	2.6
Lithuanians[a]	1.1	0.8	2.3	2.2	1.1	3.3
Turkmen[a]	1.0	0.4	1.8	1.8	0.7	3.0
Kirgiz[a]	0.9	0.4	1.6	2.6	1.5	3.7
Latvians[a]	0.5	0.4	2.0	2.0	1.1	3.0
Estonians[a]	0.4	0.3	1.8	2.0	0.7	3.3
OTHER GROUPS OVER 1 MILLION POPULATION						
Tatars[b]	2.3	0.3	1.0	0.9	0.7	1.1
Germans	0.7	0.5	0.4	0.6	0.4	0.7
Chuvash[b]	0.6	2.1	0.7	0.9	—	1.8
Jews[c]	0.5	0.6	0.7	0.6	—	1.1
Bashkir[b]	0.5	1.1	0.5	0.6	0.7	0.4
Mordvinians[b]	0.4	0.4	0.5	0.7	0.4	1.1
Poles	0.4	0.4	0.3	0.3	0.4	0.7
Other Ethnic Groups	3.9	2.0	6.3	11.3	3.8	19.0

[a]National groups with union republic status.
[b]National groups with autonomous republic status.
[c]National groups with autonomous region status.

Sources: Calculated from Goskomstat *Natsional'nyi sostav naseleniia* (Moscow: Information-Publication Center, 1989); *Izvestiia TsK KPSS*, no. 2 (1989), pp. 140–141; *Izvestiia TsK KPSS*, no. 7 (1989), p. 113.

nated to run for a seat to represent the city of Moscow but withdrew from that contest, insisting that he would accept election only from the Academy of Sciences. In this way, Sakharov forced the issue within the Academy of Sciences, resulting in a successful challenge to the top-down control of elections within that organization. Sakharov finally won his seat representing the Academy and became a highly vocal and respected advocate of democratic reform within the new CPD until his death in December 1989.

In sharp contrast to this contest, the CPSU leadership recommended exactly one hundred candidates for its one hundred allocated seats in the new representative organ; they were all accepted by a vote of the CPSU Central Committee. Although the Party leader, Gorbachev, was pressing for *demokratizatsiia* of political structures at large, he was either unwilling or unable to enforce competition within his own organization. This sent an ambiguous message to the population at large and to Party members about the Party's own intentions.

Once the new CPD convened, a new constitutional amendment abandoned the representation of public organizations for subsequent elections. That representation was deemed unfair because it enabled overrepresentation of certain citizens who could vote both in their territorial constituencies and in the designated public organizations. Furthermore, the determination of which public organizations were entitled to such special representation was becoming increasingly difficult to justify, as Soviet political life was undergoing a dramatic process of pluralization.

The constitutional amendments of 1988 also changed the institutional structures themselves (see Figures 4.1 and 4.2). An entirely new body, the CPD, was created. This large organ, with 2,250 deputies, elected from its members, on a rotating basis, a smaller bicameral Supreme Soviet. (The first rotation of members to the Supreme Soviet occurred in December 1990.) The new Supreme Soviet, like its predecessor, was

bicameral. The two chambers were the Council of the Union and the Council of Nationalities; each had 271 members. The Supreme Soviet was a working legislative body that met at least twice a year for three to four months. Its major powers included adoption of legislation and the state budget, confirmation of the prime minister and members of the Cabinet of Ministers, setting of election dates for the CPD, ratification of international treaties, and recommendation of long-term plans and federal programs to the CPD for approval. The body also could issue a type of vote of no confidence to remove the Cabinet of Ministers if the president or prime minister placed the question before it (as occurred following the August coup attempt).

The CPD had a broader, more representative mandate. It was given the power to ratify the constitution and constitutional amendments, thus acting as a sort of constituent assembly. It also approved long-term state plans and guidelines for domestic and foreign policy. The body elected members of the Supreme Soviet from its own ranks, elected the officers (chair and deputy chairs) of the Supreme Soviet, and chose the members of the Committee for Constitutional oversight. The CPD could, if it deemed it appropriate, revoke legislation passed by the Supreme Soviet.

Why were two legislative bodies created in 1988 rather than one? One explanation focuses on the size of the Soviet Union, the diversity of its population, and the complexity of the reform process. Given the ethnic complexity of Soviet society and its large population, a parliament small enough to function effectively as a deliberative body might be unable to represent the full diversity of views within the population. The Supreme Soviet is small enough to be a real working parliament but is perhaps limited in its capacity to capture the expanding plurality of views in society. The CPD, on the other hand, was too large to debate and deliberate policy effectively, but it could serve as a sort of constitutional congress, acting as a final arbiter on

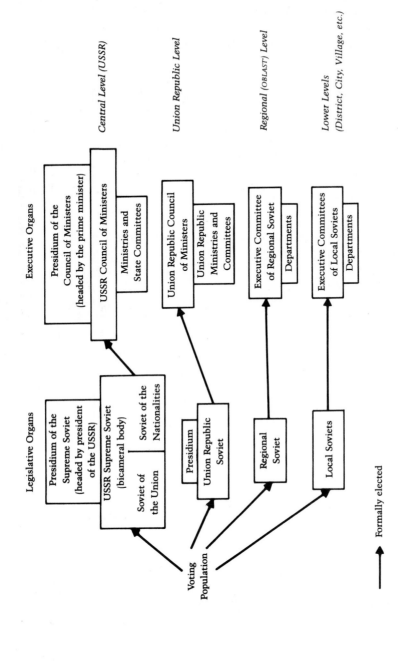

Figure 4.1   State Structures of the USSR* pre-1989

*Levels of government have been simplified for clarity of presentation.

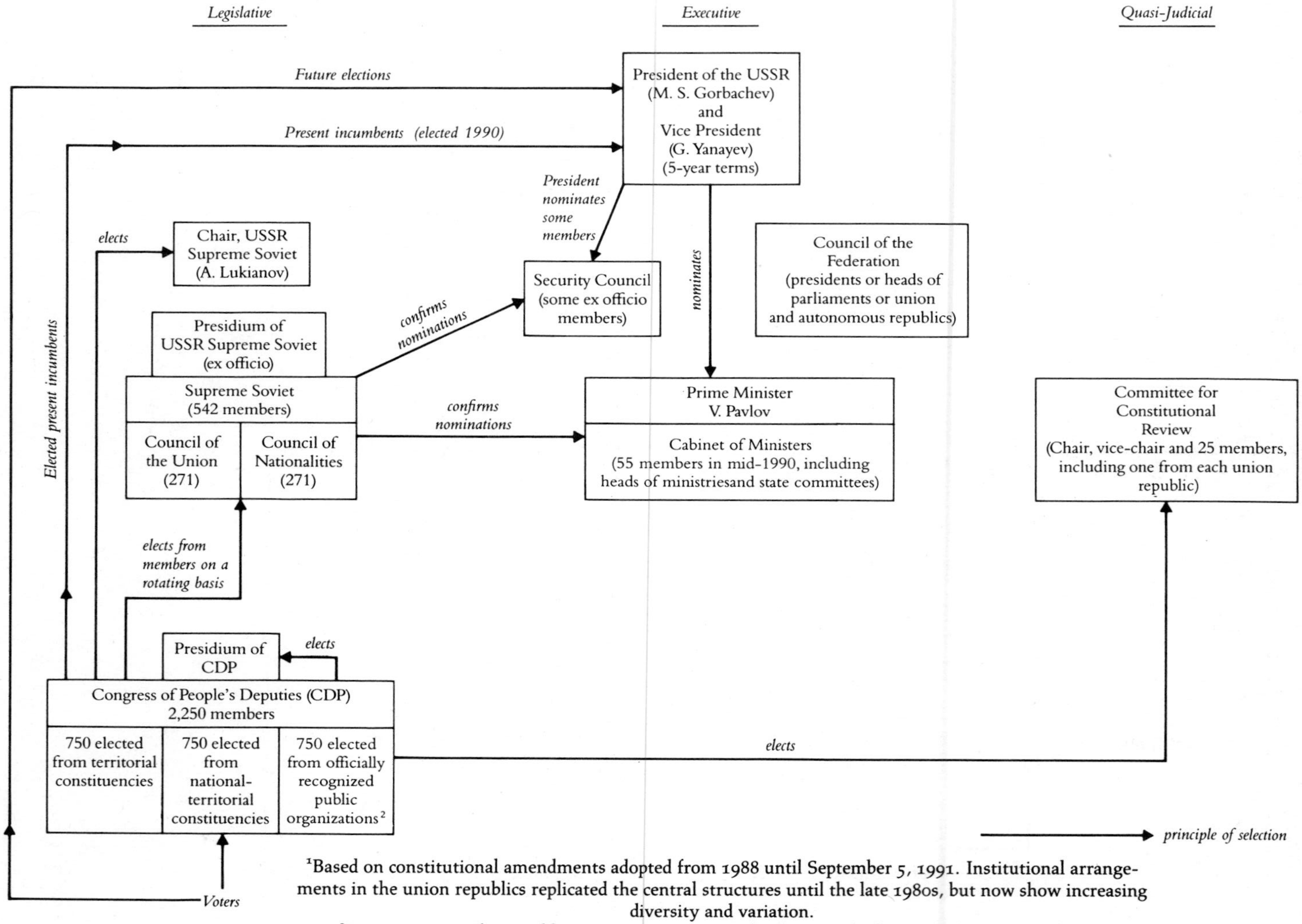

Figure 4.2   Central State Political Institutions of the USSR[1] (June 1991)

[1]Based on constitutional amendments adopted from 1988 until September 5, 1991. Institutional arrangements in the union republics replicated the central structures until the late 1980s, but now show increasing diversity and variation.

[2]Representatives from public organizations were to be eliminated when new elections were held.

decisions affecting the very essence of the reform process. Indeed, on September 2, 1991, following the failed coup, the CPD was convened in emergency session to consider the future of the government and the union. It approved suspension of some constitutional provisions to allow formation of new transitional institutions that themselves would deliberate a new constitution and oversee the process transferring numerous powers to the republics.

A second explanation for the dual structure focuses on the political advantages of the arrangement for the reform leadership. According to this view, the large CPD was more easily subject to political manipulation by a politically astute leader (the chair) than the smaller Supreme Soviet would be. Furthermore, the indirect election of the Supreme Soviet allowed the leadership some greater influence over the final composition of the smaller legislative body. Both explanations undoubtedly contain an element of truth.

The first meetings of the new CPD and Supreme Soviet in 1989 elicited intense interest among Soviet citizens, particularly because they were broadcast in full on Soviet television. For the first time in memory, elected officials engaged in heated debates in full public view. One deputy, Sergei Stankevich, a respected reform-minded historian (later elected deputy mayor of Moscow), explained:

It (the Congress) was conceived and carried out as a sort of nationwide forum allowing for the expression of the full spectrum of views currently existing in our society. This is what gave even the First Congress its great significance. It shocked the public and irreversibly changed its mentality.

To me this was the main function of the Congress—to reform public mentality, influence it and step up openness by placing on its agenda the most urgent and burning issues that are being widely discussed at home, at work and in the street.[5]

Although the overall complexion of the Congress was relatively compliant, in the late spring of 1989, an interregional group of people's deputies was initiated, soon uniting some four hundred of the more reform-minded deputies. At the other end of the political spectrum, a caucus of more conservative deputies emerged, called Soiuz (Union), and it gained increasing influence over time. Other, smaller caucuses also formed, including a group of ecologically minded deputies and a Baltic group. In the absence of a formal opposition party, these caucuses promoted more organized political debate and allowed new, younger leaders to gain visibility in the public eye. At the same time, Gorbachev, chair of the Supreme Soviet until the spring of 1990 when he was elected president of the USSR, proved effective in guiding debate within the CPD to support the general outlines of his reform agenda. Some charged Gorbachev with manipulating the CPD, but Stankevich himself notes:

The 2,250 deputies were like a turbulent sea, chaotic, and spontaneous with conflicts and clashes bursting out here and there, people forcing their way to the podium, endless deviations from the subject, and attempts to raise local issues and dwell on the points which the speaker considered vital. . . . Obviously, keeping this chaos under control required firmness on the part of the chairman. . . . Was it used to keep the debates under control or have them go a certain way?"[6]

Stankevich leaves this crucial question unanswered. He notes, however, that all too often the deputies themselves were "not prepared for organizational self-determination within the framework of the Congress." He attributes this to, among other reasons, a "misguided common-sense which prescribed traditional, reliable measures to be carried out gradually and with emphatic loyalty to the leaders of perestroika."[7] The lack of previous experience with democratic politics reinforced this tendency.

The Supreme Soviet played an active role in drafting and amending legislation. It had eight permanent commissions (four attached to each chamber), as well as fourteen committees for the

Supreme Soviet as a whole. These bodies also involved deputies in the CPD who were not part of the Supreme Soviet, thus expanding the range of views and expertise tapped. The legislative commissions and committees conducted hearings and approved drafts of legislation. They were, however, greatly hampered by the small size of their trained, paid staff (the counterpart of the U.S. congressional research staff) to assist them. While many of the deputies themselves were professionals or expert in the field in question, their capability to gather, analyze, and synthesize the massive amounts of information needed to formulate good policy was humanly limited. Furthermore, it was often difficult for deputies to gain access to information they needed, even though they were legally entitled to it; many ministries and government bodies still defensively guarded their previously secret data. So strained were the resources available to deputies that legislation on the status of the deputy passed in 1990 obligated local soviets, enterprises, and organizations in the deputy's district to provide the deputy with access to equipment such as computers and copiers, as well as to the use of secretarial services.[8]

Such arrangements were obviously inadequate. Some of the most committed deputies worked sixteen-hour days, retreating to their modest apartments or hotel rooms only for a few hours of rest, often interrupted by numerous phone calls. Other deputies did not display such a serious attitude and were chastised for failure to appear even at important sessions of the Supreme Soviet. On numerous occasions, votes had to be delayed for lack of a quorum. Nonetheless, the title "people's deputy of the USSR" conferred status on an individual, along with immunity to criminal charges (unless rescinded by the CPD itself), a modest salary, and certain limited privileges in gaining access to goods and services.

Deputies from Lithuania attended sessions only as observers from March 11, 1990 (when Lithuania declared its independence). Starting in late April 1990, they stopped participating altogether. Likewise, during 1990 and 1991 many deputies from Estonia and Latvia boycotted the meetings. This further complicated the quorum problem and led the Supreme Soviet to adopt a decree subtracting the number of such members from the number needed for a quorum.

After the first sessions of the CPD and the Supreme Soviet, the new institutions lost much of their credibility as viable organs of political reform and leadership. While the Supreme Soviet passed numerous legislative acts and the CPD adopted several constitutional amendments, the measures did not produce a noticeable improvement in the quality of life. Rather, a deterioration ensued. In the face of social and economic crisis, the CPD and Supreme Soviet appeared to large parts of the public to be increasingly ineffectual in generating legitimate and practical solutions.

Following the failed coup d'état in August 1991, first the Supreme Soviet and then the CPD were convened to deal with the crisis. The entire government (the prime minister and members of the Cabinet of Ministers) was forced to resign, and new leaders of the security and military organs were appointed. From September 2 to 5 the CPD considered what measures should be taken to prevent the central government and the union from totally collapsing. Finally, after intense pressure and manuevering by Gorbachev, who chaired the meeting, the CPD approved new transitional institutional structures. The measures had been hashed out by Gorbachev, Yel'tsin, and leaders of the other republics (excluding the Baltics, Moldova, and Georgia). Establishment of the institutions was accomplished through suspension of various constitutional provisions; the new bodies were deemed to be transitional until a new constitution and some kind of new union treaty between desirous republics could be fashioned.

The basic principle underlying the new structures involved a radical shift of power from the central to the republican governments. The CPD declared a transition period "for forming a new system of state relations based on the expression of the will of the republics and the interests of the nations." One of the major tasks of the transition period was formulation of a new union treaty "in which each state shall be able to define on its own the form of its participation."[9] In line with these principles, during the transition period the basic unit of representation in the new organs of central state power became the republic (see Figure 4.3).

During this week, the CPD, in effect, legislated itself out of office, although the deputies retained their salaries and privileges until the end of their five-year terms. The body was un-

likely to convene again. The old Supreme Soviet was also disbanded and a new Supreme Soviet was formed, based on different representative principles. The new Supreme Soviet is also bicameral, this time with a Council of the Republics and a Council of the Union. Members of both bodies are selected by the governments of the republics, rather than by the CPD or by the electorate directly. Each republic has twenty deputies in the Council of the Republics except for Russia, which has fifty-two deputies to allow representation of the various national groups within the Russian Republic. Autonomous republics or regions in other republics add one additional seat each to the appropriate republic's delegation. Deputies are to be chosen from

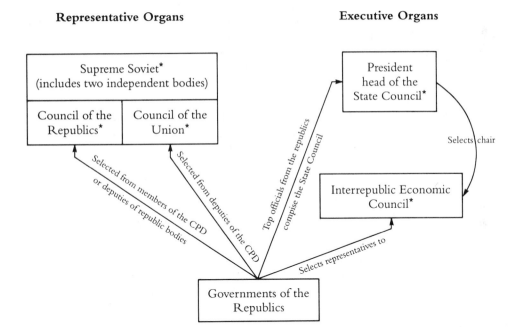

Representative Organs   **Executive Organs**

*Institutions marked with an asterisk were newly created or created in a new form by the CPD on September 5, 1991. Other institutions listed here existed previously. Some of the other bodies included in Figure 29.2 may continue to exist after Sept. 5, 1991, but at this time their status is unclear.

Figure 4.3 Transitional Governing Institutions of the USSR (as approved by the Congress of People's Deputies on September 5, 1991)*

among members of the CPD or from republic-level deputies. For adopting decisions, each republic has only one vote. The Council of the Union is selected on the basis of established proportions in the previous parliament; members must be chosen from among members of the now dormant CPD.

These two houses of the Supreme Soviet are granted joint authority to amend the constitution, to approve the union budget, and to consider the most important domestic and foreign policy issues. Decisions taken by the Council of the Union (relating to citizens' rights and freedoms, and other issues) require approval by the Council of the Republic, and the latter has authority to organize the work of central organs. Presumably this means it will decide the fate and structure of the Cabinet of Ministers, the ministries, and the state committees. The first session of the new Supreme Soviet was held in October 1991, but it was attended by representatives from only seven of the twelve remaining republics.

The new parliament faces even greater problems in generating effective and legitimate solutions to the mass of problems confronting the region than did the old structures, for its range of authority vis-à-vis the governments in the republics is highly circumscribed and poorly defined.

The Executive Organs

In March 1990, a new and important post was added to the Soviet state structures—the post of president of the USSR. Gorbachev himself pressed for its creation, arguing that a strong executive figure was needed to provide leadership for the country. In the face of some heavy opposition, the CPD adopted a constitutional amendment creating the position and subsequently elected Gorbachev as its first occupant. These were controversial decisions. Critics charged that the powerful new post could become a springboard for personal dictatorship (if

not by Gorbachev, then by a future incumbent). They also felt that the first president should be subject to popular election rather than indirect election by the CPD. Gorbachev and his supporters worried that an open national contest for the post would further polarize an already divided society and present the specter of a defeated Gorbachev but no viable alternative. Thus, the deputies were persuaded, after some questionable application of parliamentary procedure, to elect Gorbachev as the first president. Subsequent selection of the president was to be by popular election and if the post is retained, will likely be in 1992. When Gorbachev's political rival, Boris Yel'tsin, was elected president of the Russian Republic by direct popular vote on June 12, 1991, Gorbachev's failure to have received a direct popular mandate in 1990 made his claim to popular legitimacy seem even more dubious (see Table 4.3).

The new presidency was explicitly modeled after the U.S. and French presidential systems. (In the weeks preceding adoption of the proposal, articles appeared in major Soviet newspapers explaining the French and U.S. systems to the Soviet population.) Initially, the system adopted in the USSR structurally resembled the French system much more closely than the U.S., for it involved the grafting of a strong presidency onto the preexisting parliamentary structures. Like a more traditional Western European parliamentary system, the new Soviet structures had an elected parliament, which in turn approved a prime minister (nominated, in the Soviet case, by the president). In the U.S. presidential system, there is, of course, no counterpart of the prime minister.

The president was granted some impressive and, over time, increasing powers, but in many cases limits were placed on their exercise. Prior to the September 1991 changes, the president could veto legislation passed by the Supreme Soviet and recommend appointees to government posts (including the prime minister). He had extensive authority in the foreign policy

Table 4.3 Positive Evaluations of the Activities of Prominent Political and Government Figures (percent of those surveyed with a positive evaluation*)

Name of leader	Overall Percentage with a Positive Evaluation June 1990	Nov. 1990	Selected Socio-economic Groups (Nov. 1990)						
			Workers	Peasants	Scientific Personnel (Universities)	Cultural and Educational Personnel	Military Officer Corps	Students	Workers in the Party Apparatus
M. S. Gorbachev	60	25	23	30	37	18	24	31	23
B. N. Yel'tsin	72	69	73	59	70	62	64	79	33
V. A. Kriuchkov[1]	17	18	15	18	30	25	24	29	37
A. I. Luk'ianov[2]	32	25	21	26	26	29	27	18	56
G. Kh. Popov	32	29	28	8	50	36	46	40	2
N. I. Ryzhkov	62	34	34	37	37	33	33	31	54
A. A. Sobchak	58	45	46	26	67	53	55	65	12
E. Shevardnadze	66	64	61	65	71	63	76	83	72
D. T. Yazov[3]	n.a.	14	13	18	15	9	9	19	21

*Includes those replying with a "positive" evaluation and with a "mostly positive" evaluation, based on an all-Union survey conducted from October 24–November 5, 1990. The Soviet source indicates that the international standard for an adequate rating is 43 percent positive evaluation.

[1]Head of the KGB. [2]Chair of the Supreme Soviet. [3]Minister of Defense. All three individuals were involved or implicated in the 1991 coup attempt.

Source: Tsentr sotsiologicheskikh issledovanii, Akademiia obshchestvennykh nauk pri TsK KPSS, *Politicheskaia sotsiologiia: Informatsionnyi biulleten'*, II, no. 2 (Moscow, 1991) p. 87.

sphere and vast powers of decree (which were explicitly limited after the coup). The new transitional structures formed in September 1991 by the CPD left the position of the president intact, but the scope of the central government itself was greatly reduced, as were the president's powers. Furthermore, since Gorbachev was responsible for the appointment of the men who perpetrated the coup, this may also have fueled pressure to reduce his role. The exact parameters of the president's remaining legal authority are not yet clear.

Changes adopted in late 1990 created the post of vice president, a Security Council, and a new Cabinet of Ministers (replacing the former Council of Ministers). A new law on the Cabinet of Ministers was adopted on March 20, 1991.[10] The cabinet and its head, the prime minister, were made directly subordinate to the president's authority, and the prime minister became the president's chief aide but not the head of government. This moved the structures a step away from the parliamentary model and closer to a strict presidential system of the U.S. variety (albeit with stronger presidential powers and a weaker system of checks and balances than in the United States). Defenders of the new system depicted it as involving a separation of powers between the various institutions. In reality, however, it was hard to assess the potential strength of the institutional actors, since their present roles were so strongly influenced by the particular character of the incumbents. Clearly the system of checks and balances between the central organs was inadequate to prevent or topple the coup d'état attempt of August 1991; the failure of the coup was not the result of any separation of powers in the central government, but rather was brought about by the successful exertion of authority of the government of the Russian Republic.

Before September 1991, the Cabinet of Ministers was subordinate to the president, but in other regards it resembled the former Council of Ministers, which it replaced. The cabinet presided over the complex ministerial structures responsible for running the extensive network of state economic and administrative institutions. Under Brezhnev, the Council of Ministers had more than 110 members who were formally selected by the Supreme Soviet but actually were appointed under the Party's *nomenklatura* system. Membership generally has included the heads of the various ministries, chairpersons of state committees, and chairpersons of the councils of ministers of the union republics. Membership in the Cabinet of Ministers in mid-1991 was to reach fifty-five, but this time did not include chairs of republic bodies (they could participate and vote but were not regular members).

Following formation of the new legislative bodies in 1989, ministerial appointments were subject to sometimes critical scrutiny and approval by the Supreme Soviet. Each of the ministries has been responsible for overseeing a functional branch of the economy, including, for example, the Ministry of Defense, Ministry of the Electronics Industry, Ministry of Transportation Construction, Ministry of Culture, Ministry of Health, and Ministry of Energy and Electrification.

The state committees had duties cutting across the various functional branches of the economy. The most important has been Gosplan (State Planning Committee), which has been responsible for overseeing the drafting and implementation of the five-year and one-year economic plans. Gosplan was replaced by the Ministry of Economics and Prognosis in 1991 and its duties involved primarily long-term planning functions, rather than detailed oversight of the overall running of the economy. Other state committees have included the State Committee on Science and Technology, the State Committee on Prices, and the State Committee for Environmental Protection (created in 1988). Also attached to the Council of Ministers, and then the cabinet, has been the Committee for State Security (KGB). The market reform program adopted by the Supreme Soviet in 1990 implied continuing reductions in the size, and possibly the importance, of the new cabinet, since the state sector of the economy was itself to shrink. Following the failed coup in August 1991, the long-term fate of the various all-union ministries and state committees was even less certain, since many of the enterprises under their control would presumably be turned over to republic control and/or be privatized. Furthermore, the role of central economic planning is likely to decline. As of this writing it is also unclear whether the Cabinet of Ministers will continue to function and, if so, what form it will take.

The head of the Cabinet of Ministers (like the old Council of Ministers) was the prime minister. A Gorbachev protégé, Nikolai Ryzhkov, held that post from September 1985 until late 1990, when he suffered a heart attack following sharp criticism of his economic policy and numerous demands for his resignation. His successor, Valentin Pavlov, was the former minister of finance, and his appointment represented general continuity with the approach of the Ryzhkov government rather than an endorsement of a more radical pace of marketization. Pavlov's conservative convictions were evidenced in his participation in the August 1991 coup attempt. Following the failed coup and sacking of the old ministers, an economic management committee was set up to develop a transitional economic blueprint. The committee was initially chaired by Ivan Silayev, prime minister of the Russian Republic. Also on the committee was Grigorii Yavlinskii, a leading advocate of market reform. In the short-term this committee seemed to be carrying out the functions of the former prime minister.

Two additional bodies—the Presidential Council and the Council of the Federation—were also created in 1990 to advise the president. They have since been abolished. The Presidential Council proved to be a short-lived entity, in existence only from the spring of 1990 until late December 1990. Members from a wide range of backgrounds were appointed by the president, and they acted as his personal consultative committee. As a sounding board for diverse viewpoints, the Presidential Council may have served a transitional function, but its functional superfluity and somewhat arbitrary composition probably explain its early demise.

The Council of the Federation might be seen as a kind of predecessor to the State Council (discussed below) created after the August coup attempt. This body was formed ex officio rather than by personal appointment. It included the presidents or heads of the supreme soviets of the union republics and leaders of autonomous republics. It served as a forum for coordinating the activities of the various republics, ensuring the participation of their governments, and making policy recommendations to the Supreme Soviet. The Council of the Federation reflected the diverse and liberal views of the governments of the various republics, although several republics did not consistently take part in the meetings. The Baltic states maintained observer status in the body from the outset. In announcing his plan for transition to a market economy, Gorbachev noted that an interrepublican economic commission of the Council of the Federation would be created to discuss and oversee the transformation of economic relations among the republics.

Fashioned after the U.S. National Security Council, a new Security Council was appointed in March 1991 (see Table 4.4). It took over some of the consultative functions of the short-lived Presidential Council and acted in an advisory capacity to the president. The Defense Council, which was first made known in the Brezhnev years, continued to operate as well, but apparently under the supervision of the Security Council. The Defense Council had included the president, the minister of defense, and other figures associated with the military-industrial complex. It played an important role in the formulation of defense and foreign policy, although its activities were generally shrouded in secrecy. The frame of reference of the Security Council was broader, to include national defense, economic and ecological security, law and order, and emergency situations. Members were nominated by the president in consultation with the Council of the Federation and approved by the Supreme Soviet, but several members appear to have been included ex officio (for example, Minister of Defense Dmitrii Yazov; KGB head Vladimir Kriuchkov; Foreign Minister Aleksandr Bessmertnykh; and Minister of the Interior Boris Pugo). The membership of the Security Council had a conservative complexion, due to the inclusion of the above officials associated with the military-security complex. It proved to be an unreliable body as the majority of the Council's members were among the leaders of the August coup attempt (see Table 4.5). Only Vadim Bakatin (former minister of the interior, but replaced by Pugo in late 1990) was a respected liberal. He clearly was not involved in the coup attempt. He was appointed head of the KGB following the failed August coup to bring that organization under control of the reformers. Meanwhile, reform figures, including Anatolii Sobchak and Gavriil Popov, refused Gorbachev's request to serve on the Security Council following the coup attempt.

The creation of the presidency, the Security Council, and the Council of the Federation was a clear indication of the real transfer of power that occurred from the CPSU to the state organs. By mid-1990 Gorbachev's claim to leadership

Table 4.4   The Security Council of the USSR (appointed March 7, 1991)

Gennadii Yanayev,[1] Vice President of the USSR

Valentin Pavlov,[1] Prime Minister of the USSR

Vadim Bakatin

Aleksandr Bessmertnykh,[2] Foreign Minister of the USSR

Vladimir Kriuchkov,[1] Head of the KGB

Evgenii Primakov

Boris Pugo,[1] Minister of Internal Affairs

Dmitrii Yazov,[1] Minister of Defense

[1]Indicates an individual who was a leader of the failed coup d'état in August 1991.
[2]Bessmertnykh was removed from his post as foreign minister after the coup attempt based on his failure to oppose it.

Source: *Vedemosti S''ezda narodnykh deputatov SSSR i Verkhovnogo Soveta SSSR*, no. 12 (20 March 1991).

was almost entirely independent of his role as CPSU head.

His decision to retain that position until after the August coup rested, most likely, on a conviction that he could better keep the reform on course if he, rather than a conservative rival, headed that organization. He also likely believed that resigning from the Party post could lead to further polarization and intensified conflict between old Party structures and the newly invigorated state institutions.

After the August coup attempt, new executive structures were formed. As in the new Supreme Soviet, the source of representation of these organs is the republics. Two new organs were created, the State Council and the Interrepublic Economic Committee. The State Council consists of the president of the USSR and top officials of the union republics. (In this way it resembles the old Council of the Federation.) Its decisions are binding. It is not clear to what extent the president will rely on the State Council, how committed the republics will be to its success, and therefore whether it will be any more effective as an instrument of interrepublic cooperation than was the old Council of the Federation. In abolishing the position of vice president, the new mechanism gave the State Council

the power to designate a chairman to take over the president's duties, should the latter become incapacitated. The choice must be confirmed by the Supreme Soviet within three days. This measure was an effort to prevent a repeat of the August coup and develop some system of collective responsibility in the case of a leadership vacuum. The second body, the Interrepublic Economic Committee, represents the republics on an equal basis and is responsible for coordinating the implementation of economic reforms and social policy. This could prove a formidable task, not only because of the crisis nature of the problems, but due to the difficulty of achieving agreement among the remaining republic governments. The repeated restructuring of the executive organs, even before the coup attempt, suggests how complex it is to fashion effective mechanisms of governance.

The Judiciary

Traditionally, the judiciary has not formed an independent branch of government in the USSR as it does in some Western states, and the notion of separation of powers was not accepted in Soviet Marxist ideology until recently. Rather, the law was seen as an arm of the political authority

Table 4.5   Profile of the "Coup Plotters"[1]

Name	Year of Birth	Major Posts Held at Time of Coup Attempt	Date Appointed	Career Background and Previous Posts
Gennadii I. Yanayev	1937	Vice President of USSR USSR Security Council	Dec. 1990 March 1991	Komsomol, CPSU apparatus, official trade union
Vladimir A. Kruichkov	1924	Head of KGB USSR Security Council	1988 March 1991	Komsomol, diplomatic work, CPSU apparatus, KGB
Valentin S. Pavlov	1937	Prime Minister of USSR USSR Security Council	Jan. 1991 March 1991	Official in state bureaucracy
Dmitrii T. Yazov	1923	Defense Minister USSR Security Council	Dec. 1987 March 1991	Military officer (general of the army), candidate member in CPSU Politburo
Boris K. Pugo	1937	Interior Minister USSR Security Council	Dec. 1990 March 1991	Komsomol, CPSU apparatus, former head of Latvian KGB, former head of Latvian Party
Oleg D. Baklanov	1932	First Deputy Chair, Defense Council	n.a.	Factory manager, armaments specialist, state bureaucracy (Minister of the Machine-Building Industry), CPSU Secretariat
Vasilii A. Starodubtsev	1931	Chair, USSR Peasants' Union and RSFSR Agrarian Union[2]	1990	Kolkhoz chair, Novomoskovskoe Agroindustrial Association
Aleksandr Tiziakov	1926	President, USSR State Association of State-Owned Industrial, Construction, Transport, and Communications Enterprises[3]	1990	Director of the Kalinin Machine-Building Plant (an artillery factory in Sverdlovsk)

[1]The list includes the eight members of the self-declared "State Committee for the State of the Emergency in the USSR" who perpetrated the attempted coup d'état August 19–21, 1991. Others, including Anatolii Luk'ianov (chair of the USSR Supreme Soviet since March 1990) and Valerii I. Boldin (head of the presidential staff) are widely believed to have been leading figures in the coup as well. Biographical information is taken from the author's files; various issues of *Izvestiia TsK KPSS*; Elizabeth Teague, "Coup d'État Represented Naked Interests" *Report on the USSR*, 3, no. 35 (30 August 1991), pp. 1–3; and Don Van Atta, "Profile of Coup Leader Vasilii Starodubtsev," in *Ibid.*, pp. 3–5.

[2]A conservative organization set up in 1990 with the support of Yegor Ligachev. Starodubtsev openly opposed privatization of land.

[3]Involves heavy representation of the military-industrial complex in the production system.

to further the process of constructing a socialist society. Soviet Marxist thought traditionally denied the necessity for judicial review of Party or state actions.

Since the appointment of judges and procurators was part of the *nomenklatura* system, the Party exerted considerable influence over the judiciary. One of the main targets of criticism under *glasnost'* has been "telephone justice," the phenomenon of Party officials instructing judges how to rule in specific cases. While such direct political intrusion was more common in political cases than in routine criminal cases, once a suspect was officially indicted, he or she generally was convicted. Political decisions also mandated harsher sentences for certain types of criminal charges.

Khrushchev initiated a campaign for "socialist legality," which involved increasing the uniformity of procedures and the codification of civil and criminal law. This brought considerable predictability to the manner in which routine cases were handled. In some regards, Soviet legal practice resembles continental European patterns. For example, until recently there was no jury trial. Instead, the judge was assisted by two lay assessors, and the pretrial investigation took on more importance than in the United States. Unique aspects of Soviet legal practice centered on the educative and deterrent roles attributed to law, as well as on the importance of social rehabilitation and peer involvement. The accused's general character and contribution to society were considered as relevant evidence, and often coworkers or neighbors were called to testify on these matters.

As discussed previously, under *perestroika* establishment of a law-based state became a political priority. In the legal sphere, this involved a dramatic change in the attitude toward judicial organs and processes. An independent judiciary, separation of powers, presumption of innocence, and a modified form of judicial review are now officially accepted concepts. Lawyers have formed an independent association, advocating the accused's right to free selection of counsel and access for the accused's counsel to information from the pretrial investigation. Jury trials have been introduced for particular types of cases, and telephone justice has come under harsh criticism.

At the pinnacle of the state system, a new Committee of Constitutional Review began functioning in 1990. Its twenty-seven members were legal experts elected by the CPD. While the committee was not given the power of judicial review in the U.S. sense, it was granted a mandate to (1) review alleged incompatibilities between laws and the constitution; (2) review alleged incompatibilities between all-Union legislation or the all-Union constitution, on the one hand, and union republic laws or constitutions, on the other; and (3) recommend changes in legislation to bring Soviet practice more in line with constitutional requirements. The body's conclusions were given only recommendatory status, although they could be enforced by the CPD. Only in cases involving violations of human rights and freedoms was the committee given authority to declare acts null and void. As is common in some parliamentary systems, the CPD retained final authority in interpreting the constitution.

The formation of the Committee for Constitutional Review represented a major deviation from past Soviet practice in the direction of establishing a truly independent role for the judiciary. Although the committee was initially not empowered to issue opinions regarding the congruity of union republic laws and constitutions with the all-Union constitution until the latter was amended to reflect newly negotiated relations between the two levels of government, it began functioning in other spheres in January 1990. As noted in Chapter 28, in 1990 it proved its willingness to declare presidential decrees unconstitutional. The new union treaty, which was to be signed on August 20, 1991 (but was scuttled by the coup attempt), contained a provision for a new constitutional court to adjudicate jurisdictional disputes, including those between the republics, and the republics and central authorities. As of this writing the fate of this proposal and of the Committee for Constitutional Review is unclear.

Local Government

Local government in the Soviet Union consists of the elected soviets and their various executive and administrative organs, which include the soviet executive committee; various departments concerned with areas such as education, trade, health, and local industry; and standing committees, which involve broader elements of the population in soviet activities. Traditionally, these bodies have been subject to dual subordination: they were responsible not only to the local soviet but also to the higher organ in the state bureaucracy responsible for the same functional area. For example, the health department of the local soviet was ultimately answerable to the Ministry of Health, which created conflicts of interest for these local organs because local concerns at times contradicted national priorities. Furthermore, these local bodies in the soviet structure also were responsible to local Party authorities.

City governments have had extensive responsibility for services traditionally provided by the private sector in the West (e.g., housing, everyday services, and retail trade) as well as for social services such as education and health care. Despite repeated efforts in the past to give local governments greater authority to realize effective planning and coordination in these spheres, local governments have continued to be hindered by inadequate resources and by constraints and priorities established by central planning organs and ministries of productive branches. The result has been deficiencies in the development of basic communal services, retail supply networks, housing, environmental quality, spatial aspects of urban planning, and the aesthetic qualities of cities.

The dependence of local soviets on higher bodies for budgetary allocations and plan directives has denied local governments a stable and independent fiscal base. In addition, planning documents prepared by local planning organs were, in large part, a summation of the economic plans of enterprises located in the region. At the same time, local governments were reluctant to challenge the prerogatives of important economic enterprises in the region because they depended on the voluntary cooperation of enterprises to develop an integrated regional infrastructure of housing and services.

Industrial enterprises located in the area have had their own priorities—namely, fulfillment of production plans at minimal cost—and generally have been backed up by the ministry to which they were responsible. These enterprises have had far more political clout than local soviet bodies, partly because national leaders themselves generally have placed a higher priority on achieving production goals than on developing an integrated structure of communal facilities. For example, if a local chemical enterprise were polluting a reservoir in the city, the local soviet might find its own efforts ineffectual in halting the damage, as the chemical enterprise has had far stronger political support in its ministry than the local soviet has at the top.

Even before the reforms of the late 1980s, local soviet structures provided widespread opportunities for public participation in government. Women, non–Party members, and citizens of working-class or peasant background were more likely to be active at the local level than in national politics. While in some cases participation provided a mechanism to address grievances at the local level, for most Soviet citizens, participation in local government served mainly as an instrument of political socialization and perhaps legitimation. Controls on the dissemination of information, restrictions on public debate, and the dominance of societal organizations by the CPSU prevented popular mobilization from being an effective counterforce to the power of the enterprises/ministries represented in the region.

In the spring of 1990, following the first competitive local elections since the 1920s, radical reform governments were elected in Moscow, Leningrad (now St. Petersburg), Kiev, Minsk, Sverdlovsk, and some other cities. As noted previously, elections on June 12, 1991 in Moscow and Leningrad confirmed popular support for the reform-minded mayors (see Table 4.5 on public opinion surveys of attitudes toward Anatolii Sobchak, St. Petersburg's mayor, and Gavriil Popov, Moscow's mayor). While most local governments (at least in Russia) are still in relatively conservative hands, the experience in the large cities, led by popular reform leaders, could serve as powerful models for activists in other regions. The newly elected reform leaders in these cities have radical platforms that aim to strengthen local autonomy, market economic principles, and democratic accountability.

These city governments aim to alter radically existing patterns of administrative subordination. This involves the assertion of local government authority over other actors by measures such as reclaiming the control of land and physical assets from ministerial, enterprise, and Party organs (prior to September 1991). Similarly, some cities have taken measures to force compliance with environmental standards (for example, by threats to cut off water, power, and other infrastructural supplies to offending enterprises). Efforts have also been made to gain further budgetary control, economic power, and fiscal independence for city governments. Some of these claims were reinforced by provisions of the new Law on Local Government and the Local Economy, adopted in the spring of 1990 by the central Supreme Soviet.[11] Following the shift in power to the republics after the failed coup, responsibility for development of the legal structure for local governments will rest with the republics.

Effective policy response and improvement of the local quality of life are major concerns of the new governments. Examples of policies to fur-

ther these ends include privatization of key sectors of the local economy traditionally under city authority (such as housing and some communal services), the institution of a voucher system for preschool education to encourage the accountability of child care institutions and local initiative, support for nonstate (cooperative or individual) enterprises, and encouragement of a competitive market for local goods and services.

Perhaps the central feature of the new governments is their support for an actively participating public. The newly elected legislative bodies (soviets) themselves are characterized by open debate and the presentation of diverse platforms. In Moscow, for example, they have embarked on a restructuring of soviet executive organs and relations between soviet legislative and executive bodies. They also have revamped standing commissions and introduced new mechanisms to involve deputies and citizens in the process of municipal governance. The creation of independent press and electronic media, free from CPSU or government influence, has reinforced public involvement and open policy debate.

These programs challenged the hierarchical structure of traditional decision making and long-established principles operative under CPSU dominance: democratic centralism, antifactionalism, dual subordination, and the *nomenklatura* system. In many regards, the reform programs seem to be congruent with new legislation and official proclamations about local government made by President Gorbachev and other leaders. However, before the coup attempt, the central political leadership tried to reclaim some authority on the local level and reasserted the power of central directives. In late October 1990, Gavriil Popov, the new mayor of Moscow, spoke with frustration of the great obstacles facing local reform politicians:

We continue to function in a system governed by a one-party system. That democrats are in power does not mean that they wield any power. I ought honestly to tell my voters that I essentially have no real power. I don't command anything. I cannot provide a building. I cannot ensure protection for privately-run shops. I can't do a lot of things.[12]

In the aftermath of the coup, decentralization of power to the republics and suspension of CPSU activities created much more fertile ground for Popov's efforts. Nonetheless, only the future will tell us whether reformist forces can successfully mobilize public support and resources to generate viable local alternatives to the old, now largely ineffective political and economic structures.

Toward a Multiparty System?

From the early 1920s until the late 1980s, the CPSU had a virtual monopoly on political power in the USSR. In this role, it developed a broad network of institutional structures and mechanisms to ensure its dominance over other organizations (see Figure 4.4). Beginning in 1987, this system of control was subject to challenge both by internal Party reformers and by forces external to the Party. The failed coup d'état of August 19–21, 1991 marked the end of an era for the CPSU. Those events, intended by the perpetrators to protect the old system of power, ended up assuring its final collapse.

First in Russia and the Baltics, then all over the country, the Party was closed down. On August 25, 1991, after realizing the extent of betrayal among top Party figures, Gorbachev himself announced his resignation as Party leader. Top Party bodies were disbanded, and Gorbachev ordered that property of the Party be transferred to state organs. Gorbachev also issued a decree forbidding any political party or movement from organizing in the armed forces, the Ministry of Internal Affairs, the KGB, and bodies of the governmental bureaucracy. On August 29, 1991, the USSR Supreme Soviet suspended Party activities all over the USSR, pending investigation of its complicity in the failed coup d'état. Party buildings were sealed off to

prevent the destruction of incriminating evidence. Employees in Party organizations lost their jobs, although Gorbachev's decree mandated the soviets to help them find new posts or provide social guarantees to which they were legally entitled. Ironically, the former employees of the CPSU, a party that had always committed itself to full employment, would be among the first to face unemployment en masse as a result of the political and economic reform package. While remnants of the Party might survive or be reconstituted as new parties in some regions, the organization's principles were fully delegitimized and its base of organizational and economic power destroyed. Nearly seventy-four years of Communist rule had come to an end.

In this section, we examine the evolution of the CPSU since the inception of *perestroika* and follow the process of its evolution and decline. Then we look at new parties and political organizations that may provide the basis for political power in the future.

The CPSU: A Party in Decline

As of early 1991, the CPSU was still the most powerful political institution in the Soviet Union, and yet there were signs of decline. Not only had other political parties formed (although they were still small and weak compared to the CPSU), but, as noted previously, the CPSU itself was riven by dissension and threatened by unprecedented numbers of resignations. At the Twenty-eighth Party Congress in July 1990, several important changes in Party structure were adopted, the culmination of a Party reform effort initiated in 1987 under Gorbachev's leadership.

The Basic Political Structures. The most powerful organ in the CPSU (and until recently in the Soviet Union) was the Politburo, the decision-making center of the Party. Traditionally, the Politburo considered all important policy is-

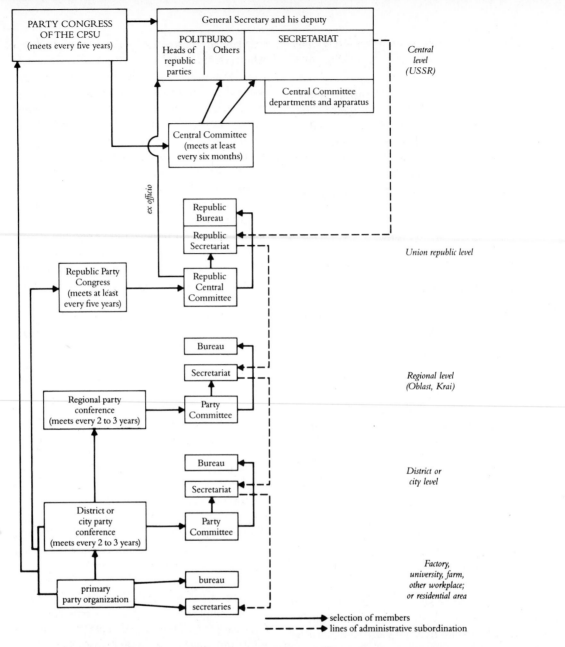

PARTY CONGRESS
OF THE CPSU
(meets every five years)

General Secretary and his deputy

POLITBURO
Heads of republic parties | Others

SECRETARIAT

Central level (USSR)

Central Committee departments and apparatus

Central Committee
(meets at least every six months)

ex officio

Republic Bureau

Republic Secretariat

Union republic level

Republic Party Congress
(meets at least every five years)

Republic Central Committee

Bureau

Secretariat

Regional level (Oblast, Krai)

Regional party conference
(meets every 2 to 3 years)

Party Committee

Bureau

Secretariat

District or city level

District or city party conference
(meets every 2 to 3 years)

Party Committee

bureau

secretaries

Factory, university, farm, other workplace; or residential area

primary party organization

→ selection of members
- - - → lines of administrative subordination

*Shows party structures up until the Party's suspension on August 29, 1991. For clarity of presentation, some administrative levels are omitted (e.g., territories, autonomous republics, etc.). Since 1989 some variations from this scheme have been introduced at the republic level and below.

Figure 4.4 Structure of the CPSU*

sues facing the country in both the foreign and domestic spheres. Under political reforms initiated in 1988, real decision-making power began to shift to state organs, including the new legislative bodies (the CPD and the Supreme Soviet) and the new executive organs (the presidency and various organs subordinate to it). These innovations brought a decline in the Party's role as policy initiator and policymaker. In July 1990, at the Twenty-eighth Party Congress, the Politburo itself was radically restructured (see Table 4.6).

Whereas previously the Politburo was a small body (fourteen full members in 1981, eleven in February 1990), the new body was considerably larger, with twenty-four full members. Probably even the old Politburo was too large to be a real working group; its working core consisted of its head (the general secretary) and three or four key advisers. Clearly, the restructured Politburo was too large to provide day-to-day guidance for the Party and the country. Thus, the increase in size embodied a change in function: the Politburo became a quasi-representative, consultative organ rather than an effective leadership core. Furthermore, the Politburo was supposed to concentrate its efforts on running the *Party's* affairs, not the country's.

The composition of the Politburo also changed dramatically. The head of each union republic Party organization sat on the Politburo. Each of these individuals was of the dominant ethnic group in his republic (these individuals were all men in 1991). Seventeen of the twenty-four Politburo members were non-Russian; there was one woman. In contrast, voting members of the previous Politburo included only three non-Russians and no women. Even more striking,

Table 4.6 The Changing Nature of the Politburo

Characteristic	February 1990	Following Twenty-eighth Party Congress (July 1990)
Political role	Leading political organ in the Soviet Union and in the CPSU; leading policymaker in the Soviet Union	Leading organ in the CPSU
Size	Eleven full members in February 1990, 7 nonvoting members	Twenty-four voting members, no nonvoting members
Membership	Heads of important Party and state bodies and several members of CPSU Secretariat	Fifteen union republic Party heads, 7 other leading state or Party officials, CPSU general secretary and his deputy
Ethnic composition of full membership	Eight Russians, 1 Belorussian, 1 Ukrainian, 1 Georgian	Seven Russians, 2 Ukrainians, 2 Latvians, 1 member from each of the other 12 union republics, 1 South Ossetian
Head	General secretary, elected by Central Committee (Mikhail Gorbachev)	General secretary and his deputy elected by Party congress (Mikhail Gorbachev, Vladimir Ivashko)
Meetings	Weekly	Monthly

only two members of the old Politburo (Gorbachev and his deputy, Vladimir Ivashko) belonged to the new body. Several prominent members of the old Politburo, including allies of Gorbachev at the time (such as Eduard Shevardnadze and Aleksandr Yakovlev), were not put forth as candidates for reelection to the new Politburo but sat on the short-lived Presidential Council (discussed earlier in this chapter). Their removal from the Politburo did not represent their personal demotion but the demotion of the Politburo itself. Its status as the highest political organ in the Soviet Union was eclipsed by the new state organs, characteristic of a general shift in power.

The new Politburo was similar to the old one in name only. The old Politburo represented the political establishment at the center. Ivan Frolov, the editor of *Pravda* (the CPSU central newspaper) and a member of the new Politburo, has explained that the new structure "underscored the Party's break with former practice, under which it was organically included in the administrative-command system and was at the top of the hierarchy."[13] Inclusion of the union republic leaders could bolster demands for decentralization to the regions, although one should keep in mind that generally it was the heads of the more orthodox loyalist Party organizations (in those republics where the Party had split) who represented the republic-level parties on the Politburo. Nonetheless, the new Politburo may have been intended to act as a counterbalance to the conservative Russian Party organization and obstructive elements in the central Party apparatus.

Under *perestroika*, the Central Committee took on increasing importance within the CPSU. Its membership was selected by the Party congress (which is normally held every five years), and thus there were limited opportunities to change its composition. Under Gorbachev's leadership, these opportunities occurred at the Twenty-seventh Party Congress in 1986 and the Twenty-eighth Party Congress in 1990. The full membership of the Central Committee reached 319 in 1981, declined to 307 in 1986, and rose to 412 in 1990.

The Central Committee has traditionally been viewed as the Who's Who of Soviet politics, as it has included the most important and powerful political figures in the country. Until the formation of the new state legislative bodies in 1989, it was the closest thing to a real parliament in the Soviet Union (but a very tame parliament indeed). Prior to *perestroika*, little information was available about its meetings, and it was doubtful whether they fulfilled any major deliberative function in the Party. Public dissension rarely emerged from Central Committee meetings, but these sessions probably did facilitate communication between the Politburo and the broader elite in the system. During periods of leadership change, the strength of support a leader had in the Central Committee influenced his prospects for retaining or gaining the top Party post. (Recall the Central Committee's removal of Khrushchev as Party leader in 1964.)

Under Gorbachev, the Central Committee took on a more active role in intra-Party debates. Gorbachev used its plenums as forums to present important reform ideas. Increasingly over time, the meetings reflected deep splits in the organization. For example, at its February 1990 meeting debate, the body endorsed Gorbachev's proposal to support the rescinding of the Party's constitutional monopoly on power only after heated debate and in April 1991, some Central Committee members voiced deep dissatisfaction with Gorbachev's leadership. These conflicts also were reported in more detail in the press than previously.

Under Brezhnev, the Central Committee included individuals from all walks of Soviet political life. First Party secretaries from the *oblast'* (regional) level were strongly represented, as were other *apparatchiki* (full-time Party workers) and officials from central and republic state structures. The new Central Committee elected in 1990 saw a marked turnover in personnel. While Gorbachev had hoped to see the election of a Central Committee of a more reformist political complexion at the July congress, this apparently did not happen. Following the massive resignations of more reformist elements from the Party in late 1990 and 1991, the CPSU again became a more homogeneous organization.

With the changes in July 1990, the Central Committee continued to elect the members of the Politburo (except the general secretary and the deputy general secretary, who were elected by the Party congress). Previously, the Central Committee usually approved nominations put forth by the Politburo itself. From July 1990, seventeen of the twenty-four members of the Politburo were ex officio members (i.e., the heads of the union republic Party organizations, as well as the CPSU general secretary and the deputy general secretary, were automatically on the Politburo). Therefore, the Central Committee had only limited ability to alter the balance of power in the Politburo.

The Central Committee also selected the CPSU Secretariat. The Secretariat was a small but important body. In July 1990 it had eleven responsible secretaries and five newly created positions for ordinary members of the Secretariat, drawn from the general membership of the Party. The Secretariat had a key role in the Party, as it headed the organization's bureaucracy. The Party bureaucracy subordinate to the Secretariat was called the Central Committee apparatus. In the late 1970s, Jerry Hough estimated that some 1,500 *apparatchiki* were working full-time in the Central Committee apparatus (this may have been an underestimation); if one included full-time Party workers at the republic, regional, and local levels, the apparatus included close to, if not over, 100,000 individuals.[14] Since 1988, the size of the Party apparatus was cut significantly in an effort to reduce overlap between state and Party functions and to increase efficiency.

In the fall of 1988, six commissions were created to involve Central Committee members more fully in the activities of the central Party organization. Each commission was headed by a member of the Secretariat, and the commissions oversaw development in broad areas such as Party affairs, ideology, agriculture, social and economic issues, legal reform, and international affairs. In October 1990, these six commissions were replaced by eleven commissions.

Each secretary supervised one or more departments of the Central Committee apparatus (the central Party bureaucracy). In 1988, the number of departments in the Central Committee apparatus was reduced from twenty to nine, but it increased to twelve in October 1990.[15] With these changes came cutbacks in staff both at the central and lower levels of the Party bureaucracy. These amounted to an estimated 30 percent between 1988 and 1990.[16] Those who lost their jobs were given preference for open positions, as well as severance pay and housing priority in new locations. Further reductions of 40 percent at the central level (from 1,493 to 603 employees) were planned.

Before the reforms, each department in the Central Committee apparatus was in charge of overseeing the fulfillment of Party policy in a specific functional area, such as education, agriculture, propaganda, or science and education. This involved several types of activity: provision of advice to the Politburo on major policy issues, supervision of state organs, and selection of personnel for important posts throughout the Party/state structure. With the reduction in the size and organizational complexity of the Party apparatus, the scope of activity of the Central Committee apparatus declined. The Party bureaucracy was no longer supposed to oversee day-to-day affairs of state organs but to deal with the broader outlines of the Party's policy. The Politburo continued to rely on the Secretariat and Central Committee apparatus for information and advice.

Even since the restructuring of the Politburo in July 1990, there was still an overlap in membership between the Politburo and the Secretariat, most notably the general secretary (Gorbachev) and his deputy (Ivashko). In early July 1990, other members of the Secretariat also sat on the Politburo. These included Aleksandr Dzasokhov (an Ossetian), in charge of ideological affairs; Galina Semenova (a Russian), in charge of women's affairs; Yegor Stroyev (a Russian), in charge of agrarian affairs; Oleg Shenin (a Russian), in charge of cadres and Party development affairs; and Gennadii Yanayev (a Russian), in charge of international affairs. Yanayev (who became one of the plotters of the August coup attempt) was nominated by Gorbachev to fill the newly created post of vice president of the Soviet Union. After some debate, he won Supreme Soviet approval in late December 1990. The heavy representation of Secretariat members among the new Politburo's non–ex officio members suggested that the Secretariat was taking over the role of the old Politburo within the Party structure (that is, serving as the real working head of the CPSU) and that the newly expanded Politburo was serving as a consultative body to ensure input from and contact with the non-Russian sections of the Party. This impression was reinforced by Ivan Frolov's statement that the new Politburo would meet once a month but the Secretariat would meet weekly.[17]

The Party congress met at least every five years. As noted earlier, the Twenty-seventh Party Congress met in February and March 1986, shortly after Gorbachev's ascension to power. The rapid pace of political change led the Party leadership to call a special Nineteenth Party Conference in June and July 1988. A kind of mini–Party congress, the conference affirmed the Party's support for a wide-ranging package of political reforms, including creation of the new CPD and Supreme Soviet. The special Party conference, however, did not make any changes in the composition of the Central Committee. In February 1990, the Central Committee plenum confirmed an early convening of the Twenty-eighth Party Congress. Normally the next congress would have been held in 1991 (five years after the regular Twenty-seventh Party Congress), but due to changes within the Party itself and its role in society, the congress was moved up.

In July 1990, delegates met in Moscow. Traditionally, the Party congress was a largely ceremonial affair, confirming decisions already made by higher Party bodies. Likewise in the past, delegate selection was controlled by higher Party organs at each stage, reflecting the circular flow of power discussed in Chapter 1. The Twenty-eighth Party Congress was different from previous congresses. For the first time since the 1920s, the delegates were elected, in large part, on a competitive basis. Splits between different strains in the Party were openly articulated on the congress floor, and top leaders, including Gorbachev, were subjected to heavy criticism. In addition, members of the old Politburo were asked to report on their activities. Most of these reports received a hostile reception from at least some portion of the delegates.

The draft CPSU platform, put forth by the February plenum of the Central Committee, competed with minority platforms (including the Democratic Platform, discussed in Chapter 3). The result was an amended version of the original Central Committee draft, which confirmed the general outlines of *perestroika* but was not radical enough to satisfy many delegates. We have previously discussed some of the positions supported by the Party congress, as well as its political ramifications. Here we wish to emphasize the qualitatively new character of this congress. The meeting was not the well-orchestrated affair of years past but a genuine forum for political conflict. Ironically, just as the congress took on a political life of its own, popular interest waned. For all the hot air and political fencing, many average citizens (members and nonmembers of the CPSU alike) saw the Party as engaged in a rearguard action to preserve its own political power.

Party structures at the lower levels (republic,

The Twenty-Eighth Congress of the CPSU

What delegates to the CPSU Congress thought[1]:

1. What sort of party should the CPSU be as a result of this Congress?

   A vanguard party   67%
   A parliamentary party   19

2. In your opinion, what is most important for strengthening the party?

   Consolidation of all
       tendencies in the party   58%
   Removal of conservatives   17
   Removal of people who
       don't believe in socialism   30
   Hard to say   1

3. What is your attitude toward the principle of democratic centralism?

   Preserve it, but strengthen
       its democratic basis   68%
   Shift to the principle
       of democratic unity   22
   It is necessary to
       preserve it unchanged   6
   Hard to say   4

4. Do you agree that in moving to a market economy we are moving toward a fuller realization of the possibilities of socialism?

   I fully agree   29%
   I mainly agree   37
   I mainly disagree   15

I don't agree   10
Hard to say   7
No answer   2

5. What is your attitude toward the theory of scientific socialism worked out by Marx, Engels, and Lenin?

   It is fully correct   12%
   It requires development
       and must be cleansed of
       distortions and dogmatism   82
   It is mistaken   3
   Hard to say   2

What the population thought about the Congress[2]:

1. What feelings do you have in connection with the Twenty-Eighth Congress of the CPSU?

   Hope   36%
   Confidence   4
   Doubt   27
   Hopelessness   18
   Indifference   15

2. Do you think that the Congress will help overcome the crisis in society?

   Yes   28%
   I doubt it   50
   No   22

[1]Based on a survey of 85 percent of the delegates to the Congress (3,986 respondents). The results are from unpublished documents provided to delegates by the Secretariat of the Congress. (*Ekspress-informatsiia no. 2*, 3 July 1990; *Ekspress-informatsiia no. 5*, 9 July 1990.) The survey was conducted by the Sociological Service of the Congress, which was operated by the Center for Sociological Research of the Academy of Social Sciences attached to the Central Committee of the CPSU.
[2]Based on a survey in eighteen regions of the USSR, June 25–27, 1990. Results reported in *Ekspress-informatsiia no. 3*, July 5, 1990.

regional, district, and city) roughly paralleled those at the top. Primary Party organizations were the base organs to which every CPSU member belonged. Larger primary Party organizations had a full-time secretary to carry out administrative tasks. Historically, primary Party organizations were usually based in the workplace or in an educational institution, but in July 1990 the policy statement passed by the CPSU congress advocated shifting

> the emphasis to creating strong and active Party branches in places of residence in view of the growing importance of election campaigns conducted in residential areas.[18]

On July 19, 1991, Russian president Boris Yel'tsin issued an edict banning activities of political parties and public organizations in state bodies and state enterprises. It was directed primarily against alleged CPSU obstruction of reform measures. At the same time, the CPSU's intention to develop residentially based organizations never had time to come to fruition.

The primary Party organization, according to democratic centralism, was subordinate to the next highest level in the Party hierarchy—generally to the city or *raion* (district) Party organs. It elected delegates to the Party conference of the city or district organization. The city or district Party conference (equivalent to the Party congress at the center) in turn selected a committee (analogous to the Central Committee), which elected a smaller body, called the bureau, and a secretariat, including a first secretary and deputy secretaries. The basic structure was replicated at each level, although the size of the full-time Party staff was progressively larger as one proceeded up the bureaucratic ladder.

A particularly important level in this hierarchy was the *oblast'*. There are more than 120 *oblasti* in the Soviet Union, and the first secretary of the Party at this level was historically a powerful political figure. Jerry Hough called these individuals "Soviet prefects," since they served as a crucial administrative link between the center and the region, analogous to the French *prefet*.[19] They traditionally were key figures in bargaining for regional interests with the central Party organizations, and many of them were members of the Central Committee itself. They also acted as mediators among various conflicting interests at the regional level and in this way learned the important political skills of bargaining and compromise. The position of *oblast'* first secretary was an important stepping-stone for those aspiring to higher Party positions.

Until the end, the CPSU remained a hierarchical structure, but several changes shifted some authority to lower levels. For example, at the Twenty-seventh Party Congress, the Party guaranteed "the freedom of setting up horizontal structures—Party clubs, councils of Party branch secretaries and other purpose-oriented professional and interest associations."[20] This marked a reversal of traditional democratic centralist policy, which sanctioned communication between Party organizations only through the hierarchical structure of formal subordination. In fact, even before this policy was approved, such linkages had been formed.

The new Party Statutes adopted in July 1990 also limited members of elected Party bodies to two consecutive terms in the same position, granted union republic Party organizations increased independence, and gave primary Party organizations more input into the selection of delegates to Party conferences and congresses at the various levels of the hierarchy. While affirming that "a decision adopted by a majority is binding on everyone," the Statutes granted the minority certain rights, including the right to uphold its position at Party meetings and in the Party press and, importantly, the right "to demand reconsideration of disputed questions in its own organization or by higher-level bodies."[21] These amendments to the Party Statutes represented an important shift in emphasis from the centralist to the democratic elements of democratic centralism, potentially reversing decades of top-down control in the Party hierarchy and undermining the circular flow of power discussed in Chapter 1.

The direct, and in many instances competitive, election of local Party officials and delegates to higher Party bodies also undermined the control of higher organs over activities of local branches. Interference from higher bodies still continued, however. For example, in elections of delegates to the Twenty-eighth Party Congress, some candidates from local primary Party organizations were disqualified because they had deposited their dues in holding accounts to prevent their use by conservative provincial or regional Party bodies. In general, many primary Party organizations demanded (and to some extent won) some control over their own budgets and the possibility of retaining a larger proportion of members' dues to support local activities. Representatives of some of the minority platforms in the CPSU (such as the Democratic Platform) suggested that a portion of Party property (buildings, publishing houses, and other assets) be turned over to splinter factions upon their withdrawal from the CPSU. In July 1990, an official of the CPSU Central Inspection Commission refuted this demand in pointed terms: "The Party's material base was created by the labor of several generations of Communists. . . . [O]ne cannot agree that anyone who leaves the CPSU has a right to demand his share of the common property. The Party is not a joint-stock company."[22] Of course Gorbachev's own decision of August 25, 1991 produced an even more radical outcome, turning Party property over to the soviets, with its future use to be decided "in strict accordance with laws of the USSR and republics on property and public associations."[23]

Functions of the Party. Several functions traditionally fulfilled by the CPSU were ceded to other organs after 1988. We have already mentioned the shift in policy-making roles from the Politburo to the new state legislative and executive bodies. Three other functions also were weakened: oversight of state bodies, ideological leadership, and personnel selection.

In the past, the Party tried to ensure state compliance with its directives through the creation of state/Party parallel organs and personnel overlap. This applied not only at the highest echelons of the Party (in the Party Secretariat) but also in each individual enterprise. Members of the primary Party organizations were to be watchdogs for the Party, making sure that Party guidelines were carried out in their workplace. Even at the best of times, this system was quite ineffective. The staff of the relevant Party organ was comparatively small and often lacked the specialized expertise necessary to evaluate the performance of the state body. In other cases, Party organs came to share interests with the state organs they were intended to oversee. (For example, Party officials in charge of agriculture shared an interest in winning increased investment for agriculture and thus were sometimes reluctant to reveal deficiencies in agricultural operations that might compromise claims for preferential treatment.) From 1988, the oversight function of the CPSU declined even further. Cutbacks in the size of the CPSU apparatus were intended to reduce the interference of Party organs in the day-to-day operations of state organs. Indeed, at the Twenty-eighth Party Congress, a dispute arose over whether the Party should even maintain primary organizations in state bodies such as the KGB and the military. At that time they were retained, but a strong minority sentiment within the Party urged their disbandment to ensure the authority and autonomy of these state organs. As noted above, Gorbachev's decree of August 25, 1991 forbid all parties from organizing in these organs.

Official Party policy confirmed the Party's role as ideological leader. In practice, however, the legitimacy of Party doctrine had declined dramatically among the population at large and even among CPSU members. The reformed CPSU hoped to lead by persuasion, not coercion. This goal was difficult to achieve because the

Party's past deceptions had induced a lack of credibility.

The Party's control over personnel selection also was under challenge. Since the early 1920s, personnel selection had been controlled through the *nomenklatura* system. The *nomenklatura* was a list of important offices and people considered eligible to fill those posts. Appointment to offices on the list was subject to Party approval, in many cases tantamount to selection by the Party itself. The *nomenklatura* included not only all important Party posts (from the local to the central level) but also many important positions in state structures, including ministries, large enterprises, educational institutions, trade unions, and the media. The CPSU Secretariat and the secretariats at lower levels of the Party were responsible for overseeing the *nomenklatura* system. The *nomenklatura* for the most important positions was in the hands of the central Secretariat, while local positions were under the control of secretariats lower in the Party hierarchy. *Nomenklatura* lists were not public, thus a certain amount of speculation surrounded their exact scope. The *nomenklatura* system allowed the elite to act as a gatekeeper to its own ranks.

Beginning in 1989, competitive elections for parliamentary posts and Party offices also began to undermine the *nomenklatura* system, which had come under more frequent public attack. Indeed, the policy statement approved by the Twenty-eighth Party Congress renounced "formalism and the *nomenklatura* approach to its personnel work." The document continued, "The bodies of state power and management enjoy full jurisdiction in making personnel decisions, and within the Party itself these matters are transferred from the top level to Party branches and all Communists."[24] Despite this commitment, some Party officials continued to obstruct the transfer of personnel selection to the electorate or responsible state organs. Many *apparatchiki* correctly believed that full implementation of this approach would threaten their own personal positions. In some cases, such as in the province of Volgograd in January 1990, even broader popular and media pressure led to the resignation of unpopular local Party leaders.

Membership and Recruitment. Just over 10 percent of the adult population of the Soviet Union were members of the CPSU in early 1989. The rate was higher among some groups and lower among others. For example, males with a university education were overrepresented, while females, who make up over 50 percent of the population, accounted for only 29.9 percent of the Party on January 1, 1989. (This represented an increase from 26.5 percent in 1981.) Manual workers, peasants, and many ethnic minorities also were underrepresented. The proportion of manual workers increased between 1981 and 1989, rising from 43.4 percent to 45.4 percent, while the proportion of peasants decreased, from 12.8 percent in 1981 to 11.4 percent in 1989.[25]

Before *perestroika*, membership in the CPSU provided certain benefits. For example, in most cases it was a prerequisite for significant upward job mobility. It also involved extra duties, such as complete political loyalty to the Party line and a time commitment for extra meetings, participation in various Party campaigns, and getting the vote out at election time. Since the late 1980s, under public pressure, the privileges of Party membership declined. Likewise, in 1990 resignations from the Party increased dramatically. Reportedly, 371,000 left the Party in the first six months of 1990,[26] but in the first half of 1991 Party membership declined by 4.2 million to 15 million members.[27] Party membership brought fewer benefits than previously, but most resignations more likely reflected a genuine frustration with the pace and scope of political reform within the CPSU. Some bemoaned the reforms as organizational suicide, while others saw the Party as putting a brake on necessary change.

The Party also found it increasingly difficult to recruit the most promising and able young people to its ranks. Youths between ages four-teen and twenty-seven were traditionally encouraged to join the Komsomol (Communist Youth League). In the past, many proceeded from there to Party membership, and many young people saw the Komsomol as a stepping-stone to career promotion. By the late 1980s, large numbers of young people avoided the Komsomol, and the organization largely lost its influence. In some regions, the Komsomol was disbanded, as individuals sought other outlets for their energies. Some joined the independent *neformal'nye* (informal groups) that push causes such as environmental protection, preservation of cultural monuments, or ethnic autonomy; others pursued nonpolitical interests such as rock music or sports. Increasingly, young adults also refused to join the Party, despite personal invitations. They refused due to personal convictions or simply because the benefits of membership were evaporating.

At the beginning of the 1990s, Party loyalists must have wondered where their future lay. The decline of communism in Eastern Europe was ominous and yet most did not want to imitate the Chinese example at Tiananmen Square. Was there no road back to 1985, before Gorbachev's unsettling reforms? Or could the CPSU transform itself into a party of a new type and still retain power? August 1991 brought answers to some of those questions as Party loyalists were forced to accept the reality of the Party's demise.

Already in late 1989, communist parties in some of the union republics had begun to form their own independent organizations, and in 1990 minority factions within the CPSU began to form new political parties. Other noncommunist groupings also sprang up. It is to these fledgling party structures we now turn.

New Parties in Formation

In 1988, more than sixty thousand independent organizations had already formed in the USSR. Dubbed *neformal'nye*, most of these groups grew up at the grassroots level and were fairly small. Some began publishing newsletters or other unofficial bulletins, which are now often sold in news kiosks, on street corners, or in pedestrian underpasses. At various times, the authorities tried to suppress some of these publications, but most have been hindered mainly by the shortage of paper and limited access to duplicating facilities. These publications represent a new form of self-publishing (*samizdat*, the Russian term previously used to describe dissident writings), which was made legal under the Press Law that went into effect in August 1990.

These new organizations concern themselves with a wide variety of issues. Among the more prominent are environmental protection, preservation of cultural monuments, national self-assertion, the formation of alternative trade unions, rehabilitation of Stalinist victims, religious freedom and the reopening of religious institutions, the expansion of *glasnost'*, and peace issues. Among the better-known groups are Memorial, concerned with rehabilitating Stalinist victims, and, on the more reactionary end, Pamiat' (Memory), a Russian patriotic association that includes xenophobic and anti-Semitic elements. (The organization might, in broad sketch, be compared to the nationalist/xenophobic National Front organizations in the United Kingdom and France.) Other groups have formed to represent the interests of particular groups in Soviet society, such as the disabled, prisoners in Afghanistan or veterans of the Afghan war, and professional groups such as lawyers, musicians, or initiators of cooperatives.[28] Some independent organizations have a broader political purpose, proposing programs and philosophies as alternatives to the prevailing system.

The diversity of interests represented by the new groups, as well as their regional and ethnic fragmentation, has made it hard to develop unified structures throughout the country. Some of the new groups do, however, have branches in several cities, or even in several republics. For example, in 1990 the Social-Ecological Union linked more than 140 environmental groups in at least nine cities. Similar umbrella organizations bring together economic cooperatives, independent trade unionists, lawyers, and consumer interests.

In the non-Russian regions, popular front organizations formed in 1988 and 1989 in most union republics and some autonomous republics to unite forces seeking greater national sovereignty, cultural and linguistic revival, and in some cases outright independence from the Soviet Union. For example, Sajudis, the Lithuanian movement for restructuring, spearheaded the movement for Lithuanian national sovereignty and independence and was heavily represented in the new Lithuanian parliament elected in February 1990. Similar movements in other republics have included the Latvian People's Front (Awakening), the Estonian People's Front, the Armenian National Movement, Rukh (the Ukrainian People's Movement for Restructuring), and the Moldovan Democratic Movement in Support of Restructuring. In opposition to the separatist platforms of these groups, internationalist (Interfront) movements formed in the Baltics, Uzbekistan, and Moldavia. Largely made up of ethnic Russians, these organizations have purported to represent the interests of national minorities within the republic in question and often have maintained cooperative relationships with those central economic ministries whose enterprises employ Russian workers and represent an outpost of continued central control.

On October 9, 1990, the Supreme Soviet adopted a law on societal associations that established the legal framework for the formation and operation of political parties in the Soviet Union. The law went into effect on January 1, 1991. It specifically states that "parties are equal before the law" (Article 16).[29] The same article establishes that those serving in the military or in law

enforcement organs must be guided by the law in carrying out their duties; they are not bound by decisions of political parties or associations. This provision was controversial because it definitively undermined the CPSU's traditional requirement of Party discipline from its members and entrenched the dominance of state authority over CPSU policy in the actions of the state's coercive organs.

Even before this law was adopted, especially following removal of the CPSU's constitutional monopoly on power in the spring of 1990, several groups constituted themselves as political parties. A new party system is present only in embryo, however, and many of the fledging parties now in existence may be ephemeral. These new parties emerged both from splinter groups in the CPSU and from outside the CPSU.

Out of the CPSU itself came regional communist parties, independent of the CPSU, in several of the union republics. These stood alongside the regional (loyalist) branches of the CPSU itself until the CPSU's dissolution following the August coup attempt. For example, in Lithuania, there is an independent Lithuanian Communist Party formed (renamed the Democratic Labor Party of Lithuania in December 1990) alongside the Lithuanian Communist Party based on the CPSU platform. The CPSU also split in Latvia and Estonia. In the Russian Republic, the recently created Russian Communist Party (part of the CPSU) had a strongly conservative complexion, and significant portions of the CPSU membership in Russia broke from the republic affiliate of the CPSU. Boris Yel'tsin left the CPSU in 1990 and said that he would not associate himself with any other party.

In addition to these regional parties, splinters within the CPSU formed to unite people from various regions of the country (including non-Russians) on a programmatic base. In this context, we have already mentioned the Democratic Platform, representing the more radically democratic wing of the Party, which formed the basis for the new Republican Party discussed previously.

In the summer of 1991, a group of leading reform figures, including Eduard Shevardnadze (who quit the CPSU in early July 1991), Gavriil Popov (the mayor of Moscow) and Anatolii Sobchak (the mayor of Leningrad, now St. Petersburg), joined forces to form the Movement for Democratic Reform. The new organization was presumably intended to unite "democratic" forces from inside and outside the Communist Party all across the USSR, and it was generally assumed that eventually the movement would transform itself into a political party that could provide a base of support for its popular leaders. Gorbachev's reaction to the formation of the organization was positive.

Following the failed coup d'état of August 1991, there were questions about the viability of such an "all-Union" movement (since it was unclear what type of political union might continue to exist). On the other hand, since Gorbachev had resigned from his CPSU post and recommended dissolution of the central Party organs, the possibility also arose that he might somehow associate himself with the new movement. The relationship of the new movement to other democratic parties (e.g., the Democratic Party of Russia, the Social Democratic Party, and the Republican Party, discussed elsewhere in this section) was also unclear, as these groups had initially hesitated to link themselves with a grouping so closely associated even with the reform wing of the CPSU. In August 1991, Aleksandr Rutskoi, the vice president of Russia, headed a new Democratic Party of Russian Communists, a progressive formation within the CPSU. This initiative was viewed as divisive by parts of the CPSU leadership. However, with the end of CPSU dominance and with the political vacuum left by its demise, the formation of a united democratic movement (including some former CPSU members) seemed even more important and at the same time more feasible than previously.

With the fall of the CPSU, one could also expect conservative elements in the former Party to organize themselves into one or more new parties, based on remnants of the old Party structure. Already before the coup attempt, Nina Andreyeva, who claimed authorship of the controversial pro-Stalinist letter published in 1988 in *Sovetskaia Rossiia*, was involved in forming a "Bolshevik Platform" group in the CPSU in July 1991; earlier she had raised the possibility of forming a new communist party of "Leninist Bolsheviks." Some evidence also indicated that for months before the coup, officials in some Party bodies had been transferring Party funds to non-Party or foreign bank accounts or to dummy organizations to prepare for the eventuality of future confiscation of Party property. These resources, if they escaped public scrutiny, could provide a financial base for new conservative or neo-Stalinist organizations.

Numerous other organizations have roots largely outside the CPSU. The original popular front organizations in the various union republics formed the basis for new regional parties or coalitions of parties with somewhat differing programs. In the Russian Republic, nationalism does not provide such a clear unifying principle for the new parties, so a considerable fragmentation already exists, producing a confusing mosaic that could hardly be characterized as a real multiparty system. The new associations are organizationally and numerically weak, they overlap in both program and membership (even some prominent individuals are associated with more than one organization), and they are internally split.

Some Soviet commentators attribute the fragmentation of parties to the fact that no clear socioeconomic base (except ethnic identification) exists for party cleavages. Parties have tended to form around broad ideological-cultural principles rather than on the basis of shared material

Source: *Moscow News*, no. 34 (September 2–9, 1990),
p. 6.

Statues of Lenin have been ubiquitous in the Soviet
Union. In this cartoon, Lenin, previously the guiding figure, now looks down in dismay as Soviet
citizens seek a new direction.

support from the initiators and members of economic cooperatives (because they see such parties as supportive of private property and economic independence from the state). Manual
workers also are beginning to form their own
organizations, which may ultimately become a
new variety of workers' parties. Indeed, one
might expect an array of workers' parties to
emerge, some basing themselves on a revival of
"true" Marxist principles and others rejecting
Marxism in some measure and modeling themselves more closely after the Polish Solidarity
movement or Western labor or social democratic
parties.

For example, from April 30 to May 2, 1990,
the first congress of the independent workers'
movement and organizations convened in No-
vokuznetsk, with representatives from fifty-
eight organizations in forty-six cities. Some of
the organizations urged delegates to withdraw
from the CPSU and form a new party. That
position was rejected by the congress and a Confederation of Labor, not a political party, was
formed. Some of the organizations represented
at the congress later expressed support for the
Democratic Party of Russia, founded in May
1990.[31] Discontent among workers, crystallizing
in the miners' strikes of 1989, 1990, and 1991,
lay the groundwork for an independent trade
union movement and perhaps a new noncommunist workers' party.[32]

The United Front of Workers (UFW) in Russia
could form the core of a more orthodox Leninist
workers' party. Likewise, the Marxist Workers'
Party–Party of the Dictatorship of the Proletariat (as well as several other small parties) lays
claim to the true Marxist-Leninist heritage.
Founded on March 25, 1990, this party purports
to represent workers and reportedly has members in sixty industrial centers, including St.
Petersburg, Moscow, Riga (Latvia), Donetsk
(Ukraine), Minsk (Belorussia), and Kishinev
(Moldova). Its platform is distinctly antimarket
and proposes a genuine "dictatorship of the proletariat," involving elimination of the *nomen-*

interests.[30] In this view, new economic relations
based on the emergence of diverse property
forms (e.g., private or cooperative) should facilitate the formation of such shared socioeconomic
interests and thus, in the long term, help to give
the party system a clearer shape.

Only a few of the emerging parties can claim
a relatively clear socioeconomic base. For example, certain of the liberal democratic parties
(such as the Constitutional Democrats) receive

klatura, the realization of real self-management for workers, and the hiring of managers by workers.[33] If a market economic system is successfully introduced in the Soviet Union, the dislocations it would engender could encourage a further realignment of working-class interests.

With the foregoing exceptions, most new political parties lack a clear socioeconomic base of support. They have tended to form around notable figures and to articulate opposition to the old structures more effectively than they advocate a clear alternative. Aleksandr Meerovich has identified some key issues that divide the numerous parties.[34] Earlier, a particularly divisive issue was the attitude toward the CPSU. Some of the new associations saw the CPSU as susceptible to reform and therefore saw an alliance with the more democratic elements in the Party as a useful strategy. Members of other parties believed the CPSU to be beyond saving and saw the only hope in the formation of a broad coalition of forces opposing the CPSU. Now this issue is less important.

Another division centers on the attitude toward market reform. Even among those who favor market reform, there are differences over the proper way to achieve the transition: will it require the use of authoritarian methods to suppress the inevitable opposition, or should adherence to democratic methods take precedence over all else? Others are critical of market reform altogether, but here the motivations vary widely. Various neo-Stalinists see market economics as a threat to long-established Soviet principles, while some working-class elements see it as further undermining real working-class power.

Out of the maze of divisions, we can tentatively identify certain dominant strains within the numerous new party movements. A large number of the new organizations, which Meerovich calls the "democratic mainstream,"[35] support traditional Western liberal values of individual civil liberties, market economics, rule of law, and multiparty competition (see Table 4.7).

People adhering to this view self-consciously call themselves "democrats." To be sure, there are nuances in this spectrum, ranging from social democratic sentiments (in the Swedish sense) through more classical liberalism (such as that represented by the German Free Democratic Party) to neoconservatism (of the Thatcher variety). We do not mean to suggest a direct correlation or parallel between these Western positions and the new Soviet parties, but rather to indicate that this democratic mainstream appears united mainly by its opposition to the illiberalism of the past Soviet system. As the party system develops, undoubtedly numerous important divisions, in some ways not unlike those that exist in Western party systems, will emerge within this mainstream. Attributes of Russian and other national cultures in the USSR, as well as the effects of over seventy years of Communist rule, also will influence the specific ideologies and programs that emerge along this spectrum. What makes the entire spectrum within the democratic mainstream radical in the present Soviet context is its unambiguous rejection of past collectivism, single-party rule, and state economic monopoly.

Within this democratic mainstream, some of the most prominent parties in early 1991 were the Democratic Union, the Democratic Party of Russia under the leadership of Nikolai Travkin, and various social democratic parties. Emphasizing the link to the liberal tradition (more conservative on a Western Left-Right spectrum) are the Constitutional Democrats and the Liberal-Democratic Party of the USSR. Groups splintering from the former CPSU, such as the Republic Party and the Movement for Democratic Reform, also fall into the democratic mainstream.

The Democratic Union, formed early in 1988, was one of the first groups to declare itself an opposition party. Since its initiation, its platform has challenged the leading role of the CPSU, opposed the socialist foundations of the prevailing system, and urged resistance to compulsory military service. In 1989 and 1990, local author-

Table 4.7   Support for Political Parties
(Based on All-Union Survey conducted from October 24 to November 5, 1990)

Do you support the following parties and movements?

	Yes, I support	Indifferent	No, I don't	Hard to say	No answer
CPSU-LINKED					
CPSU	34%	13%	28%	17%	8%
Communist Party of the RSFSR	18	14	26	28	14
United Front of Workers	8	15	21	40	6
DEMOCRATIC MAINSTREAM					
Green Alternative	26	11	17	30	16
Democratic Party of Russia	15	16	20	36	13
Memorial	10	13	22	37	18
Social Democratic Party of Russia	7	17	21	39	19
Christian Democratic Party	4	17	24	38	17
CONSERVATIVE PATRIOTIC					
Pamiat'	6	12	31	33	18
Monarchists	1	13	37	32	17
OTHER					
Confederation of Anarcho-Syndicalists	1	14	32	35	18

Source: Tsentr sotsiologicheskikh issledovanii, Akademiia obshchestvennykh nauk pri TsK KPSS, *Politicheskaia sotsiolo-giia: Informatsionnyi biulleten'*, no. 2 (II), Moscow, 1991, p. 74. Categories are the author's.

ities repeatedly denied the Democratic Union authorization to hold public rallies and demonstrations, and the Democratic Union repeatedly thwarted the prohibitions in various cities throughout the Soviet Union.[36] The Democratic Union has, over time, been plagued by internal factionalism and splits.

The Democratic Party of Russia is one of the largest and most visible of the new parties and has won seats in some local governments throughout Russia. The leadership of this group has come in part from former CPSU members, although the party itself is anticommunist. In many ways, it shares much in common with a certain segment in the former Democratic Platform.

The Constitutional Democrats are the self-proclaimed heirs of the prerevolutionary Cadets. Formed on October 21, 1989, but constituted as a political party in May 1990, the group bases itself largely on Western principles of human rights, individual liberties, and constitutional rule. In 1991, branches existed or were forming in several Soviet cities both in the Russian Republic and outside of it, including Moscow, St. Petersburg, Irkutsk, Rovno, Riga, Smolensk, and Khar'kov.[37]

A significant portion of the "democratic mainstream" in Russia is united in the Democratic Russia movement (as distinct from the Democratic Party of Russia), which held its founding congress in October 1990. This organization provides a kind of umbrella for several political parties committed to a noncommunist reform path and also involving strong assertions of sovereignty for the Russian Republic. The movement has not issued its own programmatic documents, but has provided a base of support for Yel'tsin and other reform figures. Parties such as the Democratic Party of Russia, the Social Democratic Party of Russia, and the Republican Party (the former Democratic Platform in the CPSU) have been involved in the movement.

Other political groupings center on cultural, environmental, and religious themes. In Russia, "patriotic" parties emphasize the cultural, environmental, and political decline of the Russian nation. This type of patriotic sentiment can take on a variety of political shadings—from anti-Semitic and neofascist to a politics of cultural and environmental renewal. Other parties are religiously based. There are at least three Christian Democratic organizations in the Russian Republic alone. An all-Union Green Party also has been formed.

This discussion demonstrates the fragmentation among opposition parties in the USSR. In early 1991, there were an estimated five hundred political parties in existence in the USSR, more than twenty organized nationwide. Efforts are under way to build coalitions between groups with similar platforms. Unifying tendencies should be reinforced when the parties face new elections, although regional fragmentation is likely to increase following the events of August 1991. The electoral system, based predominantly on single-member (winner-take-all) districts, should encourage some consolidation in the party structure. (Union republics may, however, adopt diverse electoral systems. The October 1990 elections in Georgia were based in part on a proportional representation system.) Nonetheless, most parts of the former Soviet Union lack experience with competitive democracy, as the political practice of the past seventy years has instead emphasized correctness of ideology. The tradition of ideological politics, even if rejected overtly by many of the new parties, may predispose their adherents to favor purity of doctrine over politics as the art of the possible. This may well make bargaining, compromise, and coalition building more difficult to achieve.

You may have noticed that in this chapter we have not discussed the present status of the "Union" itself. The basis for center-periphery relations in the Soviet Union is still in great flux. While the Baltic states have been granted independence and the other republics have gained virtual autonomy in shaping their own political and institutional arrangements, as of this writing no firm agreement has been reached between the republics and the center regarding the appropriate relationships among the various levels of government. Along with the question of economic reform, this is the hottest political issue in the early 1990s. No doubt by the time this book is in your hands, present institutional and constitutional arrangements defining the parameters of the Union will have been fundamentally altered. In the last chapter, we treat this problem for what it now is—a major socioeconomic and political crisis. It is to this theme and to other dilemmas characterizing the state-society relationship that we turn in the last chapter of this section.

Notes

1. Stephen White, *Gorbachev in Power* (Cambridge: Cambridge University Press, 1990), p. 46.

2. These statistics are based on unpublished materials distributed by the Soviet Embassy in Ottawa,

Canada. Slight inconsistencies with data on peasants and worker representations in Table 4.1 likely reflect slightly different criteria for defining these categories.

3. See Michael Urban, *More Power to the Soviets: The Democratic Revolution in the USSR* (Hants, England: Edward Elgar, 1990), chapter 5.

4. Ibid.

5. Sergei Stankevich, *Perestroika through the Eyes of a People's Deputy* (Moscow: Novosti, 1990), p. 43.

6. Ibid., pp. 44–45.

7. Ibid., p. 31.

8. For a summary of the law, see Dawn Mann, "Supreme Soviet Adopts Laws on the Status of People's Deputies," *Report on the USSR* 2, no. 39 (28 September 1990), pp. 1–4.

9. "Postanovlenie S"ezda narodnykh deputatov SSSR," *Izvestiia*, 6 September 1991, p. 2.

10. See "O Kabinete ministrov SSSR," *Izvestiia*, 27 March 1991, p. 2; and for a general discussion of the new executive bodies see Alexander Rahr, "Further Restructuring of the Soviet Political System," *Report on the USSR* 3, no. 14 (5 April 1991), pp. 1–4.

11. Zakon Soiuza Sovetskikh Sotsialisticheskikh Respublik, "Ob obshchikh nachalakh mestnogo samoupravleniia i mestnogo Khoziaistva v SSSR," *Vedemosti S"ezda narodnykh deputatov SSSR i Verkhovnogo Soveta SSSR*, no. 16 (18 April 1990), pp. 319–330.

12. *Moscow News*, no. 42 (28 October–4 November 1990), p. 7.

13. *Report on the USSR* 2, no. 30 (27 July 1990), p. 23.

14. Jerry Hough and Merle Fainsod, *How the Soviet Union Is Governed* (Cambridge, Mass.: Harvard University Press, 1979), pp. 424, 496.

15. *Report on the USSR* 2, no. 42 (19 October 1990), pp. 37–38.

16. Stephen White, *Gorbachev in Power*, pp. 35–36.

17. Cited in *Report on the USSR* 2, no. 3 (27 July 1990), p. 23.

18. "Towards a Humane, Democratic Socialism (Policy Statement of the 28th Congress of the CPSU)," in *Documents and Materials: 28th Congress of the Communist Party of the Soviet Union* (Moscow: Novosti, 1990), p. 93.

19. Jerry Hough, *The Soviet Prefects: The Local Party Organs in Industrial Decision-Making* (Cambridge, Mass.: Harvard University Press, 1969).

20. "Towards a Humane, Democratic Socialism," p. 93.

21. *Pravda*, 18 July 1990, pp. 1–2, trans. in *Current Digest of the Soviet Press* (hereafter *CDSP*) 42, no. 14 (1990), p. 15.

22. Report by A. A. Nizovtseva, *Pravda*, 4 July 1990, p. 4, trans. (condensed) in *CDSP* 42, no. 28 (1990), p. 11.

23. "Texts of Gorbachev's Decrees on the Party," *New York Times*, 25 August 1991, p. 14.

24. "Towards a Humane, Democratic Socialism," p. 92.

25. "KPSS v tsifrakh," *Izvestiia TsK KPSS*, no. 2 (1989), pp. 138–140.

26. Celestine Bohlen, "Top Soviet Committee Faces Irrelevance," *New York Times*, 9 October 1990, p. A3.

27. "O proekte novoi programmy KPSS," *Izvestiia*, 26 July 1991, p. 2.

28. For a sample listing of independent groups, see *Neformal'niye: A Guide to Independent Organizations and Contacts in the Soviet Union* (Seattle: World without War Council, 1990).

29. Zakon Soiuza Sovetskikh Sotsialisticheskikh Respublik, "Ob obshchestvennykh ob"edineniiakh," *Vedemosti S"ezda narodnykh deputatov SSSR i Verkhovnogo Soveta SSSR*, no. 42 (17 October 1990), p. 1030.

30. This point and the discussion that follows are derived in part from the insightful analysis by Aleksandr Meerovich, "The Emergence of Russian Multiparty Politics," *Report on the USSR* 2, no. 34 (24 August 1990), pp. 8–16.

31. See *Izvestiia*, 8 May 1990, p. 3, trans. in *CDSP* 42, no. 19 (1990), p. 26.

32. See *Sovetskaia Rossiia*, 17 May 1990, p. 4, trans. in *CDSP* 42, no. 19 (1990), p. 26.

33. From an interview with Iu. Leonov, in *Argumenty i fakty*, no. 14 (7–13 April 1990), p. 8, trans. in *CDSP* 42, no. 14 (1990), p. 27.

34. Meerovich, "The Emergence of Russian Multiparty Politics."

35. Ibid., p. 13.

36. A decree issued by the Presidium of the Supreme Soviet on July 28, 1988, required application, ten days in advance, to the local soviet executive committee for permission to hold a meeting, rally, or demonstration. The committee could deny the application if "the purpose of holding it is at variance with the USSR Constitution or Union- and autonomous-republic Constitutions or if it threatens public order or the safety of citizens." From the text of the decree, published in *Izvestiia*, 29 July 1988, p. 2, trans. in *CDSP* 40, no. 30 (1988), p. 15.

37. This information is based on documents issued by the Party under the title "Paket programmnykh dokumentov: Soiuz Konstitutsionnykh Demokratov," Moscow, 1989, as well as from the weekly newspaper of the group, *Grazhdanskoe dostoinstvo*, no. 14 (April 1990), p. 4; and no. 15 (April 1990), p. 4. I am grateful to Tatiana Patera for this material.

C H A P T E R

5

Crisis of the System:
Social and
Economic Problems

Two problems of crisis proportions faced the Soviet leadership and population by the end of 1990, and a third one loomed on the horizon. First, the economic collapse had become so serious as to evoke fears of food shortages, famine, food riots, and even civil conflict in the coming winter. Second, "separatism mania" threatened the very existence of the Soviet Union, as sentiments for independence grew in some union republics and declarations of sovereignty were issued by soviets at all levels of the system, down to the boroughs of individual cities. On November 23, 1990, Gorbachev himself, in alarming terms, raised the prospect of national disintegration. He reassured the public that he personally had no aspirations to institute a dictatorship but implied that the impetus might come from other quarters if measures were not taken immediately to meet the crisis.[1]

In the fall of 1990, the political leadership had presented marketization of the economy as the cardinal solution to prevent both economic collapse and national disintegration. It was hoped that liberalization of economic control, encouragement of diverse property forms (private, cooperative, joint-stock, and state owned), and joint ventures with foreign entrepreneurs could revive the incentive to work and instill a new vitality and responsiveness to consumer demand in the economic sphere. Likewise, the market would provide a new "glue" for the Soviet federation, linking the various republics by economic self-interest rather than through central coercion.

Attractive as this vision was in theory, in practice the medicine might, in the short term, simply aggravate the illness. Furthermore, as we discuss later in this chapter, the shift to a market system proved difficult to implement. A necessary concomitant of real market reform was the breakdown of the central economic structures (already occurring in late 1990). This in turn reinforced the centrifugal tendencies that were already tearing the union apart. A market reform could provoke even further social unrest in the face of the high unemployment and soaring inflation that would almost inevitably accompany it. Thus, a third specter loomed. Would broader segments of the long-vaunted working class, faced with yet further hardship in the form of job insecurity and a declining standard of living, join the Soviet miners in demanding a fundamental transformation of political and economic power? If so, to what end and with what effects? If the strike weapon were used by the working class in concerted fashion, it could plunge the country into an even deeper economic crisis and place an immense obstacle in the path of any leader intent on remaking the economy.

It is to these difficult issues that we now turn.

First we examine more closely the economic dilemma and the alternatives proposed to address it in 1990 and 1991. Then we examine the rise of ethnonationalism and its challenge to the continued existence of the Soviet Union. Finally, we consider the problems of social discontent, with particular attention to working-class attitudes and the potential for working-class unrest in the face of major systemic crisis.

Economic Reform and the Economic Crisis

The economic downturn seemed to intensify as *perestroika* proceeded. In 1990 national income declined 11 percent and industrial output was down 1.2 percent. In the first quarter of 1991, these indicators fell by 10 and 5 percent respectively. Projections for 1992 indicated a possible 20 percent decline in production.[2] Declines also occurred in labor productivity, capital investment, and housing construction (see Table 5.1). The effects were visible to the Soviet public. Consumer goods were in increasingly short supply; even the most basic food items such as cheese, butter, eggs, vegetable oil, baby food, milk, and bread were, at least intermittently, unavailable. Rationing of sugar, soap, meat, and other staples was widespread, affecting even Moscow and St. Petersburg. Shortages resulted from several factors: declines in production, panic buying and hoarding in response to fear of future price increases and shortages, and diversion of goods to the underground economy. We explore some of these points further later in this chapter.

As Soviet citizens found shelves in state stores empty in 1990 and 1991, they increasingly had to turn to other outlets. As was traditional in the Soviet system, packets of food often were distributed at the workplace in exchange for rubles and special coupons. But the nonstate sector took on increasing importance, with correspondingly higher prices. Whereas most food prices were still heavily subsidized in state stores, prices at the peasant markets, in consumer cooperatives, and in other unofficial outlets were responding to the mandates of supply and demand. These prices varied from place to place and time to time, but prices were generally higher than in previous years, often too high for the average citizen to afford (see Table 5.2).[3] The average income of blue- and white-collar workers increased by 8.9 percent between June 1989 and June 1990 (to 257 rubles per month), but this was hardly adequate to offset increases in prices at these nonsubsidized markets.

In the first half of 1990, prices in state stores increased an estimated 5 percent for nonfood consumer goods and 1 percent for food products. Unfortunately, supplies were short in these stores, and thus the low prices offered little advantage. Meanwhile, prices in the peasant markets went up dramatically. In April 1991, state prices were raised by an average of 170 percent. Starvation was uncommon (a few cases were reported in Central Asia in 1990), but many citizens probably did suffer from nutritional deficiencies. Soviet authorities assured the population that food supplies were adequate. They pointed to hoarding and a breakdown in the distribution system as causes of the problem. These explanations did not assuage people's fears, and as winter approached in 1991, even the leadership expressed concern about supplies.

Why had *perestroika* produced a decline in economic performance rather than an improvement? Before we attempt to answer this question, we need to explore the problem of economic reform in broader terms and in historical context.

Economic Reform: Experience and Options

In examining economic reform in the Soviet Union, we should distinguish between two distinct approaches that were applied in the Soviet bloc up until the advent of *perestroika*. The first approach was incremental administrative re-

Table 5.1   Soviet Economic Performance, 1989–1990
(percentage increase over previous corresponding period)

	1989	First Quarter 1990	First Half 1990	1990 (Overall)
Gross national product	3.0	−1.0	−1.0	−2.0
Net material product produced	2.4	−2.0	−2.0	−4.0
Industrial production	1.7	−2.2	−0.7	−1.2
Labor productivity	2.3	−2.2	−1.5	−3.0
Capital investment	0.6	−0.9	−3.0	
Including:				
Central state sources	—	−27.0	−23.0	
Enterprises' own funds	—	12.0	12.0	
Retail trade turnover (state and cooperative)	8.1	11.3	12.3	
Housing	−3.0	−9.0	−6.0	

Sources: *Ekonomika i zhizn'*, no. 6 (1990), pp. 15–19; no. 18 (1990), pp. 15–18; no. 32 (1990), pp. 15–18; Ted Tedstrom, "Economic Slide Continues," *Report on the USSR* 2, no. 37 (14 September 1990), p. 10; NATO Economic Committee, *1991 Report on the State of the Soviet Economy* (Brussels: NATO, March 1991), p. 26.

form. This strategy describes all of the post-Stalinist reforms undertaken by the Soviet leadership (the Khrushchev reforms, the Kosygin reforms of 1965, and subsequent changes under Brezhnev and Andropov). A leading U.S. economist, Gertrude Schroeder, has referred to these efforts as the "treadmill of reforms."[4] Indeed, in the first three or four years of Gorbachev's leadership, it was not clear whether he could break the pattern. This approach retained the basic parameters of central planning but tampered with the incentive system for economic enterprises and allowed them some autonomy in fulfilling goals set by central organs.

The second approach involved introduction of a regulated market economy. Before the collapse of communist power, this strategy was attempted in only one Soviet bloc country (Hungary) in any systematic manner, as well as in China. Hungary embarked on its New Economic Mechanism (NEM) in 1968, but it was only a qualified success. Despite the efforts of the Hun-

garian leaders to implement a comprehensive reform package, some elements of the old command administrative system remained in force: most prices were still subject to some form of regulation, inefficient enterprises often were subsidized to prevent bankruptcy, guarantees of job security continued to make the firing of unproductive workers difficult, and old managers often were retained, hindering the rise of more technically skilled personnel.

Although the Hungarian reform was the most radical approach in the Soviet bloc until the collapse of communist rule in Eastern Europe, it was still only a halfway house between the old centralized planning system and a true regulated market economy. It resulted in a hybrid economy that realized only some of the benefits of a competitive system, but at the same time limited some of the costs of marketization, such as high unemployment and rampant inflation. Although the Hungarian model proved successful in improving the supply of consumer goods and

Table 5.2   Market Prices on Food Products in Several Soviet Cities, October 26–30, 1990 (in rubles per kilogram)*

	Leningrad	Riga (Latvia)	Tashkent (Uzbekistan)	Cheliabinsk (Urals Region)
Pork	20–25	10–15	8	10
Beef	20–25	8–10	9	10–13
Mutton	14–15	5–11	12	9
Potatoes	1.5	0.70	1	0.60
Tomatoes	5–6	3–5	2	3
Cucumbers	7–8	—	3	—
Garlic	2–3	3	4	5
Onions	0.80–1	1.5–3	—	—
Carrots	1.5	1–1.5	1	1.5
Cabbage	3–4	0.60	0.60	—
Apples	3–5	2–5	3	5–6
Pears	8–10	4–7	5	5
Grapes	5–6	4.20–8	2.50	5
Plums	5–6	—	—	2.50
Peaches	—	25	—	—

*The average monthly wage in the middle of 1990 was 257 rubles.

Source: *Argumenty i fakty*, no. 44 (November 1990), p. 7.

raising agricultural production, its performance in other areas was less enviable. Growth rates were unimpressive, and per capita foreign debt levels were among the highest in the Soviet bloc. Hungarian industry failed to meet international standards, so its products remained uncompetitive. By many measures, Hungarian economic performance was indistinguishable from that of its more orthodox neighbor, the GDR.

Thus, post-Stalinist reform efforts prior to *perestroika* (and in the early years of *perestroika*) suffered the weaknesses of "half measures." Incremental administrative reform adjusted the existing structures but did not replace them. As noted in Chapter 2, however, there were seemingly insurmountable difficulties involved in constructing a consistent and effective

set of measures that would also facilitate an accurate information flow to planners. Consequently, this type of reform produced only minimal improvement in economic performance. The Hungarian NEM suffered from a different variant of the same problem, as failure to accept the full consequences of the market approach (unemployment, plant closures, and price increases) led to retention of many of the negative consequences of the old central planning system. U.S. economist Marshall Goldman has aptly explained the difficulty with such partial reform efforts:

To reform gradually, the Soviets would have to find ways to integrate the central planning process and the market, each of which leads to different and sometimes contradictory allocation results. In effect, they would have to deal with an economy heading in two different directions at once. A story still being told in Moscow about the effort made to improve Moscow's traffic illustrates the fear of a collision. "The British have an efficient system; let's switch traffic to the left side of the road," argued one Moscow authority. A wiser head warned that the switch might be too confusing if made at once. Instead, he proposed that only trucks and taxis with the most experienced drivers move to the left during the first stage of the experiment. Passenger automobiles would continue on the right side of the road for another six months, so they could prepare themselves at which time they would move to the left.[5]

Most of the incremental administrative reforms (and, to a large extent, the Hungarian semimarket reform) evoked analogous conflicts.

In Gorbachev's early years in office (1986 to 1989), he made general references to enterprise autonomy, market forces, flexible prices, and financial incentives, but it was still not clear whether his reform package implied a real break from the past system of administrative reform and, if so, whether it would merely replicate the Hungarian effort or move beyond it. Some legislation passed between 1986 and 1989 indicated that Gorbachev was willing to discard elements of previous economic orthodoxy. For example, the Law on Cooperatives and the Law on Individual Enterprise permitted an expanded nonstate sector operating largely on market principles. The 1987 Law on the State Enterprise gave state firms more control over choice of output, methods of production, and use of profits. But the implementation of even these steps was spotty, and obstacles were placed to their realization by still-powerful elements of the state and Party bureaucracies. Meanwhile, economic performance continued to deteriorate.

The Failure of Perestroika *and the Turn to Market Reform*

Why did the economic reforms of *perestroika* fail so miserably up to 1991? If economic re-

forms prior to 1985 had not brought marked improvement to the Soviet economy, they also did not trigger economic decline. Yet since 1985, Gorbachev's *perestroika* did produce a downturn. The reasons are multiple, and it is difficult to assign a weight to each in explaining the failure. Policy blunders surely played a role. For example, in the early phases of *perestroika*, monetary imbalance was fed by the antialcohol campaign, which reduced government revenues and also limited the sale of a commodity that, in the past, had helped to absorb excess consumer demand. (Moonshine production also contributed to a sugar shortage, one of the first items to be rationed in many parts of the Soviet Union.) Increased enterprise autonomy allowed enterprises to raise wages without necessarily achieving commensurate improvements in output or productivity. Lack of restraint in government spending reinforced the monetary imbalance. Consequently, a pattern that had characterized previous Soviet policy was aggravated even further—too much money was circulating, and there were too few goods to purchase. In the past, the government had proclaimed its commitment to improving supplies of consumer goods, but without implementing a real shift in production priorities. Popular support for the reform program waned when it became clear that no immediate benefits would accrue to the average shopper. It was only in 1990 that significant cutbacks in new projects and capital investments were planned to divert all available resources to satisfy consumer needs. By that time, the center had lost so much control over the production and distribution system that it became hard to make central priorities stick.

Measures to allow enterprises more autonomy in determining their output structure (put into effect in 1987 in many branches) allowed near-monopolistic producers of some items to lower the quality of production and reduce the mix of products produced, thus aggravating shortages of basic items such as soap. At the same time, incentives for innovative or productive work were not sufficiently improved. Inconsistencies and fluctuations in central economic policies also made enterprises unwilling to take initiatives, even in areas where they were permitted. In general, the reform program articulated up until late 1990 was characterized by half measures. Unlike past half reforms, however, the early measures destabilized existing patterns sufficiently to cause significant new strains on the economic system. The early measures neither allowed a full-scale transition to a market economy nor maintained the traditional plan directives, which in the past had allowed the economy to muddle along, even at a relatively slow and inefficient pace.

Symptomatic of this hesitancy was the failure to implement any major change in the price system. Gorbachev and his colleagues in the leadership viewed the more radical step of freeing some prices to respond to market demand with ambivalence. They undoubtedly feared that price increases on basic items would fuel inflation and trigger popular unrest (such as occurred in Poland in 1980). In addition, they failed to conduct a systematic reassessment of state-set prices, even though this might have helped bring them into a more realistic relationship with supply and demand. While market price signals were weak, enterprises were expected to use their new independence to respond to real needs in the economy. In practice, the newly granted rights of enterprises were not always used to achieve the optimal use of resources or to respond to societal demands. Some enterprises were using their expanded autonomy to raise prices de facto by, for example, altering product mix to produce higher-priced (but not necessarily better) commodities. The enterprise tried to improve its own position (through hoarding, wage increases, and a reduction in product mix), since the status of traditional success indicators had been undermined.

Other reasons for the economic decline were largely political in nature. State ministries and Party *apparatchiki* (particularly at the regional and local levels) resisted efforts to decentralize economic authority to the enterprises, for these measures threatened their own positions and authority. Since enterprises were still largely dependent on other state organs for supplies of materials, they often had to accede to demands from ministries to supply output. Up until 1990, the weight of so-called state orders continued to dominate enterprise production in most sectors. In the Soviet media, there were even charges (largely unproved) that conservative officials sought to sabotage *perestroika* by stockpiling and hoarding key goods to invoke a crisis in the economy.

In the late summer of 1990, there was a general consensus that some more decisive measures, extending even beyond the model of the Hungarian NEM, were needed to deal with the economic crisis. Reform economists had been harping on market reform for some time, and the commitment to marketization by the new noncommunist governments in Eastern Europe may have made this option seem more viable. Gorbachev himself, supported by the CPSU Central Committee and the Supreme Soviet, confirmed his commitment to bring about a transition to a regulated market economy. This was a historic decision by any measure, even if its method of implementation was hazy and its realization difficult. The decision implied acceptance of the failure of the traditional central planning model and its replacement by a decentralized system and nonstate enterprises. Whereas in the past the market was described as anarchic and unresponsive to social needs, now it was presented as a mechanism to increase order, efficiency, and responsiveness.

In August through October 1990, two alternative strategies for realizing this transition were hotly debated in the Soviet Union. The more conservative variant, supported by then-prime minister Nikolai Ryzhkov, foresaw a gradual evolution to market principles, preceded by measures to try to stabilize the monetary and production systems. An alternative variant,

Gorbachev tells a joke about himself:

"They say that Mitterrand has one hundred lovers. One has AIDS, but he doesn't know which one. Bush has one hundred bodyguards. One is a terrorist, but he doesn't know which one. Gorbachev has one hundred economic advisers. One is smart, but he doesn't know which one."

The *New York Times* reported that "the joke was warmly received by members of the Soviet Parliament who were listening."

Source: "The Humor of Gorbachev," *New York Times*, 29 November 1990, p. A20.

called the five-hundred-day or Shatalin plan (referred to in Chapter 3), was supported by more radical economists, the newly elected leader of the Russian Republic (Boris Yel'tsin), and the governments of several other union republics. This plan resembled, in many regards, the "shock therapy" prescribed by the Polish government since early 1990.

Gorbachev was unusually ambivalent and inconsistent in expressing his preference for one plan over the other. While he had characteristically altered his position in light of changing political currents, for the first time he seemed to be genuinely unable to make up his mind about the radical Shatalin plan. He was probably also under considerable pressure from conservative elements in the state/Party apparatus to resist the radical impulse, which would, if effective, undermine their power.

Finally, after several delays and false starts, Gorbachev came forward with his own compromise program in October 1990. He affirmed the goals of the Shatalin plan but was reluctant to accept the tremendous costs associated with the shock therapy. He tried to weave a path between Ryzhkov's go-slow strategy and the Shatalin approach. In his plan, in contrast to the Shatalin variant, subsidies in some industries were to remain in place for some time, and prices would

be freed only gradually and only on some goods. While the Shatalin plan emphasized decentralization of economic decision making to the republics, under Gorbachev's plan, greater economic powers would remain with the central authorities (banking, energy, defense, and security), while other, yet undefined powers would be devolved to the individual union republics on the basis of negotiations. The five-hundred-day timetable, which was intended to force a steady pace of reform, was abandoned in favor of a loosely defined blueprint for implementing the plan.

Gorbachev sought a middle way, a road that would lead to a regulated market system, but without the drastic social upheavals that were already evident in Poland and that might well unravel the remaining thread of national unity in the Soviet Union. Ironically, immediately following the announcement of Gorbachev's plan and its approval by the Supreme Soviet, protests from the heads of some republics (most notably from Yel'tsin of the Russian Republic) suggested that perhaps too little common ground remained between the center and the periphery to allow the plan to be tested.

Could Gorbachev's compromise plan overcome the crisis? By mid-1991 it was evident that even this moderate approach would not be fully implemented and could not break the stalemate in authority between the center and the republics. Gorbachev had stepped back onto the "treadmill of reforms." Why was it so hard for the reform leadership in Moscow to bite the bullet and push a rapid transition to a market economy, as the Shatalin plan had laid out? What were the difficulties involved in instituting an effective transition program?

Problems of a Transition to a Regulated Market

The basic hallmark of administrative reform is the maintenance of a controlled price system, which in turn implies considerable central control over what should be produced. By the same token, a good indicator of true movement toward a market economy is the freeing of most prices from central control. Despite several false starts, by the middle of 1991 the Soviet leadership had taken only the most tentative and hesitant steps in this direction. Proposals to raise prices on bread in the summer of 1990 were quickly scuttled in the face of widespread protests. A decree issued by Gorbachev in November 1990 commanded the release of prices on certain luxury items. It was immediately countermanded by the leadership in several union republics (including Russia) and never really took effect. Only in April 1991 were significant price increases implemented.

Why is price reform so important and so difficult? Operation of a market economy assumes that prices respond to forces of supply and demand. Thus, the shortage of a particular item leads to a rise in price, stimulating other producers to enter the fray. In a country with pervasive shortages of nearly all goods, introduction of a market system is likely to produce immediate and dramatic increases in prices. When prices on scarce goods are kept low by virtue of state control (as they traditionally have been in the USSR), the pent-up demand takes the form of long lines or *blat* (the use of special influence or contacts to get preferred access to goods or services). Once prices are freed, the lines will shrink (and finally dissolve), but prices will soar. Theoretically, these high prices should attract other producers, resulting in an increase in supply of the scarce commodity, thus leading to a normalization of prices.

This process takes some time, especially in an economy with a productive structure ill-suited to meet consumer demands. Further, the normalization of prices assumes the entry of new producers and the existence of competition in the production of a given commodity. In the Soviet Union, this is a problem because the central planning system has encouraged the formation of very large enterprises that in many cases virtually monopolize production of a given product. If prices are freed, these monopolistic producers have little incentive to lower prices on their products or to respond to consumer demand. Competition must be generated by breaking up these large, semimonopolistic enterprises or by creating new enterprises. But in an economy where nearly all productive assets are owned by the state, where do these new enterprises come from? While foreign investment or joint ventures with foreign companies could play a much-touted but minimal role, fundamentally what is required is the splitting up of the large state monopolies. The procedure for doing this is unclear. Most fledgling entrepreneurs, such as those allowed by the Law on Cooperatives, would be too small to offer serious competition.

Assuming that competing enterprises could somehow be formed, another problem would arise. Competition should force firms to increase efficiency and productivity in the use of labor, capital, and material resources. The discipline of the market should push the least efficient and least responsive enterprises out of business. This, in turn, would throw workers out of their jobs, at least temporarily. Under these conditions, in the short term the number of unemployed persons could grow very large. Not only would workers lose their jobs due to bankruptcies, but existing enterprises would have to fire large numbers of inefficient or redundant employees to lower production costs and increase productivity. Some level of unemployment is a corollary of any real market system, but the transition from a centrally planned to a competitive market system could produce exceedingly high levels of unemployment for several years. (For the Soviet Union, projections of unemployment under market reform range from six million to sixty million.)

As this discussion suggests, transition to a competitive market might induce unacceptable social consequences. It was, in part, these effects that Gorbachev and opponents of the Shatalin plan feared.

The realization of market reform faces other obstacles. First, how can this transition from a top-heavy, highly bureaucratized system to a mixed ownership and decentralized market system be facilitated? The number of purely technical problems involved in the transition is overwhelming. For example, how can the giant enterprises be broken up? What agency will be responsible for selling off state enterprises and property to new owners? (One has to guard against reinforcing or creating a bureaucratic monolith that would itself become an obstacle to further reform.) What will be the mechanism for the transfer of state property into private hands? Who shall be allowed to buy the state's assets, and where will the money come from? What kind of banking system shall be established and how? How can the ruble be given increased credibility as a currency, and how can it be made convertible in the international market without destabilizing the internal monetary situation and inducing public panic? (Without free convertibility of the currency, foreign investors could not easily remove profits from the country; thus, they had a reduced incentive to invest.)

Other problems center on the pricing system. How can the system of centrally fixed (often artificially low) prices be transformed into a system of freely fluctuating prices that will respond to the forces of supply and demand? If the shift is made all at once, it could trigger extreme inflation, even on the most basic necessities. If the transition is made gradually, the government will have to continue subsidizing important sectors of the economy that continue to receive low prices.

This raises the question of the immense Soviet budget deficit, which underlies the imbalance in the money supply (too much money chasing too few goods). How can the state budget be cut back, while at the same time maintaining a social network that can shield the most vulnerable segments of the population from the destabilizing effects (inflation and unemployment) of the transition to the market economy? Even if these specific questions can be answered, where should the reform start? Should the government first try to stabilize the monetary situation and then free prices, or vice versa? What will be the effects of each approach?

These and other problems allow no easy solution, and even Western economists, committed as most were to the market approach, could offer only theoretical assistance. In articulating *perestroika*, Gorbachev himself had probably underestimated the inherent difficulty of the task that faced the Soviet leadership in their efforts to remake the economy. Probably any leadership team would have found the goal of major structural change in the Soviet economy impossible to achieve without major breaches. The experience of the Eastern European countries since their revolutions in 1989 and 1990 reinforces this claim, for not one of these economies has found an easy recipe for reform.

Furthermore, not everyone has supported the market approach. Successful marketization, with its concomitant destatization of the economy, would imply the reduction or even abolition of many state ministries, as state enterprises would be replaced by a variety of ownership forms. Those ministries that formed part of the military-industrial complex stood to lose the most, as under the old system, they had the ear of the leadership and held the purse strings of the state budget. Until *perestroika*, military production and its associated infrastructure had priority access to scarce resources of all types. Concessions to the West in arms reduction and the release of Eastern Europe from Soviet control already had engendered resentment among elements within the military. Gorbachev's apparent willingness to destatize the economy, reorient production toward nonmilitary needs,

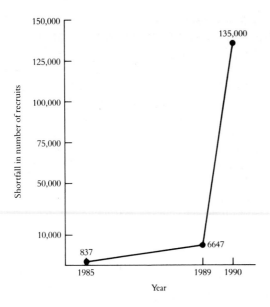

Sources: "Final Draft Figures Revealed," *Report on the USSR* 3, no. 7 (26 April 1991), p. 33; and *Pravitel'stvennyi vestnik*, no. 8 (February 1991), p. 2.

Figure 5.1   Shortfalls in Military Draft Recruitment in the USSR

disempower the ministerial structure, and tolerate separatist initiatives in the republics threatened the very rationale and foundation of this military-industrial coalition. In 1990, when some republic governments began to sanction resistance to the military draft and to develop alternative military service, this further angered the military leadership. (See Figures 5.1 and 5.2.)

Opposition to marketization has come not only from these elements and parts of the Party apparatus that have stood to lose from the change, but also from substantial segments of the population. Public support is necessary if the population is to accept the sacrifices required during the transition period. Even the proponents of market reform acknowledge that inflation and massive unemployment are inevitable

side effects of the strategy. These hardships, on top of the evident decline in the standard of living that has occurred since 1985, scarcely increase popular confidence in the government. Opinion polls, although not always producing consistent results, have shown the population deeply split on the issue of market reform. (See Table 5.3) Substantial portions of the population still prefer rationing of scarce goods over high prices for a more abundant supply. There are also strong sentiments against the increased differentials in income that are already developing as a result of a small but prosperous cooperative sector. Even among those who affirmed the desirability of market reform, there is undoubtedly widespread misunderstanding about its meaning and consequences. Many who supported the market strategy probably feel that they have little more to lose; they consider paying high prices for real goods preferable to facing empty state stores with mythically low prices. But might not this support dry up quickly once it becomes apparent that the market reform will not bring a quick improvement in life but more likely a decline?

The Polish shock therapy, begun by that government in 1990, offers little consolation. At the outset, public support for the radical program of the Polish government, led by Tadeusz Mazowiecki, was high. This support evaporated in the face of spiraling inflation and a falling standard of living. The political effects were dramatic. When the first free elections were held in Poland in November 1990, Mazowiecki came in third with only 18 percent of the vote (lagging behind Lech Walesa, but also behind the maverick Polish-Canadian businessman Stanislaw Tyminski, who had left Poland in 1969 and returned only in 1990 with promises of a quick economic fix). This example has hardly made the Soviet population and leadership anxious to emulate the brutally radical pace of the Polish market reform. If support for the reform dried up that quickly in Poland, one could expect even worse consequences in the Soviet Union, where there

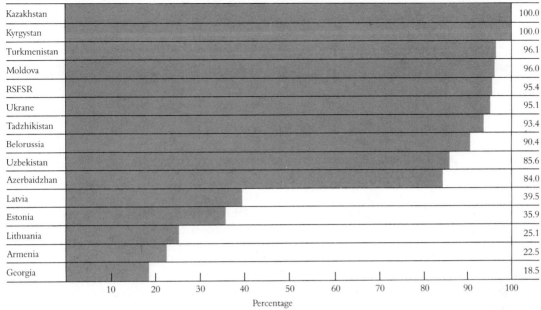

Percent of Recruits Actually Appearing for Duty

Republic	Percentage
Kazakhstan	100.0
Kyrgystan	100.0
Turkmenistan	96.1
Moldova	96.0
RSFSR	95.4
Ukrane	95.1
Tadzhikistan	93.4
Belorussia	90.4
Uzbekistan	85.6
Azerbaidzhan	84.0
Latvia	39.5
Estonia	35.9
Lithuania	25.1
Armenia	22.5
Georgia	18.5

Percentage

Source: "Final Draft Figures Revealed," *Report on the USSR* 3, no. 7 (26 April 1991), p. 33.

Figure 5.2   Military Draft Recruitment by Republic (1990)

was only minimal support for the government at the outset. These concerns suggest that a third major crisis might be looming on the Soviet horizon. Even if a market economy could be successfully introduced, it might elicit even greater popular unrest, particularly among the industrial working class. If the market reform did not materialize, the results might be the same.

On another level, the rise of regionalism and ethnic nationalism in 1990 also complicated the reform effort and produced a further downturn in economic performance and further shortages of consumer goods. As the various union republics and other subunits in the system declared sovereignty or independence, foreign investors were understandably concerned; they could not be sure that contracts concluded with one level of government would be honored by another. The sovereign republics also began to restrict exports to other regions, despite plan mandates. Real and imagined shortages led some local soviets to allow the sale of goods only to residents with the proper identification. Fearing future shortages themselves, local producers and authorities held on to their products, hoping to barter them for desired commodities elsewhere.

One example occurred in November 1990, when several agricultural districts announced that they would no longer supply milk to Moscow, as designated by the economic plan. A wave of panic buying began, as city authorities tried to reassure residents that a supply could be found with the aid of foreign partners. There was speculation that conservative leaders in outlying areas were using this weapon to under-

Table 5.3   The Political Mood of the Population
(Based on All-Union Survey conducted from October 24 to November 5, 1990)

1. DO YOU BELIEVE IN THE SUCCESS OF *PERESTROIKA*?

Yes, unconditionally	9%
More likely yes	20
More likely no	19
No	33
Hard to say	18
No answer	2

2. DO YOU SUPPORT THE TRANSITION TO A MARKET ECONOMY?

Yes	30%
More likely yes	18
More likely no	10
No	24
Hard to say	18

3. WHAT IS YOUR ATTITUDE TOWARD COOPERATIVES?

Fully positive	4%
Positive, but not to all	45
Negative to the majority	26
Fully negative	22
Hard to say	3

4. WHAT IS YOUR ATTITUDE TOWARD THE DEVELOPMENT OF A PRIVATE SECTOR IN THE ECONOMY?

It should prevail	24%
It should be permitted on a small scale	44
It shouldn't exist	13
Hard to say	16
No answer	5

5. DO YOU CONSIDER THAT YOU MAY LOSE YOUR JOB DURING THE TRANSITION TO THE MARKET ECONOMY?

Yes	44%
No	34
Hard to say	20
No answer	2

6. HOW DO YOU EVALUATE THE ACTIVITY OF THE GOVERNMENT OF THE USSR AT THE PRESENT MOMENT?

Positively	6%
Mostly positively	9
Mostly negatively	25
Negatively	40
Hard to say	19
No answer	1

7. DO YOU BELIEVE THE CPSU IS A FORCE CAPABLE OF LEADING THE COUNTRY OUT OF THE CRISIS SITUATION?

Yes	15%
More likely yes	9
More likely not	18
No	46
My position is unclear	12

Source: Tsentr sotsiologicheskikh issledovanii, Akademiia obshchestvennykh nauk pri TsK KPSS, *Politicheskaia sotsiologiia: Informatsionnyi biulleten'*, no. 2 (II), Moscow, 1991, pp. 67–73.

Totals may not add up to 100 percent due to rounding.

mine the radical reformist government elected in Moscow in the spring of 1990. An equally likely explanation interpreted the action as a response to the city of Moscow's own policies limiting the sale of certain commodities to Moscow residents. Thus, protectionist policies spiraled into the destruction of orderly trade relationships.

In late 1990, Ukraine announced the introduction of its own "currency," coupons (issued with the paycheck of residents) that had to accompany ruble payment when certain goods were purchased. Local governments in other parts of the country implemented similar policies, while other republics (for example, Estonia) had already made plans to introduce their own

Crisis of the System: Social and Economic Problems / 5

currencies. In some cases, customs controls were set up at the borders between republics (see the box in the next column).

Such measures snowballed, so that by the end of 1990, economic anarchy threatened. While the old mechanisms of production and distribution were being undermined by assertions of local control, a new mechanism was not yet in place. Optimistically, one might interpret this process of local protectionism as the beginnings of a market, for even in late 1990, it was leading to the conclusion of contracts between enterprises, regions, and republics for the exchange of needed commodities. These contracts were, however, largely barter arrangements, since the credibility of the ruble as a medium of such interenterprise, interrepublic, and interregional exchange had been undermined. Nonetheless, these fledgling commodity exchanges (*birzhy*) have enabled goods to seek their own value, suggesting some responsiveness to forces of supply and demand.

By late 1991, no method had been found to regularize trade, and the ruble continued to lose value. Barter relationships proliferated, placing some sectors in a weak bargaining position. For example, how could public service institutions (schools and universities, transport systems, health care facilities), which do not have a tangible product to offer, participate in this type of exchange? Barter trade also denied economic managers the flexibility required to respond to the complex interdependencies of a modern economy. Following the failed coup in August 1991, some republics became even more intent on establishing their own currencies so that they could gain more control over monetary policy and shield themselves from problems in other parts of the country. This approach had some merit, but it could further complicate interrepublic trade relationships. Would republics accept each other's currencies or would they demand payment in hard currency? If the latter occurred, shortages of hard currency would further reinforce existing obstacles to regularized interrepublic trade. It was these and other prob-

A Comedy Called the Parade of Sovereignties (1990)

By Francis X. Clines

"On what authority are you stopping me?" the Latvian motorist asked the new Estonian border guard who flagged him down on the road, exemplifying in a simple confrontation the ultimate questions haunting the Soviet Union. . . .

The border guard worked hard in the rain at establishing Estonia's latest expression of its attempted independence—28 fully operative customs posts opened on its own authority in the past two weeks. They are to keep local commodities from leaching east into the Russian republic and south into Latvia, Estonia's erstwhile Baltic ally in bucking Moscow's authority. . . .

"I will open my trunk and show you I have no Estonian meat or milk, but I want to know on what authority you are demanding this," the Latvian said with a persistence that could have been rated felonious a few years ago.

The customs guard, Alvar Vallau, did his best, clearing his throat, squaring his shoulders, which bore the latest slender insignia of separatist authority. Finally he had to summon someone from the nearby trailer office.

It turned out to be a policeman who came out frowning in the rain, buttoning a familiar gray tunic, that of the Soviet police. Instantly the driver obeyed, showing his license and opening his trunk. There was sideline laughter in the twilight world of Estonian sovereignty as Soviet authority still had its role to play.

lems that had to be addressed by the new Inter-republic Economic Commission that was established by the CPD in early September 1991. Despite the need for quick action as a hungry winter quickly approached, when this chapter went to press ten republics had agreed to only the bare outlines of a cooperative economic strategy. Several alternative proposals had been put forth by reform economists (including Yavlinskii and Shatalin); these reflected varying degrees of economic coordination between the republics and the center. Without some seemingly workable agreement, major Western aid (except emergency food and humanitarian assistance) was likely to be limited.

Meanwhile, efforts to bring the runaway money supply under control were unsuccessful, and the government seemed unable to exercise restraint in its monetary policy (See cartoon below). A monetary reform in January 1991 was aimed at removing large ruble notes from circulation and thus reducing excess money in the system, but its sudden and irregular method of implementation fueled public discontent. In April 1991, major price increases (planned the previous year) were finally implemented. On average, state prices rose 180 percent while the average Soviet worker was compensated with only an additional sixty-ruble supplement (approximately 20 percent of average monthly pay) (see Table 5.4). The new state prices were still centrally regulated and did not fluctuate with supply and demand on most items (except, for example, fresh produce). Because supplies of goods in state stores continue to be grossly inadequate, consumers increasingly have had to turn to alternative suppliers (peasant markets, cooperatives, black market trade, or informal barter arrangements). In these sectors, prices do fluctuate with supply and demand and have spi-

ЭМИССИЯ ДЕНЕГ В СССР (НА 1991 г. — ПО ОЦЕННАМ ЭКОНОМИСТОВ).

Source: *Argumenty i fakty*, no. 8, 1991, p. 2.

Emission of Money in the USSR (1991 figures based on Estimates of Economists).

Balloons: 11.5 billion rubles in 1988, 18 billion in 1989, 25 billion in 1990, 50 billion in 1991.

Table 5.4   Changes in Retail Prices on Selected Goods in State Stores
(in rubles and kopecks)

	Previous Retail Price*	New Retail Price* (April 1991)	Percentage Change
Beef	2–00	7–00	350%
Mutton	1–90	6–00	315
Pork	1–90	5–30	278
Milk	0–28	0–50	179
Butter	3–60	10–00	278
Cheese	3–20	6–40	200
Eggs	1–30	2–60	200
Flour	0–46	1–40	304
Rice	0–88	2–20	250
Sugar	0–85	2–00	235
Tea	9–60	18–00	188
Rye bread	0–12	0–48	400
Men's T-shirt	1–34	4–70	350
Men's suit (50% wool)	107–00	245–00	229
Women's cotton dress	11–30	26–00	230
Children's sweater (wool)	12–50	59–00	472
Sofa bed	188–00	346–00	184
Refrigerator	250–00	430–00	172
Color TV	755–00	1218–00	161
Radio	135–00	207–00	153

*Per kilogram for food items, and per unit for nonfood items.

Source: *Pravitel'stvennyi vestnik*, no. 13 (March 1991), p. 11.

raled to higher and higher levels as the state retail trade has collapsed. Demonstrations and strikes protesting the price increases have occurred throughout the USSR; even formerly complacent Belorussia was affected, as thousands of workers in Minsk joined protest marches. Demonstrators targeted not only the price increases, but also demanded the resignation of Gorbachev and the holding of new multiparty elections to the Belorussian Supreme Soviet. As *Izvestiia* interpreted the events:

The price "spark" set off a powder keg. . . . Promises had been made that prices would increase by 50 percent at the most and that the government would without fail consult with the people about what to raise prices on, and now neither of these things happened.[6]

Resentment in Belorussia was linked to the disruption of normal economic ties that had resulted from the assertions of sovereignty by the republics:

As soon as the "parade of sovereignties" began, when the republics obtained some degree of independence, everything started to fall apart. The disruptions had an especially acute effect in Belorussia. In the past three or four years, the industrial giants were constantly on the verge of shutting down. . . . A crisis situation arose, with several thousand machines piling up in the yard of the tractor plant, unable to be shipped out to customers because of missing parts; the same thing happened at the two automotive plants, at the motorbike plant, and at the automation-lines plant.[7]

In April 1991, the government (for the second time) radically adjusted one of three official rates of currency exchange that are available to tourists in the USSR: one U.S. dollar was now worth slightly more than twenty-seven rubles. (The year before the rate had been raised to approximately six rubles for one dollar, in contrast to the previous official tourist rate, which fluctuated at approximately .62 rubles per dollar.) This change was a tentative step toward free convertibility of the ruble, for the new exchange rate approximated the black market rate, which was closer to reflecting the true market value of the ruble. On the one hand the move undermined black market currency trade, but on the other generated new problems that are probably inevitable consequences of any transition to ruble convertibility. Anyone holding foreign (hard) currency or having contact with Western tourists would have a distinct advantage in the marketplace. Not only would he or she have access to special hard currency shops, but also could easily become wealthy by Soviet standards. A dual economy (one part operating with hard currency exchange, the other with ruble trade) could easily develop and thus dramatically increase the gap between the "haves" and "have-nots" and elicit resentment toward the reform process. In mid-1991 efforts were made at some Soviet borders and airports to restrict the imports of hard currency and goods by Soviet citizens, most likely an effort to limit the growth of this dual economy. Here again, however, attempts to reduce the social dislocations engendered by reform measures might instead serve to prolong the agony by hindering the rapid transition from the old to a new economic system.

Beginning in December 1990 and more intensely following the August 1991 coup attempt, Gorbachev and other Soviet leaders requested economic aid (in the first order, food aid) from Western countries. Germany had begun sending aid earlier; in late 1990 U.S. president George Bush and other Western leaders promised increased credits and technical assistance. With the Soviet crackdown in Lithuania in January 1991, however, most Western governments withheld the promised aid; they wondered whether the assistance would further or hinder the reform and used its reinstatement as a carrot to encourage a return to a more reformist path. After Gorbachev again shifted course in the spring of 1991, the Group of Seven (uniting the major Western industrialized nations) heard Gorbachev's appeals and made further commitments of technical assistance and credits in July 1991. Some Western critics found the response to the Soviet request inadequate and laid blame at the feet of the Western leaders for the August crisis. Would more substantial commitments from the West have strengthened Gorbachev's authority in dealing with crisis and averted the coup attempt? This seems unlikely, since the impetus for the coup was the scheduled signing of the draft union treaty on August 20, 1991, an issue largely unrelated to Western aid.

After the coup attempt, the aid question surfaced again, but with a new urgency. The economic decline was continuing unabated, and failure to produce some positive results might elicit another, this time more successful coup attempt, possibly with greater popular support. Furthermore, the post-coup leadership at the center and in various republics seemed more committed to market reform than previously, and this sparked the interest of the Western countries. Would the republics be able to conclude an economic agreement that would assure the Western leaders that aid could be effectively utilized? And would the leaders of the republics and the renewed leadership in the central Soviet organs have the political will and popular support to make such a market reform work? The "August days" had generated hope, but as autumn leaves began to fall, doubts again began to mount. Would the unresolved economic crisis sooner or latter, indeed, allow the coup plotters a second chance?

The Crisis of Nationalities

Since 1989 the most difficult and disruptive social challenge confronting the Soviet leadership has been the ethnic diversity of the population. For many years before the advent of *perestroika*, Western scholars identified nationality conflict as the greatest potential threat to Soviet stability. For this reason, most Western experts believed that future Soviet leaders would balk at real political liberalization, the lifting of censorship, or any credible notion of democratization, precisely because such a loosening of control could release a Pandora's box of national rivalries and demands for secession. In allowing *glasnost'* to extend to discussion of national relations in the USSR, Gorbachev did precisely what Western scholars had considered unlikely. He had apparently underestimated the depth and pervasiveness of national resentment underlying the apparent sea of calm, however, and *glasnost'* did indeed lead to the upheaval Western scholars had predicted.

The National Composition of the USSR

As noted previously, there are more than one hundred ethnic groups in the Soviet Union, twenty-two of which have populations of one million or more (see Table 5.5). The dominant group, the Russians, made up about 51 percent of the population in 1989, when the last census was taken. The next largest group, the Ukrainians, accounted for more than 15 percent of the Soviet population in 1989. They are ethnically similar to the Russians (both are of Slavic background), but they have a distinct language, culture, and history. The Russian-dominated leadership has sometimes placed trusted Ukrainians (especially the more Russianized Ukrainians from the eastern part of the republic) and Belorussians (also Slavs) in key political posts in regions populated by ethnic groups that are culturally less similar to the Russians. Nonetheless, particularly in western Ukraine (annexed to the USSR only in 1940), a desire for greater autonomy or independence, as well as resentment of Russian dominance, was expressed in unofficial *samizdat* writings even before the advent of *perestroika* and *glasnost'*.

Ukrainian grievances were symbolized by the collectivization campaign of the 1930s, which resulted in severe famine in Ukraine in 1932–33. The campaign was seen by many Ukrainians not only as a vehicle of enforcing Soviet power but also as a manifestation of Russian intrusion and exploitation. The suppression of the Ukrainian Catholic (Uniate) Church in 1944–45 was another concrete source of resentment, as was the perceived effort of the Soviet authorities to impose the Russian language. Under Gorbachev's leadership, methods of implementing collectivization and suppression of the Uniate Church have been officially repudiated. The Uniate Church is now undergoing a process of restoration.

Other European groups include the Baltic peoples of Estonia, Latvia, and Lithuania, making up 0.36 percent, 0.51 percent, and 1.07 percent of the Soviet population, respectively, in 1989. These areas were forcibly integrated into the Soviet Union in 1940 on the basis of the secret Molotov-Ribbentrop pact concluded between the Soviet Union and Nazi Germany in 1939.

Table 5.5 Share of Nationalities of Union Republic Status in Total Population of the Soviet Union, 1959, 1970, 1979, and 1989 (in percent)

	1959	1970	1979	1989
SLAVS				
Russians	54.6%	53.4%	52.4%	50.99%
Ukrainians	17.8	16.9	16.2	15.45
Belorussians	3.8	3.7	3.6	3.51
Total	76.2	74.0	72.2	69.95
CENTRAL ASIANS				
Uzbeks	2.88	3.8	4.75	5.84
Kazakhs	1.73	2.19	2.50	2.85
Tadzhiks	0.67	0.88	1.11	1.48
Turkmen	0.48	0.63	0.77	0.95
Kirgiz	0.46	0.60	0.73	0.89
Total	6.22	8.10	9.86	12.01
GROUPS OF TRANSCAUCASIA				
Azeris	1.41	1.81	2.09	2.38
Armenians	1.33	1.47	1.58	1.62
Georgians	1.29	1.34	1.36	1.39
Total	4.03	4.62	5.03	5.39
BALTIC GROUPS				
Lithuanians	1.11	1.10	1.09	1.07
Latvians	0.67	0.59	0.55	0.51
Estonians	0.47	0.42	0.39	0.36
Total	2.25	2.11	2.03	1.94
OTHER				
Moldavians	1.06	1.12	1.13	1.17

Sources: Data for 1959, 1970, and 1979 from Ann Sheehy, "The National Composition of the Population of the USSR According to the Census of 1979," *Radio Liberty Research Bulletin*, no. 123/80 (27 March 1980), p. 14; data for 1989 calculated from Goskomstat, *Natsional'nyi sostav naseleniia* (Moscow: Information-Publication Center, 1989).

Columns do not add up to 100 percent because groups without union republic status are not included.

Between the two world wars, these nations each enjoyed independent statehood and were represented in the League of Nations. Estonia and Latvia, in particular, had high levels of education and a higher standard of living than Russia.

The Baltic peoples have a strong sense of national identity, are resentful of their forcible inclusion in the USSR, and have been relatively resistant to pressure from the regime to assimilate the Russian-dominated culture. The atmosphere and point of reference in Baltic cities is distinctly Western European. The Estonian language is enough like Finnish to allow access to Western news broadcasts and television images through the Finnish media. Both the Estonians and the Latvians are predominantly Protestant, which also sets them apart from the orthodox tradition of neighboring Russia. The Lithuanians are largely of Roman Catholic heritage and have had close historical links with Poland.

Like the Baltic peoples, the Georgians and the Armenians (both in the Transcaucasian region) and the Moldavians (on the Romanian border) also have a strong sense of national identity. The Georgians were integrated into the Russian empire in 1801, but they enjoyed independence from 1918 to 1921.

There are several Islamic groups in the Soviet Union, making up 11.6 percent of the population in 1959 and 16.5 percent in 1979. These regions were colonized by tsarist Russia in the nineteenth century. At that time, the individual Islamic groups had no clearly defined sense of national identity. Over the past decades, their proportion of the total Soviet population has grown considerably (due to high birthrates) in comparison to the more urbanized European population. The Islamic peoples inhabit Azerbaidzhan (in Transcaucasia) and the five republics of Central Asia (including Kazakhstan, parts of which are highly Russianized). The Soviet government has had the greatest difficulty in assimilating these groups because of their cultural, linguistic, and religious distinctiveness, as well as their strong ties to the traditional Islamic family and community. Yet Soviet authorities have seen their inclusion in the Soviet mosaic as of strategic importance, while also providing a demonstration of the Soviet Union's ability to forge a multiethnic state.

In addition to the groups discussed here (all of which have enjoyed union republic status), numerous other national groups inhabit the USSR. Groups without union republic status but with populations over one million in 1989 included the Tatars, Germans, Chuvash, Bashkir, Jews, Mordvinians, and Poles. The Tatars, an Islamic group that accounts for over 2 percent of the Soviet population, were granted the status of an autonomous republic (a lower-level territorial-administrative designation) rather than a union republic because they are concentrated in the midst of the Russian Republic. In 1990 and 1991, the Tatars, the Bashkirs, and other groups have demanded union republic status, correctly realizing that this would imply certain benefits in terms of cultural and linguistic rights. Other small population groups also have demanded an upgrading of their territorial-administrative status or, in the case of the Gagauz (a Christianized Turkic group that resides in Moldova), formation of a separate administrative unit where previously none has existed.

One ethnic group that has posed a particular dilemma for the Soviet leadership in recent years is the Jews, who are geographically dispersed throughout the USSR. As a group, the Jews are highly urbanized and linguistically and culturally assimilated; few practice their religion actively. Nonetheless, individuals of Jewish descent have carried evidence of their heritage in internal passports stamped "Jewish." (All Soviet citizens have had their nationality stamped in their internal passports.)

In the 1930s, the proportions of Jews in the Party, the most prestigious occupations, and higher education were substantially higher than their proportion in the population as a whole. As John Armstrong has pointed out, the regime needed this group's skills, skills that were scarce in the years following the revolution.[8] Once the economy stabilized, the regime set up obstacles to the educational and career advancement of Jews; general educational levels had risen, and there were enough qualified candidates for privileged posts among ethnic Russians and other Slavic groups. Jews were no longer needed for their specific skills, and the regime made an effort to eliminate the overrepresentation of Jews in privileged posts. Nonetheless, based on their proportion of the total Soviet population, Jews are still relatively overrepresented among professional groups such as doctors, lawyers, and artists, although admission of Jews to these professions has been restricted.

Anti-Semitic sentiments have traditionally been fairly strong among the Russian population and have received vocal expression under the influence of *glasnost'*. In 1990, evidence of anti-Semitism in the form of graffiti and public statements by activists in organizations such as Pamiat' raised fears of pogroms or violent actions against Soviet Jews. For the first time, in October 1990, a Soviet court convicted an individual (a member of Pamiat') with fanning ethnic enmity by disrupting a writers' union meeting with anti-Semitic slogans in January 1990. This judgment indicated that the Soviet government was increasingly concerned with ethnic extremism in general and anti-Semitism in particular.[9]

Under international pressure, the Soviet authorities allowed more than 240,000 Jews to emigrate between 1970 and 1980, but after 1980, with the deterioration of superpower relations, the Soviets again restricted the issuance of exit permits (from a high of about 51,000 in 1979 to fewer than 1,000 in 1984).[10] The regime apparently feared that other ethnic minorities would demand similar emigration rights. In addition, it disliked committing educational resources to a group with a high level of emigration. Even so, Jews were among the few Soviet citizens allowed to emigrate at all, which may have in-

creased popular resentment against Jews even further.

Since the late 1980s, Soviet authorities have removed most obstacles to Jewish emigration. Nonetheless, a long waiting period often is required, since direct airline flights between the USSR and Israel have not been allowed by the Soviet government. Despite establishment of consular relations with Israel, the Soviet government faces continued pressure from its Arab allies to restrict Jewish emigration. At the same time, the U.S. government has made the granting of trade advantages associated with most-favored-nation status dependent on Soviet adoption of a liberal emigration law. In December 1990, President Bush lifted some trade and credit restrictions to facilitate Soviet import of food supplies even before passage of the Emigration Law on May 20, 1991. Most provisions of the law were to go into effect in January 1993.

With the general easing of travel and emigration restrictions and with the economic crisis, some Soviet intellectuals fear that a serious brain drain could ensue. Massive emigration could appeal to non-Jewish groups as well, threatening the scientific and technological capability of the country and also reducing the influence of the scientific intelligentsia on policy. In late 1990, government officials in Poland and other Eastern European countries braced themselves for a possible influx of discontented Soviet citizens, which by fall 1991 had not occurred.

Ethnic Heterogeneity. Not only are there numerous different national groups in the USSR, but there is also a lack of ethnic homogeneity in most regions of the country. In 1989, about 20 percent of Soviet citizens lived in regions not inhabited primarily by their own ethnic group. In most union republics, there are large ethnic minorities (including Russians outside the Russian Republic). The least ethnically homogeneous regions are Latvia, where only 52 percent of the population is Latvian, and Kazakhstan, where Kazakhs account for only 40 percent of the population. On the opposite end, some 93 percent of the inhabitants of the Armenian Republic are Armenian, although only two-thirds of Soviet Armenians actually reside in the Armenian Republic (see Table 5.6).

In most non-Russian regions (but especially in areas such as the Baltics and Kazakhstan), the in-migration of Russian workers to fill jobs created by the development of new industrial facilities has further offset the weight of the titular nationality (see Table 5.7). In these cases, the Russian immigrants usually have settled in urban areas; thus, in many of the non-Russian republics, the indigenous group is more weakly represented in the cities than in the countryside. In Central Asia, in particular, Russian immigrants generally enjoy a higher standard of living and have higher levels of education than the titular nationality in the republic.

Perception is sometimes as important as fact. The *perceived* advantages of Russians and the imposition of Russian in-migration are sources of deep discontent in most non-Russian regions. Thus, the ethnic mix in particular areas, an inherently difficult problem, is reinforced by local resentment of the Russian presence. This resentment is usually directed at new immigrants, and longtime Russian residents often are seen as "one of us."[11] Hostility toward Russians, along with new immigration controls put in place by some republic governments, seems to be reducing rates of Russian in-migration and increasing rates of Russian out-migration from some areas (but as of mid-1991 not to any large extent from, for example, the Baltic states).

In late 1990, Russian residents in some parts of Central Asia, the Caucasus, and Moldavia feared for their physical safety. While these fears had a real foundation in some cases, they also served to justify intervention by the center, whose real motive was the suppression of indigenous movements for independence. In addition, the complex ethnic mix that characterizes most parts of the USSR, along with an involved history of real or imagined grievances, makes simple decentralization of power to ethnically based republics or other territorial-administrative units a difficult route for managing interethnic tensions.

Policies and Grievances

Up until the advent of *glasnost'*, Soviet authorities used several strategies to reduce the risk of ethnic unrest. Coercion played a significant role, as incipient nationalist groups were suppressed and censorship limited the dissemination of divisive propaganda. But the apparent success of the Soviet authorities in maintaining ethnic stability up until the late 1980s was not only the result of repressive methods. The strategies pursued served in some ways to encourage ethnic accommodation, while at the same time laying the foundation for the present crisis.

Federalism. In Chapter 2, we discussed the importance of federalism in addressing national diversity in the Soviet Union. There, we emphasized that, on the one hand, federalism was an important mechanism for managing ethnic conflict, while, on the other hand, it laid the foundation for the "new nationalism" of the indigenous ethnic elites who rose through the republic-level structures. In addition, federalism gave a concrete geographic focus to the expression of national demands once *glasnost'* created the opportunity for such expression. Since political-administrative units (union republics, autonomous republics, and so forth) already existed as legal and legitimate political entities, these same units usually formed the basis for demands for sovereignty and autonomy. Soviet federalism, along with other measures (such as the mandatory inclusion of nationality in each Soviet citizen's passport and implicit quotas for ethnic groups in certain institutions) reinforced ethnicity as a basis for self-identity.

In the discussion that preceded the drafting of

Table 5.6   Ethnic Composition of the Union Republics, 1989 (listed from most to least homogeneous)

	Population (000's)	Three Largest Ethnic Groups (% of republic's population)	% of Titular Nationality Living in Its Own Republic
Armenia	3,304	Armenians (93.3%) Azeris (2.6) Kurds (1.7)	66.6%
Azerbaidzhan	7,020	Azeris (82.6) Russians (5.6) Armenians (5.6)	85.3
Russia	147,002	Russians (81.5) Tatars (3.8) Ukrainians (3.0)	82.6
Lithuania	3,673	Lithuanians (79.6) Russians (9.4) Poles (7.0)	95.3
Belorussia	10,149	Belorussians (77.8) Russians (13.2) Poles (4.1)	78.7
Ukraine	51,449	Ukrainians (72.6) Russians (22.0) Jews (0.9)	84.7
Turkmenistan	3,512	Turkmen (71.9) Russians (9.5) Uzbeks (9.0)	92.9
Uzbekistan	19,808	Uzbeks (71.3%) Russians (8.3) Tadzhiks (4.7)	84.6%

*This represents the first time a non-Slavic group has been in the top 3.

Source: Calculated from Goskomstat, *Natsional'nyi sostav naseleniia* (Moscow: Information-Publication Center, 1989).

the 1977 Soviet constitution, there was some suggestion that the federal system should be disbanded in favor of a unitary structure. The federal structure was, however, retained. By that time, Soviet authorities had come to accept that ethnic identification and diversity are permanent features of Soviet life and that they must continue to have institutional expression. In late 1990, Gorbachev proposed a new draft union treaty to renew Soviet federalism, but by then commitment to maintaining any kind of feder-

ation was already weak in many parts of the Soviet Union.

Economic and Investment Policy. In the early decades of Soviet rule, relatively high levels of investment in the more backward regions of the USSR were rooted in the Marxist belief that industrialization, urbanization, and economic equality would reduce ethnic consciousness by forging a deeper awareness of common class in-

	Population (000's)	Three Largest Ethnic Groups (% of republic's population)	% of Titular Nationality Living in Its Own Republic
Georgia	5,396	Georgians (70.2) Armenians (8.1) Russians (6.3)	95.1
Moldavia (Moldova)	4,332	Moldavians (64.4) Ukrainians (13.8) Russians (12.9)	83.2
Tadzhikistan	5,090	Tadzhiks (62.2) Uzbeks (23.5) Russians (7.6)	75.1
Estonia	1,556	Estonians (61.5) Russians (30.3) Ukrainians (3.1)	93.8
Kirgizia (Kyrgystan)	4,258	Kirgiz (52.3) Russians (21.5) Uzbeks (12.9)	88.0
Latvia	2,667	Latvians (52.0) Russians (34.0) Belorussians (4.5)	95.1
Kazakhstan	16,463	Kazakhs (39.7) Russians (37.8) Germans (5.8)	80.3
USSR Total	285,689	Russians (50.99) Ukrainians (15.45) Uzbeks (5.84)*	N/A

terests. The standard of living and levels of education and industrialization in Central Asia (the most backward region) did rise significantly. At the same time, investment was inadequate to bring the more backward areas up to the same standard of living and levels of industrialization/ urbanization as the more advanced sections of the country.

During the Brezhnev years and up to the present, the commitment to regional equalization has declined, as the leadership has become more concerned with shaping economic investment decisions to meet the needs of the national economy as a whole. As the USSR entered the 1970s, investment funds were scarcer and natural resources were becoming more expensive to exploit, since the most easily accessible deposits were near depletion. Thus, the regime was under pressure to pursue development projects with the highest perceived payoffs. A particular priority was the development of the rich deposits of mineral and fuel resources in Siberia. This has been a costly commitment because of the harsh natural conditions, which require the use

Table 5.7 Estonians' Share of Total Population of
the Estonian Republic, 1922–89*

	Total Population	Percentage Share of Estonians
1922[a]	1,107,100	87.7
1934[a]	1,126,400	88.2
1939[b]	1,134,400	95.5
1945[b]	854,000	97.3
1959	1,196,791	74.6
1970	1,356,079	68.2
1979	1,464,476	64.7
1989	1,565,662	61.5

*Please note that the decline in the Latvian share of the
total population of Latvia would be even more dramatic,
while the decline in Lithuania is much less dramatic.
[a]Census data using pre-1945 borders.
[b]Estimates using circumscribed post-1945 borders.

Source: Riina Kionka, "Migration to and from Estonia,"
Report on the USSR 2, no. 37 (14 September 1990), p. 21.

of special technology and equipment, as well as
the payment of higher wages to lure workers to
remote regions with an inhospitable climate. In
many ways, Central Asia suffered most from
this gradual shift in priorities, and by the mid-
to late 1980s, that region lagged farther behind
most European sections of the USSR in terms of
investment and levels of consumption and industrial growth than it had twenty to thirty
years earlier.[12]

Patterns of demographic growth introduced
an additional dimension to regional investment
decisions (see Table 5.8). In the Brezhnev years
and up until the present (or until the real institution of market reform), the most economically
developed sections, in the European portion of
the USSR, have generally suffered from a labor
shortage. This is aggravated by low birthrates
among the more highly urbanized Russians and
European peoples. Housing shortages and high
rates of female employment have contributed to
the declining birthrates. In contrast, the Muslim

population groups of Central Asia and Kazakhstan (and to a lesser degree Azerbaidzhan) are
reproducing at a much higher rate. This reflects
a more agrarian life-style and maintenance of
traditional family and cultural norms. In these
republics, the economic infrastructure has been
inadequate to absorb the growing population.
Thus, in 1990, the highest levels of unemployment in the USSR were in heavily populated
pockets in Central Asia (for example, the Osh
region of Kyrgystan). The demographic shift has
brought with it serious economic dislocations.
Valuable labor resources have not been located
where they were needed, and ethnic tensions
have resulted from the intense social problems
present in those localities.

In the past, the leadership faced several policy
options in dealing with the demographic imbalance. More industrial and agricultural investment could be directed to Central Asia and Kazakhstan to take advantage of the labor surplus.
However, the area is low in water resources. To
solve this problem, a major diversion of several
Siberian rivers, from north to south, was proposed and discussed throughout the 1980s.
Many experts criticized this as a costly and ecologically risky affair. In addition, its financing
would divert resources from other important
projects, such as the development of the rich
natural resource potential of Siberia. Shortly
after the Twenty-seventh Party Congress in
1986, the project was, at least for the time being,
dropped, despite strong support for it from Central Asian political elites. Policies directed toward interregional equalization seem even less
likely as a market reform is instituted and as
power shifts from the center to the republics.
Even if central authorities might like to offer
preferential treatment to win the support of
some regions for a renewed federation, such advantages probably would be resisted by other
republics that would have to foot the bill.

Another option to deal with demographic imbalance was relocation of Central Asian labor to
the European part of the country or to Siberia,

Crisis of the System: Social and Economic Problems / **5**

Table 5.8   Data on Nationalities with Union Republic Status, 1989

National Group	Group's Share of Total USSR Population (%)	1989 Population as % of 1979 Population	1989 Population as % of 1959 Population
Russians	50.99%	105.6%	127.7%
Ukrainians	15.45	104.2	118.5
Uzbeks	5.84	134.0	277.0
Belorussians	3.51	106.0	126.8
Kazakhs	2.85	124.1	225.0
Azeris	2.38	124.0	231.0
Armenians	1.62	111.5	166.0
Tadzhiks	1.48	145.5	302.0
Georgians	1.39	111.6	148.0
Moldavians	1.17	113.0	151.5
Lithuanians	1.07	107.6	131.9
Turkmen	0.95	134.0	271.0
Kirgiz	0.89	132.8	261.0
Latvians	0.51	101.4	104.2
Estonians	0.36	100.7	103.8

Sources: Calculated from Goskomstat, *Natsional'nyi sostav naseleniia* (Moscow: Information-Publication Center, 1989); Ann Sheehy, "The National Composition of the Population of the USSR According to the Census of 1979," *Radio Liberty Research Bulletin*, no. 123/80 (27 March 1980), p. 10.

where jobs have generally been plentiful. The Central Asian groups have been reluctant to move, however, partially because of their strong ties to their traditional communities. The post-Stalinist leadership has been unwilling to engage in forced relocation, and efforts to develop incentive structures to encourage voluntary population movement have had little success. In present political circumstances, which are characterized by high levels of interethnic tension and intraethnic solidarity, these options seem even less viable. In addition, introduction of a market reform would reduce job opportunities and increase unemployment in all of the republics.

Perhaps more realistic than efforts to relocate surplus labor from Central Asia would be job retraining programs that could help to qualify portions of the indigenous population for positions vacated by out-migrating Russians or for jobs created by a market reform. Unfortunately, the leadership in these republics is even less experienced in taking such innovative steps than the leaders of the European republics, where job retraining is still only in the planning stages.

Economic development policies have produced tensions in other parts of the country as well, including the Russian Republic. Since local populations in Russia have had little, if any, input in determining development plans for their regions, they too see themselves as victims of centralization. The centralized ministries are blamed for elevating narrow-minded, materialistic departmental interests above the integrity

An Ethnic Hot Spot: The Osh Region of Kirgizia

Beginning on June 4, 1990, skirmishes began between the Kirgiz and Uzbeks, two of the Islamic groups in Central Asia. Soviet troops had to intervene to stop the conflict, leaving at least 115 people dead in the span of one week. Why have two ethnic groups that share a common religious and linguistic background come to blows?

A high unemployment rate and a housing shortage in the region provide the backdrop to the incidents. Economic reforms in the Soviet Union in the late 1980s legitimized diverse property forms. In the Kirgizia republic (later renamed Kyrgystan) a homesteading plan was initiated to allocate plots. While the Uzbeks account for only 12 percent of the entire population of Kirgizia, in the Osh region, which borders Uzbekistan, they represent more than one-third of the residents. The awarding of the building plots entirely to Kirgiz residents touched off violent demonstrations against the Kirgiz authorities, whom the Uzbeks blamed for favoritism toward the Kirgiz population. Large bands of Uzbeks tried to enter the Osh region from Uzbekistan to support their countrymen but were for the most part stopped. Soviet troops were used along the border and in Osh. Apparently not trained for such events, the troops fired not only tear gas but also machine guns to break up the demonstration and to prevent the takeover of government and Party buildings. The violence also spread to Frunze, the capital of Kirgizia where Uzbek students had to be evacuated.

---

of the national environment and the maintenance of the fundamental cultural values of the population. Decisions to construct industrial facilities or power plants often have resulted in ecological and aesthetic damage, and benefits for the local population (e.g., shops, recreational facilities, and housing) have generally come last. This context explains the importance of environmental protests in the early years of *perestroika*. Frequent targets of popular disapproval have been decisions to construct nuclear power plants, water diversion and hydroelectric projects, biochemical facilities, and heavily polluting industrial enterprises. One might interpret this as a Soviet variant of the NIMBY (not in my backyard) phenomenon.

For many national minority groups (in the Russian Republic and in other republics), decisions made by centrally dominated industrial ministries are seen as an attack on basic cultural values (including the value of the native land and nature). These decisions were particularly resented when they brought the infusion of Russian workers, as discussed previously. Independent ecological movements also have been closely linked to national self-assertion. The Chernobyl nuclear power accident (which occurred in Ukraine but also contaminated large parts of Belorussia) elicited popular skepticism not only toward nuclear power but also toward official reassurances about the ecological safety of production. It almost certainly increased popular support among Ukrainians and Belorussians for republic sovereignty and regional economic control.

Environmental deterioration was among the first issues addressed by Baltic activists because it symbolized so well the intrusion of a Russian-dominated "empire" into the "space" of the Baltic peoples. Particular targets of criticism in Lithuania were the Ignalina nuclear power plant (which operates with Chernobyl-type reactors), the Mazeikiai oil refinery, and chemical fertilizer plants in Jonava and Kedainiai. In Estonia, ecologists have cited the destructive effects of oil shale and phosphorite mining, along with high air pollution levels. Similar protests have occurred in other republics—for example, the widespread opposition to nuclear power in

Ukraine, Armenia, and the Tatar autonomous republic. In Kazakhstan, activists have demanded a halt to underground nuclear testing in the Semipalatinsk region. In other Central Asian republics, a dramatic fall in the water level of the Aral Sea is a major focus of concern. (Wasteful use of irrigation water removed from the rivers that feed the sea is largely responsible for the drop. This irrigation system in turn supports the cotton monoculture of the region, seen by some as an expression of Moscow's colonial posture vis-à-vis Central Asia.)

These, along with hundreds of other ecological protests at the local level, brought dozens of plant closures, as the political leadership realized that the intensity of popular sentiment demanded some response. Shortfalls in production resulting from these shutdowns led Gorbachev to reopen many of the offending facilities in late 1990. Thus, these closures did not address the root causes of environmental deterioration in the USSR. More important to our discussion here, they also did not dampen the desire of many ethnic minorities for more control over local development.

Cultural Policy. In the past, the Soviet leadership also dealt with ethnic diversity through cultural policy. The Leninist formula, "national in form, socialist in concept," meant encouragement of traditional ethnic folk arts, music, and dress and discouragement of nationalistic, separatist, or religious sentiments. "Asymmetrical bilingualism," or what some call Russification, involved efforts to encourage national minorities to learn Russian as a second language. However, very few ethnic Russians (only 3.5 percent in 1979 and 4.0 percent in 1989) claimed knowledge of a second Soviet language (excluding German). Russians preferred to take up Western languages such as English, French, or German. Nonetheless, minority languages have survived. Media broadcasts and book publishing continue in all the major languages (those of the union republics), and primary and secondary education is generally available in the indigenous language in the union republics, with Russian as a required part of the curriculum. In some republics (especially Ukraine and Belorussia) from the late 1960s to the late 1980s, the proportion of the titular nationality attending these native-language schools declined. Because Russian has been the common language in the USSR, a facility with it has been necessary for upward mobility.

The smaller national groups without union republic status see their linguistic traditions as seriously threatened. Since the late 1950s, there has been a decline in indigenous-language schooling for these groups. Increasingly, the indigenous language has been taught as a secondary subject, with Russian as the predominant instructional medium.[13]

While the majority of non-Russians still regard the languages of their own ethnic group as their first language, the number of non-Russians claiming knowledge of Russian as a second language has generally increased over time (see Table 5.9). In the 1989 census, about three-quarters of the total Soviet population claimed knowledge of Russian as its first or second language. Some groups—most notably the Estonians, the Azeris, the Georgians, and some of the Central Asian peoples—have been more resistant to Russification than others. According to the official Soviet census of 1989, knowledge of Russian as a second language declined among those claiming Estonian as their first language, from 29 percent in 1970 to 24.2 percent in 1979, though some of the respondents may have been unwilling to admit to knowledge of Russian. In 1989, the figure for Estonians increased to 33.8 percent, while the proportion of Lithuanians claiming knowledge of Russian declined from 52.1 percent in 1979 to 37.9 percent in 1989. Knowledge of Russian among Uzbeks (the largest indigenous group in Central Asia) reportedly increased from 14.5 percent in 1970 to 49.3 percent in 1979, a 361 percent gain. These figures say more about statistical distortion than they

Table 5.9   Linguistic Affiliation of Nationalities of Union Republic Status, 1970, 1979, and 1989

	Percentage Regarding Language of Nationality as Native Tongue		Percentage Claiming a Good Knowledge of Russian as a Second Language		
	1979	1989	1970	1979	1989
Russians	99.8%	99.8%	—	0.1%	0.1%
Ukrainians	82.8	81.1	36.3	49.8	56.2
Belorussians	74.2	70.9	49.0	57.0	54.7
Uzbeks	98.5	98.3	14.5	49.3	23.8
Kazakhs	97.5	97.0	41.8	52.3	60.4
Tadzhiks	97.8	97.7	15.4	29.6	27.7
Turkmen	98.7	98.5	15.4	25.4	27.8
Kirgiz	97.9	97.8	19.1	29.3	35.2
Azeris	97.8	97.6	16.6	29.5	34.4
Armenians	90.7	91.6	30.1	38.6	47.1
Georgians	98.3	98.2	21.3	26.7	33.1
Lithuanians	97.9	97.7	35.9	52.1	37.9
Latvians	95.0	94.8	45.2	56.7	64.4
Estonians	95.3	95.5	29.0	24.2	33.8
Moldavians	93.2	91.6	36.1	47.4	53.8

Sources: *Rahva Hääl*, 19 September 1989; 1979 census results; Ann Sheehy, "Russian Share of Soviet Population Down to 50.8 Percent," *Report on the USSR* 1, no. 42 (20 October 1989), p. 3; Ann Sheehy, "Language Affiliation Data from the Census of 1979," *Radio Liberty Research Bulletin*, no. 130/80 (2 April 1980), p. 13; Goskomstat, *Natsional'nyi sostav naseleniia* (Moscow: Information/Publication Center, 1989).

do about levels of Russification. The claimed level of knowledge of Russian decreased to a more realistic 23.8 percent in the 1989 census, suggesting that census takers may have inflated the numbers in 1979 to satisfy the hopes, expectations, and perhaps demands of their superiors.

Language was a contentious issue in 1989 and 1990 in the USSR. By the end of 1990, every republic had declared the language of the titular nationality to be the state language, although with some distinctions. In some cases, as in the Baltic states, this implied that official communications should be shifted from Russian to Es-

tonian, Latvian, or Lithuanian within a given time frame. On a symbolic level, these policies embodied the desire for cultural preservation and national independence. On a practical level, they require that Russian residents in these republics learn to communicate in the indigenous language. This in turn will necessitate the development and availability of instructional materials and facilities to teach these languages. The laws will weaken the de facto requirement of Russian fluency for job promotion. In some other republics, the concrete implications of the change in state language are less clearly drawn out. Hot debates sometimes have ensued about the status of the Russian language. In most cases, it has finally been agreed that Russian alone, or Russian in combination with the indigenous language, will continue to be the language of international communication, for even in a sharply decentralized or fragmented version of the USSR, it is hard to see how anything could continue to function without some kind of lingua franca.

Other disputes about language also emerged in the late 1980s. For example, in many regions under Soviet control, the script for the various national languages is transliterated into the Cyrillic (Russian) alphabet. Thus, Moldavian, essentially the same language as Romanian, was written in Cyrillic letters, while, across the border, Romanian continued to be written in Roman letters. Not surprisingly, nationalist spokespersons demanded, and won, a return to the Roman alphabet. Old place-names also have been restored—for example, Moldavia is now called Moldova, and cities in several republics have taken back or are considering a return to old names. This phenomenon has not been limited to the non-Russian regions. In 1990, numerous streets and squares in Moscow were given their prerevolutionary names and many cities reclaimed their old names (a delight for capitalist mapmakers but a horror for Soviet bureaucrats). Although such changes are largely symbolic, they can be highly contentious and threatening to some minority groups within a republic.

Soviet cultural policy has helped both to maintain and to weaken minority languages and culture. Thus, linguistic demands and cultural symbols have become a key rallying point for ethnic revivalism in the 1990s.

The Eruption of Ethnic Demands and Conflicts

Ethnic complexity, combined with resentment of central (Russian-led) dominance, has produced a complex morass of national tensions within the USSR. Some of the conflicts are clearly directed at the center and involve explicit demands for national independence. Here the clearest case was the Lithuanian declaration of independence of March 11, 1990. The newly elected Lithuanian parliament made the declaration just before the CPD adopted constitutional amendments establishing the new post of president of the USSR and a law defining a lengthy and restrictive mechanism for secession from the union. Advocates of independence feared that the new presidential powers might be used to reverse the trend of liberalization that had allowed separatist sentiments to assert themselves. They believed that the Lithuanian government should seize the opportunity while the window of freedom was still open. Gorbachev and the central reform leadership viewed the declaration of independence as precipitous and provocative, as it immediately raised the stakes in the brewing conflict over the distribution of power between the center and periphery.

Although the two other Baltic republics were more restrained in pushing their claims for independence, the Gorbachev government used the Lithuanian example to demonstrate Moscow's willingness to use its resources to impede the realization of the Lithuanian goal. Initially, the center exerted political and economic pressure, but in January 1991, it used military force as well. Under pressure from a partial economic blockade imposed by Moscow on April 18, 1990, the Lithuanian government temporarily suspended the declaration to facilitate negotiations with the central authorities. By the end of 1990, these on-again, off-again talks had produced few concrete results. The Lithuanian government continued to assert its claim to independence, while the Soviet government continued to assert its authority within the republic.

More cautious in their approach, the Estonian, Latvian, Georgian, and Armenian republics also affirmed their commitment to independence. By the end of 1990, all of the other union republics had issued declarations of sovereignty (see Table 3.5), asserting in various degrees their right to establish their own constitutional order, control their economic assets and natural resources, and in some cases (as for Ukraine) establish independent armies and currencies. In March 1991, six republics (the Baltic republics, Georgia, Armenia, and Moldova) boycotted a national referendum that affirmed preservation of the USSR as a "renewed federation of equal sovereign republics."

Following the failed coup d'état of August 1991, several other republics declared independence, including some, like the Central Asia republics, that might have been thought unlikely candidates a month earlier (see Table 3.5). As noted in Chapter 3, motives for the declarations varied. On the one extreme, the Baltic declarations represented genuine attempts to achieve independent statehood; independence involved a radical rejection of Soviet institutions and Communist power. Independence of the Baltic states (Lithuania, Estonia, and Latvia) was recognized by Soviet authorities on September 6, 1991. The declaration issued by the government of Uzbekistan, the most populous of the Central Asian republics, provides a contrasting case. During August 19–21 the actions of Uzbek president Islam Karimov reinforced the coup attempt. On September 14, following the failed coup and the suspension of CPSU activities by the CPD, the Communist Party in Uzbekistan (also headed by Karimov) changed its name to the Popular Democratic Party of Uzbekistan. Uzbekistan's declaration of independence was apparently a measure to protect the existing leadership from the disturbing radicalization in Moscow; the old power structure might well be preserved, at least temporarily, under a new, nationalist mantle. In short, the declaration of independence represented an effort to conserve old power relationships, rather than to nurture new ones. Furthermore, there was little evidence that the Uzbek leadership could (or even intended to) realize its declared independence. This republic, with its largely cotton monoculture, is too economically dependent on regions

of the USSR to make independence feasible, at least in the short term. In the longer term, reform oppositionists (organized, for example, in a nationalist group, Birlik) might well push the old leadership out; then, the impetus for independence might sprout from the ground up. In Georgia, yet a different situation existed. Here, the urge for independence was likely genuine, but its realization might well involve an attempt by the new noncommunist leadership (headed by Gamsakhurdia) to keep in place a quasi-authoritarian nationalist government. While former dissident Gamsakhurdia was directly elected by the population in late 1990, subsequent actions suggest serious deviations from democratic control; in particular, Georgian authorities have responded harshly to demands for autonomy made by national minorities residing in the republic (e.g., the South Ossetians). Following the August coup attempt, thousands of demonstrators demanded Gamsakhurdia's resignation, leading to intermittent clashes in the streets of Tbilisi.

As these examples suggest, the very notions of sovereignty and independence are disputed political concepts in the USSR. Central authorities, regional elites, democratic reformers, and fervent nationalists all appropriate them for their own purposes. Their goals need not be congruent with a larger process of democratization and economic reform. At the same time, the numerous declarations have made it difficult to define exactly what (if anything) constitutes the USSR, especially since the August 1991 coup attempt (see Figure 5.3).

Sovereignty, Federation, or Independence? By 1990, three general models were put forth for the future of the republics and the Union. First, Gorbachev and the central authorities hoped to retain a revamped federal system with a strong center and strong republics. The second position, put forth most vocally by the government of the Russian Republic, advocated a union of truly sovereign states (comparable, perhaps, to pro-

Souce: "Kakim zhe on budet, novyi soiuz?" *Izvestiia*, 6 September 1991, p. 1.

Figure 5.3   Depiction of the "Future New Union" by the Soviet Newspaper *Izvestiia* on
September 6, 1991

posals for Quebec's sovereignty association with Canada). This conception assumed a confederative model rather than a federal one, for ultimate authority would rest with the republics, not the center. Finally, advocates of outright independence in particular republics (e.g., the Baltics and Georgia) based their claims on the illegitimate nature of their inclusion in the USSR and on the right of democratic self-determination.

The collision between these diverging conceptions was not only theoretical but also immediate and practical, for in numerous large and small ways, each government tried to implement its position through legal enactments and specific policies. These decisions put the central government on a collision course with the republics over economic policy. At the same time, efforts by the would-be sovereign or independent states to establish autonomous spheres of action were constantly thwarted by the central authorities.

Gorbachev operated on the premise that the de facto status quo, whatever its historical origins, must provide the starting point for any redefinition of interrepublic ties. In this view, it was unrealistic, and would be unfair to the numerous parties involved, to presume a tabula rasa in defining the new relationships. At a minimum, a long period of difficult negotiation would be required to disentangle and redefine the web of connections linking the republics to each other. These ties were not only legal, political, and ideological, but also involved, in Gorbachev's view, complex economic dependencies that could not easily be severed.

At the opposite extreme, the would-be breakaway republics saw no legitimate legal foundation for their forcible inclusion in the USSR. They could point to both Leninist doctrine and provisions of the Soviet constitution in defending their right to independence. With democratically elected governments in place (the 1989–90 elections in the Baltic states were the most democratic of any in the USSR), the moral claim to independence seemed irrefutable. Most democratic states of the West had never recognized the legitimacy of the initial Soviet takeover in these areas. In 1990, however, unwilling to risk a destabilization of the now friendly Gorbachev regime, these same nations refused to grant diplomatic recognition to the elected Baltic governments (except Iceland, which recognized Lithuania before the failed coup of 1991). This pursuit of Realpolitik by the Western nations was an unexpected blow to the new Baltic leaders. The Soviet authorities no longer seemed to have a monopoly on moral hypocrisy and double standards.

Facing the collapse of all consensus on the state of the Union, in November 1990 Gorbachev finally came forth with a draft for a new union treaty, which, he hoped, would provide the basis for a renewed and voluntary federation of the republics.[14] To emphasize the voluntary nature of the federation and the equality of all republics, Gorbachev proposed the name Union of Sovereign Soviet Republics to replace Union of Soviet Socialist Republics. (The acronym, USSR or SSSR in Russian, could be retained.) The draft granted certain powers (e.g., regarding foreign policy and defense) to the central government; others were to be shared by the center and the republics, and still others were delegated to the republics. The proposed treaty would have provided the basis for a true federal structure. Just as the draft treaty was presented, the leaders of several union republics declared it unacceptable. Some, such as the Baltic governments, stated that they would not sign under any conditions. Leaders of other republics (e.g., Russia) objected to the broad scope of powers granted to the central government and demanded complete republic control over natural resources, economic assets, and economic policy. Gorbachev set a stern public tone for the debate in declaring that secession of any republic from the Union could lead to bloodshed.[15] In early December 1990, the chair of the Supreme Soviet's Council of Nationalities, Rafik Nishanov, indicated that even republics that did not approve the treaty would be part of the Union by virtue of the 1922 treaty, which was still in effect.[16] Statements such as these conveyed an ambiguous message. Military action in the Baltics in January 1991 indicated that the central authorities might be prepared to impose their viewpoint.

As noted in Chapter 3, the holding of an all-Union referendum on March 17, 1991 represented an effort to break this impasse by establishing popular legitimacy for Gorbachev's initiatives to renew the federation. While the referendum did not immediately serve that purpose, the nine republics that had participated in it soon emerged as those most willing to construct some sort of new union. Beginning in April 1991, the center and those nine republics (Russia, Ukraine, Belorussia, Azerbaidzhan, and the five Central Asian republics) pursued a new round of negotiations. Gorbachev was now strikingly more accommodating to republic demands. The republics had forced his hand by passing their own policy programs and forging a whole series of interrepublic (largely bilateral) agreements without regard for the center's preferences. By August, a new draft treaty was for-

Crisis of the System: Social and Economic Problems / **5**

mulated, and on August 20, 1991, five republics (Russia, Kazakhstan, Uzbekistan, Belorussia, and Tadzhikistan) were ready to sign. The hope and expectation was that in the fall the other four (Ukraine, Azerbaidzhan, Turkmenia, and Kyrgystan) would join as well, and that even Armenia might reconsider its position. The draft union treaty, published in *Izvestiia* on August 15, 1991, laid the foundation for a radical alteration in center-republic relations, and met many of the demands initially put forward by the Baltic states in 1989. (By 1991, the Baltic states' agendas had been so radicalized that signing the proposed treaty was out of the question.) The document granted most powers in the domestic sphere to the republics, leaving control over defense, foreign policy, security, major economic instruments (currency and gold reserves), and infrastructural sectors (such as the unified communication networks and nuclear energy) in the hands of the center. New institutional structures were outlined, including a constitutional court to adjudicate center-republic disputes. The CPD was to be abolished and a new Supreme Soviet formed, including direct representation of the republic governments. Indeed, the treaty involved transformation of the Union from "administrative federalism" to confederation.

In theory, those republics not signing the treaty were still considered part of the Union (as indicated earlier by Nishanov—although of course the Baltics and Moldova were not even in the union in 1922). "Most-favored" status, in trade and economic relations, was to prevail between the signatory republics, in an effort to lure those on the fence (Armenia, Georgia, and Moldova) to join the new union. In practice, it was unclear how resistant republics would be handled, but some expected greater tolerance. Indeed the future coup plotters may have interpreted the treaty's minimalist approach as implying a real capitulation of central authority over the defiant republics. This was almost certainly the trigger for the August 19 coup attempt.

Following the failed coup, the draft treaty was shelved. For diverse reasons, central authority lost legitimacy, the republics were even more suspicious of central control, and radical reformers, favoring an even further decentralization of power, were on the ascendancy. As discussed above, "independence mania" followed in the footsteps of the earlier "sovereignty mania." It fell to Gorbachev, Yel'tsin, and Nazarbaev (of Kazakhstan) to try to piece the shattered Union back together, at the same time that they acknowledged the inevitability of independence of the Baltic states. These leaders, and many observers, feared that without some mechanism of accommodation and cooperation, the former Soviet Union could become the site of economic catastrophe and civil strife. The negotiations to form a new set of transitional institutions (discussed in Chapter 4) and to construct cooperative economic arrangements (discussed above) resulted from this concern. While it was perhaps too soon to speak of the end of the Soviet Union, any future union would certainly be a different one; this time, ironically, embodying some more genuine variant of the principles of national self-determination mouthed by Lenin and of republic sovereignty contained in the 1977 Soviet constitution. At the same time, the process of decentralization and national self-determination might easily become decoupled from the progress of democratization and market reform. In a last gasp of activity, on September 5, 1991, the CPD passed a declaration of human rights and freedoms, which was to apply to all of the sovereign republics. Despite the noble intentions, if the center had lost its capability to control the centrifugal forces of nationalism and separatism, so it most likely would not be able to enforce the declaration of rights. Under Gorbachev's leadership (except in late 1990 and early 1991), the central government had been a force pushing *glasnost'* and *demokratizatsiia* in the periphery. After the 1991 coup attempt, it was doubtful whether central authorities or anyone else could impose on the republics even a minimal standard for democratic procedures, individual and minority rights, and reduced state control of the economy.

Interethnic Conflicts. As mentioned previously, many areas of the USSR have a complex ethnic mix. While this need not lead to interethnic tension, in many cases it has. Some of these conflicts are historically rooted, such as the conflict over the autonomous region of Nagorno-Karabakh. Other conflicts were more clearly aggravated by policy failures in the Soviet period. For example, some groups, such as the Crimean Tatars, the Checheno-Ingush, and the Volga Germans, were forcibly moved from their homelands during World War II (under accusations of treason and sympathy to the Germans). In most cases, the present Soviet government has rehabilitated these populations and tried to facilitate their relocation to their previous homelands. This has in turn elicited opposition from present residents, who fear displacement. In other cases, shortages of housing, high unemployment, and generally difficult economic conditions have fueled tension. Charges of ethnic favoritism or discrimination in the allocation of scarce goods have sparked violent ethnic clashes between resident populations or against in-migrants (for example, in 1989 and 1990 in the Osh region of Kirgizia, in the Fergana Valley in Uzbekistan, and in Dushanbe in Tadzhikistan). Other tensions have emerged as a result of declarations of sovereignty and independence. For example, a portion of the Russian population in several republics has formed its own organizations to defend its linguistic, economic, and cultural interests. Such conflicts have been particularly important in the Baltic region, but they have largely been manifested on a political level.

These types of interethnic strife reflect intense emotion and deep mistrust directed at both other groups and the political leaders. The lack of confidence in local authorities puts the latter in a weak position to mediate conflicts. In some cases, for example in the Baltics and in Georgia, nationalist leaders either control the government or have great leverage in it, but these leaders may not enjoy the confidence of ethnic minorities in these republics. Soviet troops have frequently been called in to quell outbreaks of interethnic violence, particularly in Armenia and Azerbaidzhan in relation to the Nagorno-Karabakh dispute, in Moldavia, Georgia, and Central Asia.

In some instances, nationalist leaders have claimed (but found it difficult to prove) that central authorities have deliberately provoked nationality conflict to justify central intervention to suppress independence movements. In Tbilisi on April 23, 1989, Soviet troops attacked Georgian demonstrators, leading to numerous casualties and injuries. Subsequent investigations carried out by a commission of the Supreme Soviet and in the Georgian Republic itself sought to identify the authorities responsible for issuing the order to use violence against the demonstrators. While Gorbachev's role remains unclear, top party and military officials at both the central and local levels have been implicated. This occurrence helped to intensify, rather than weaken, support for Georgian independence.

Resentment against central authority, poor policy performance, and long-standing national rivalries interact to produce seemingly intransigent problems of interethnic relations. These problems not only make reconstruction of the "union" difficult, but they also complicate every other issue the political leaders wish to address. Furthermore, they will pose continuing problems for republic-level leaders as they gain greater autonomy from the center.

The Work Force and Worker Discontent

Up until the late 1980s, Soviet trade unions were official organizations, structured to include both managerial and blue-collar workers in particular

Рис. А. Сырцова.

Source: *Argumenty i fakty*, no. 44 (November 1990), p. 7.

Top: "Room of Laughter"
The sign on the ground: "Groceries."

sectors of the economy. The trade unions were expected to mobilize the work force in support of regime goals and to provide certain services and minimal protections to the working population. The workplace was a primary focus of social activity, since many leisure activities, public-education campaigns, and day-care, housing, and vacation facilities were organized through it and the associated trade unions. Workers were (and still are) free to change their workplace, a real as well as a theoretical possibility, since there traditionally have been labor shortages in many sectors of the economy. Job mobility has been inhibited mainly by the difficulty in finding satisfactory housing and the restrictions placed on relocation to particularly desirable areas such as Moscow. To move to such places, permits have been required to control, though rather unsuccessfully, the growth of urban conglomerates. In contrast, enterprises in Siberia have offered higher wages and other material incentives. In

the pre-Gorbachev period, levels of labor mobility caused political leaders concern about the costs of job turnover, but the regime did not resort to coercive measures to restrict freedom of movement to most regions in the USSR.

During the Brezhnev period, evidence of worker discontent was largely inferential, though occasional strikes were reported through unofficial channels (e.g., in 1976 among port workers in Riga, in 1977 at a rubber goods factory in Kaunas, and in 1980 at the Togliatti automobile plant).[17] Strikes that did occur were met by a combination of repression, local concession, and censorship. Although workers tended to be less visibly active than intellectuals in dissident circles, in the late 1970s worker involvement increased markedly.[18] Nonetheless, contact and linkages between blue-collar workers and intellectuals have generally been weaker in the USSR than in, for example, Poland. In the Soviet Union, the working class has a relatively weak tradition of independent trade union organization (unlike the situation in Eastern European countries such as the GDR, Poland, and Czechoslovakia). Efforts in 1977 and 1978 to form an independent trade union in Moscow and elsewhere met with severe repression.

Lacking political outlets, workers prior to *glasnost'* expressed their alienation in indirect forms. Levels of labor productivity in Soviet firms has been consistently lower than in the West, perhaps in part because the government's commitment to job security did not allow the manager to exert effective pressure on workers. Job security was an important part of the implicit social contract, and workers were hard to fire. Low productivity and high levels of alcoholism and absenteeism were indirect expressions of job dissatisfaction. (Alcohol abuse is, however, a long-standing element of Russian culture that affects all strata of society.)

The regime responded to these labor problems with intermittent discipline campaigns, particularly during Andropov's short period of rule, beginning in November 1982, up to the first years of *perestroika*. The Party/state also repeatedly attempted to improve worker incentives and supplies of consumer goods to raise motivation levels. For example, experiments with a brigade system made groups of workers collectively responsible for a certain portion of the production process. Individual wage levels then reflected the brigade council's assessment of contribution, bringing peer pressure to bear. In another experiment called the Shchekino method, initiated in the late 1960s in Tula, managers were allowed to release or transfer unneeded labor resources and to increase the wages of the remaining work force accordingly as long as specified output levels were achieved and plan requirements fulfilled. Experiments of this type met with resistance from some managers, who felt under increased pressure to raise productivity with fewer labor resources. Overall, state efforts to stimulate commitment through improved incentives were largely unsuccessful. In addition, despite some false starts under *perestroika*, efforts to initiate genuine worker involvement in production decisions were avoided.

Workers are simultaneously consumers. The difficulty in finding desirable or high-quality goods has contributed to an almost institutionalized system of corruption throughout Soviet society, involving both the elite and the average clerk or truck driver. Under Brezhnev, and to some extent still, top officials commonly used state materials and labor to build private *dachas* or to renovate their apartments.[19] Contacts and access to various types of commodities are still important for the average worker as well. For example, truck drivers may sell state-owned gasoline, or employees may steal choice goods and materials from state shops and enterprises. Although this type of "second economy" and black market activity became more widespread in late 1990 with the breakdown of established distribution networks, it was an important part of the average worker's reality prior to *perestroika*. Contacts and access were as important as wage

levels, making it difficult for the authorities to motivate productive activity simply through differential pay scales.

Female workers have faced added strains. Soviet women achieved virtual equality in educational opportunity by the end of the Stalinist period, and by the 1980s, 86 percent of Soviet working-age women were in the labor force. Women continued to occupy lower-status and lower-paid jobs, however, particularly in sectors such as retail trade, education, health, culture, and administration.[20] Even the apparent exceptions prove the rule. In 1975, 75 percent of Soviet physicians were female, but Soviet doctors enjoyed a much lower status than their Western counterparts, and higher administrative and scientific posts in the medical profession were more often filled by men. This pattern was replicated throughout the occupational structure. In 1979–80, 80 percent of Soviet teachers, but only 32 percent of directors of secondary schools, were women.[21] Soviet women have been more likely than their Western counterparts to hold lower- and middle-level posts in traditionally male fields such as economics and engineering.

The burden on Soviet working women has been heavier because of the slow change in sex roles and poor supplies of consumer goods. Women still have the primary responsibility for child care and housework, duties that are more time-consuming in the USSR due to long lines and shortages at food outlets, the lack of labor-saving devices (such as dishwashers and automatic washing machines), and inadequate services (such as laundries and carry-out restaurants). Soviet studies in the late Brezhnev period indicated that women spent more than twice as much time as men on housework and a third less time on self-education and cultural pursuits.[22] Many Soviet women would prefer to work fewer hours and have more time to devote to family and home matters, and Gorbachev's own statements indicate a preference for this type of traditional definition of sex roles.[23]

Until the summer of 1989, the working class remained relatively complacent. With the miners' strikes in the summers of 1989 and 1990 and the spring of 1991, however, warning signals were issued. Initially greeted by Gorbachev in 1989 as a sign that the working class would help challenge the lethargy and inertia of the old elite, it soon became evident that the miners' demands would be difficult to meet and that their strikes could paralyze other sectors of the economy. This specter stimulated the central leadership to make wide-ranging promises to the miners in the summer of 1989. By mid-1990, most of these had not been kept, and further warning strikes ensued.

In the autumn of 1989, the Supreme Soviet passed legislation allowing a limited right to strike: strikes could occur only after two separate conciliation boards had sought a resolution; they could be suspended for two months; and wildcat strikes and strikes in certain essential sectors of the economy (energy, transport, communications, and defense) were banned entirely. Despite these restrictions, this legislation created room for expanded legal expression of workers' demands, a tendency reinforced by the formation of several independent organizations representing working-class interests. Independent trade union organizations sprang up, and in May 1990 representatives from several of the new groups met to form a Confederation of Labor. An independent union of coal miners also was formed in 1990.[24]

For the most part, these initiatives supported the trend toward increasing democratization of the political structures, a decline of Party influence, and decentralization of economic control, although there were some notable exceptions as well as internal contradictions and ambiguities. Some incipient links developed between urban intellectuals and various working-class groups, but most workers' organizations shared a commitment to defending workers' interests on their own terms. They rejected previous orthodoxy, which maintained that a vanguard party or an enlightened intelligentsia could interpret working-class interests better than the workers themselves.

The demands of the miners in 1989, 1990, and 1991 foreshadowed the contradictions that are likely to plague the workers' movement in the coming months and years. Conditions in Soviet mines are, in many cases, extremely difficult and hazardous, as indicated by the average casualty rate of eight hundred deaths per year in the mining industry (compared to fifty-five deaths in the United States in 1988). Although miners receive high wages by Soviet standards, the supply of goods in mining towns is often so poor that the wage levels offer little advantage. Housing is in short supply, and the average life expectancy of a miner in 1988 was forty-eight years, compared to the average male life expectancy in the USSR of sixty-five years.[25]

In 1989, some of the miners' demands focused on improved safety in the pits and better working conditions, better supplies of goods, extended vacations, and improved housing. Even at this stage, however, a political dimension was evident. Workers wanted self-financing and self-management of the mines, believing this would enable their more rational management, technological upgrading, and possibilities of export of output to foreign buyers (for receipt of hard currency, which would in turn allow the import of technologically advanced equipment from abroad). Miners in the Donetsk region of Ukraine, where several mines were slated by the ministry for mothballing due to unprofitable operating conditions, were particularly intent on gaining this control to ensure the continued operation of the pits. The workers also demanded the closure of or restrictions on the lucrative cooperative (private) enterprises that had sprung up in the area, apparently in the belief that they were based largely on speculation and unjustified profit seeking. On the one hand, these demands suggest that the miners are sympathetic and supportive of many elements of the government's reform package, particularly decentralization of economic control to the enterprise level. On the other hand, the miners are resistant to the inegalitarian implications of privatization, symbolized by the cooperative (private) sector.

In 1990, the positions of the miners were radicalized even further when they demanded removal of all Party influence from economic and government affairs, nationalization of Party property, and formation of an independent trade union movement. In 1991, miners' demands included calls for Gorbachev's resignation, a transfer of power to the Council of the Federation, recognition of the legality of the Baltic votes on independence, and a ban on political party activity in the army and in state organs. During the August 1991 coup attempt, miners were among the few groups that heeded Yel'tsin's call for a general strike in opposition to the putsch. Other groups either didn't hear the appeal (due to media censorship), responded passively, or expressed their belief that the economic costs of a work stoppage would be too damaging to the already enfeebled economy.

In terms of economic policy, miners in western Siberia had, in 1990, come out in support of the Shatalin plan and miners generally have supported the more radical economic program of the Yel'tsin government in the Russian Republic, again indicative of at least theoretical support for marketization of the economy. One wonders how the miners (and workers in general) will react if new market pressures, in a reformed system, force certain enterprises into bankruptcy or produce augmented wage differentials. Is the apparent support for a market economy based on a misplaced faith in the benign nature of its impact? Already miners have suffered some disappointments in learning that export to hard-currency markets is not automatic, even

with central controls lifted, since much of the Soviet coal is of too low a quality to be acceptable to these buyers.[26] In spring 1991, an agreement was reached between Yel'tsin and Gorbachev to turn control of the mines in Russia over to the Russian Republic.

Government estimates indicate that 9.4 million person-days of labor were lost in the first quarter of 1990 due to strikes, although most strike activity (with the notable exception of the miners' unrest) in 1989 and 1990 was related to ethnic disputes rather than workplace grievances as such.[27] Apparently the miners' example in the summer of 1989 led other groups to realize the efficacy of the strike weapon. It became a powerful pressure tactic in the dispute between Armenians and Azeris, in the Baltics, and in localized ethnic disputes in Central Asia. In the first quarter of 1991, 1.169 million person-days of labor were lost to strikes; of these, a little less than half were lost in the Russian Republic and most of the other half in Ukraine. The situation worsened dramatically in the second quarter of 1991, with widespread miners' strikes in those two republics.[28] (See Figure 5.4.)

Nonetheless, by late 1991, workers (other than coal miners) had risen up only intermittently to protest the failures of *perestroika* or the perils of the promised market. But the potential for disruption was evident, particularly when significant portions of the population might be predisposed to see economic hardship as rooted in ethnic discrimination.

CPSU conservatives attempted to rally working-class support to help maintain their influence in the political system. The somewhat restructured official trade union organizations have opposed price hikes and have attempted to maintain control over services such as distribution of housing, food, and vacation vouchers. Like the miners' organizations, they have favored restrictions on the cooperative sector. The United Front of Workers (UFW), formed in Leningrad in 1989, was supported by the conserva-

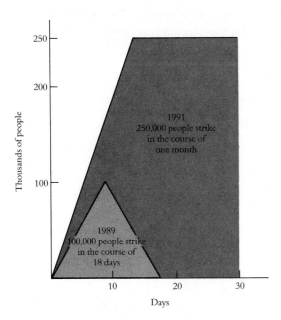

Source: *Kommersant*, no. 13 (25 March 1991), p. 31.

Figure 5.4   Miners' Strikes in the USSR
1989–1991

tive Leningrad Party organization, whose leaders had suffered serious defeats in the CPD elections in the spring of 1989.[29] This organization defends some of the more traditional Soviet conceptions of working-class power that were discussed in Chapter 3. Neo-Stalinists such as Nina Andreyeva (the alleged author of the famous Andreyeva letter discussed in Chapter 3) have been invited to address the group.

The UFW opposes private ownership, unequal wage policies, and price increases. It supports guaranteed quotas for working-class representation in the soviets and elections based in productive units rather than territorial constituencies. The organization also has links with the Interfront organizations that have formed in non-Russian areas to represent the interests of largely Russian minorities who favor maintenance of some central control in the economy.

Because they feel threatened by decentralizing nationalist policies, these Russian workers have looked to continued ties with the center for support. Although these types of conservative workers' organizations at least nominally have attracted the support of hundreds of thousands of workers throughout the country, they have not generally been successful in getting their supporters elected to public office.

There are many potential cleavages in the working class. As we have seen, some are rooted in diverse ideological conceptions, national identification, and geographic location. In addition, splits may result from different skill levels and employment in different sectors of the economy. Highly skilled male workers will find their labor more marketable in a reformed economic system than will unskilled assembly-line laborers. In particular, electricians, plumbers, and carpenters may be able to sell their skills to new cooperative or private enterprises more easily than semi-skilled and unskilled workers. As experience in other countries has indicated, women often are among the first to be laid off. This may be particularly important as the bloated white-collar sectors in the ministerial and enterprise structures are trimmed.

Those workers who are most vulnerable to layoffs (unskilled blue- and white-collar workers) are likely to resist the effects of market reform most strongly (see Table 5.10). They may, therefore, also be more susceptible to mobilization by conservative officials attempting to maintain a political foothold in the evolving economic and political system. In contrast, the highly skilled segments of the working class may find their interests served by the increasing wage differentials and competitive environment. At this writing, it seems likely that movement toward market reform will be accelerated. If it is not, other dynamics will set the fault lines within the working-class movement.

In the final section of this chapter, we suggest some of the most likely future scenarios for the

Table 5.10 The Distribution of the Population by Total Average per Capita Income, 1985, 1988, 1989

Average Total Income per Month (in rubles)	Number of People (annual average in millions)			Percent of Total		
	1985	1988	1989	1985	1988	1989
Up to 75	49.6	36.0	31.7	17.9%	12.6%	11.1%
75–100	54.8	44.7	39.2	19.8	15.7	13.7
100–125	53.6	50.2	46.3	19.3	17.6	16.1
125–150	41.7	44.9	43.5	15.0	15.7	15.2
150–175	28.9	35.0	36.1	10.4	12.2	12.6
175–200	18.6	25.7	27.4	6.7	9.0	9.5
200–250	19.0	28.8	33.8	6.9	10.1	11.8
250–300	7.2	12.6	16.4	2.6	4.4	5.7
300–350	2.7	5.3	7.7	1.0	1.9	2.7
350–400	1.1	2.3	3.6	0.4	0.8	1.2
Over 400			1.0			0.4
Total Population	277.2	285.5	286.7	100	100	100

Source: *Argumenty i fakty*, no. 45 (November 1990), p. 1.

USSR as they appear in the autumn of 1991. When you read this, consider which, if any, have become even more probable in the interim.

Will the USSR Survive?

In 1970, the Soviet dissident/émigré Andrei Amalrik wrote a book titled *Will the Soviet Union Survive Until 1984?* While the timing and parts of the argument were off, the question was prescient,[30] for in September 1991, the country seemed on the verge of disintegration. Will the USSR continue to exist into the twenty-first century, and, if so, in what form?

When I drafted this chapter in the summer of 1991, I wrote "one scenario that seems probable in mid-1991 is a movement toward a more authoritarian center." The move to authoritarianism might have occurred in different ways. One possibility was that Gorbachev himself would

continue to concentrate power into his own hands, to act as a motor for implementation of a market economic strategy. In late 1990, even some reformers felt that stronger central control was needed to overcome the multiple obstacles facing the country as it tried to address the problems of national disintegration and economic collapse. Following the events in Lithuania in January 1991, most reformers saw the shift to authoritarianism in less benign terms. They became even more disillusioned with and distrustful of Gorbachev and feared that concentration of power, even in his hands, could mark a real setback for the reform program. With Gorbachev's overtures to the "democrats" and republic leaders in April 1991, a conservative usurpation by Gorbachev himself again seemed less likely, but the specter of a military coup remained.

The coup attempt, of course, occurred, following sharp warnings from former Gorbachev aides, Eduard Shevardnadze and Aleksandr Yakovlev.

Some people speculated that the military had shrewdly realized that the legitimacy of the regime, particularly abroad, was enhanced by Gorbachev's continuance in the presidency. In the early months of 1991, the top military brass, leaders of the security organs, and Party conservatives seemed willing to give Gorbachev a last chance to "save" the nation (and their power). In late 1990 and early 1991, increased visibility and power for the military were concessions Gorbachev offered to win this support. With Gorbachev's shift in spring 1991 and the imminent signing of the union treaty, the support of the conservative forces finally broke.

The haunting fear of a coup was finally realized. The conservative coup d'état occurred, was met, and was defeated. The routing of the putsch attempt marked the beginning of a new, but in many ways equally uncertain, era. The conservative forces had proven themselves unable to exert control over the increasingly politicized population, and they had no program to offer the country. The security forces were themselves already too divided to force the issue. For Gorbachev, the Rubicon had been crossed. The embattled leader emerged from the experience momentarily dazed but with an intensified commitment to market reform and to cooperation with the more radical "democratic" forces. The immobilizing fear of a conservative backlash waned. But what would the aftermath of the failed coup finally bring?

In the autumn of 1991 emotions swayed from hope to apprehension. On the one hand, the prospect of continued *demokratizatsiia* with marketization of the economy again seemed viable and even probable, at least in some of the European republics. The scenario outlined in the agreements of early September 1991 (supported by Gorbachev, Yel'tsin, and the CPD) involved just such a vision. Each republic would be able to determine its own level of involvement in any further union, some committed to political cooperation, others only to economic cooperation (perhaps on a model of the European Community). The Baltics had already been allowed to opt out of the political union, but might come to see some economic cooperation as both necessary and beneficial. Was this "ideal" outcome likely to be achieved? Could the USSR move, relatively peacefully, toward becoming a real confederation of sovereign democratic states?

There were some grounds for optimism in September 1991. After all, the immediate crisis (the coup attempt and its disorienting aftermath) had been overcome with relative civility and minimal violence. It seemed, at least in Russia (and probably in Ukraine and Belorussia) that a critical portion of the population was capable of acting autonomously to prevent any lapse into authoritarian rule. The "democratic" forces were more united than ever before and the conservative leadership core was being purged. The powerful structure of the CPSU was being dismantled. But questions remained. Could the economic crisis be overcome, at least sufficiently to prevent any number of dire outcomes (a repeat putsch, civil strife, starvation, mass emigration, national chauvinism and ethnic violence) that might themselves threaten the democratic experiment? Time was short as a long winter approached. Would the leaders in the republics be motivated to act, now that they had the formal authority to do so? Would the new institutional structures gain enough legitimacy to win popular support and enforce the sacrifices necessary to make economic reform work? Or would authoritarianism rear its head in some republics, just as democratic forces seemed to be winning out elsewhere? How could these conflicting tendencies be accommodated? Only great finesse, political will, and tolerance on the part of the leadership, both at the republic and central levels, could facilitate a positive outcome. Successful achievement of the interconnected political and economic tasks would not allow many more political mistakes—a tall order for any leadership group, especially one just learning the fundamentals of negotiation, compromise, and bargaining. The fragile political balance between the various actors in the new post-coup compromise remained susceptible to easy disruption in the face of the looming economic decline.

A less pleasing scenario involved a continued progression of economic decline and national disintegration. In September 1991, it seemed that some kind of accommodation could be reached between the Slavic and Central Asian republics (although at that time Ukraine seemed to be resisting the economic and perhaps the political union). But would this hold, especially if conservative power structures were retained in some republics (Central Asia) and overturned in others? What about the Transcaucasian republics? Already in September, quasi-authoritarian structures seemed to be emerging in Georgia and Azerbaidzhan (elections for president in early September included only one candidate and voting methods resembled pre-*perestroika* patterns). Ethnic strife threatened to continue its violent turn in some regions (Nagorno-Karabakh and South Ossetia). Who could protect minority rights? Would the Yugoslav pattern replicate itself in these regions? A corollary of the breakup of the USSR could be what Gorbachev himself had warned against—regional pockets of bloodshed, civil strife and disorder—or, less likely but not impossible, all-out civil war. Could the USSR's nuclear arsenal be kept under firm central control? Did the formation of national guards and defense ministries in the individual republics set the stage for the use of violence to resolve political conflicts there? Finally, would increasing disorder, anarchy, and civil unrest loose yet another coup attempt, this time better organized than the last?

When Gorbachev was awarded the Nobel Peace Prize in 1990, some resentful Soviets quickly retorted, "He surely didn't win the Nobel Prize for Economics." The question in mid-1991 was could any leadership crew maintain at least a modicum of peace as the USSR unraveled and moved from a now ruthlessly condemned past into an unknown future? Would the hopes for a new, more democratic, more prosperous USSR suffer a premature death? Could the collapse of the old USSR give birth to a series of new, more legitimate national entities? Or would the forced consensus of the past give rise to unrestrained assertions of conflicting and irreconcilable claims, manageable, if at all, only by a reassertion of new forms of dictatorship?

The "August days" have left all of these questions still unanswered, although the balance seems to have shifted in favor of the more optimistic variant. The old statues, flags, and place-names of the Communist period are falling and are being restored to their prerevolutionary modes. But clearly the prerevolutionary past symbolized by those names and images does not provide a signpost for the future. The new revolutionaries of the 1990s have a fairly clear goal—to throw off the Communist past and realize some variant of Western democracy and capitalism combined with national self-determination. But the path to reach this goal is dimly lit and fraught with hazards.

As this is written, the pendulum swings from hope to resignation, both for the region's inhabitants and for "experts" trying to gauge events from a critical distance. Proud smiles graced Moscow faces on August 22, 1991 following the defeat of the coup d'état. As subtly as summer has changed to fall, euphoria has given way to old realities. The shortening days of autumn warn that time is running out for the triumphant reformers. Everything has changed, and yet nothing has changed. The stark and drab routines of shortage, corruption, and disorder are still the staples of daily life.

Crisis of the System: Social and Economic Problems / **5**

Notes

1. *New York Times*, 24 November 1990, p. 3.

2. "Antikrizisnaia programma," *Izvestiia*, 22 April 1991, p. 1.

3. The popular Soviet weekly *Argumenty i fakty* reported "market" prices in various cities on a regular basis in 1990. See, for example, no. 44 (November 1990), p. 7.

4. Gertrude E. Schroeder, "The Soviet Economy on a Treadmill of 'Reforms,'" in *Soviet Economy in the 1980s: Problems and Prospects*, ed. U.S. Congress, Joint Economic Committee (Washington: GPO, 1979), p. 312.

5. Marshall I. Goldman, "Gorbachev and Economic Reform," *Foreign Affairs*, Fall 1985, p. 64.

6. "Just What Happened in Belorussia?" *Izvestiia*, 15 April 1991, p. 2., trans. (condensed) in *Current Digest of the Soviet Press* (hereafter *CDSP*) 43, no. 15 (1991), p. 10.

7. Ibid.

8. John Armstrong, "Mobilized and Proletarian Diasporas," *American Political Science Review* 70 (1976), p. 403.

9. Francis X. Clines, "Soviets Jail Man for Anti-Semitic Threats," *New York Times*, 13 October 1990, p. 3.

10. John L. Scherer, "A Note on Soviet Jewish Emigration 1971–1984," *Soviet Jewish Affairs* 15, no. 2 (1985), p. 42.

11. Rasma Karklins, *Ethnic Relations in the USSR: The Perspective from Below* (Boston: George Allen & Unwin, 1986).

12. See data in Gertrude E. Schroeder, "Nationalities and the Soviet Economy," in *The Nationalities Factor in Soviet Politics and Society*, ed. Lubomyr Hajda and Mark Beissinger (Boulder, Colo.: Westview Press, 1990), especially pp. 51 and 53.

13. See Barbara A. Anderson and Brian D. Silver, "Some Factors in the Linguistic and Ethnic Russification of Soviet Nationalities: Is Everyone Becoming Russian?" in *The Nationalities Factor in Soviet Politics and Society*, ed. Lubomyr Hajda and Mark Beissinger (Boulder, Colo.: Westview Press, 1990), p. 106.

14. *Izvestiia*, 24 November 1990, pp. 1–2.

15. Francis X. Clines, "Gorbachev's Plan for a New Union: A Central Government Still in Charge," *New York Times*, 25 November 1990, p. 166.

16. See "Parliament Supports the Conception of the Union Treaty," *Izvestiia*, 4 December 1990, trans. in *CDSP* 42, no. 49 (1990), p. 12.

17. See Elizabeth Teague, *Solidarity and the Soviet Worker: The Impact of the Polish Events of 1980 on Soviet Internal Politics* (London: Croom Helm, 1988), especially chapter 3.

18. See Frederick C. Barghoorn, "Regime-Dissenter Relations after Khrushchev: Some Observations," in *Pluralism in the Soviet Union: Essays in Honour of H. Gordon Skilling*, ed. Susan Gross Solomon (New York: St. Martin's Press, 1982), pp. 139–147.

19. See a discussion of this in Arkady Shevchenko, *Breaking with Moscow* (New York: Alfred A. Knopf, 1985), p. 148. Under *glasnost'*, revelations about high-level corruption have become frequent in the Soviet press.

20. David Lane, *Soviet Society Under Perestroika* (Boston: Unwin Hyman, 1990), p. 217.

21. Gail Warshofsky Lapidus, "Introduction: Women, Work, and Family: New Soviet Perspectives," in *Women, Work, and Family in the Soviet Union*, ed. Gail Warshofsky Lapidus (Armont, N.Y.: M. W. Sharpe, 1982), p. xxii.

22. E. V. Gruzdeva and E. S. Chertikhina, "Soviet Women: Problems of Work and Daily Life," in *Rabochii klass i sovremennyi mir*, no. 6 (1982), trans. in *Soviet Sociology* 14, nos. 1–3 (1985–86), p. 163.

23. Mikhail S. Gorbachev, *Perestroika: New Thinking for Our Country and the World* (New York: Harper & Row, 1987), p. 117.

24. On this, see Elizabeth Teague, "Soviet Workers Find a Voice," *Report on the USSR* 2, no. 28 (13 July 1990), pp. 14–15.

25. Margaret Jacobs, "The Hard Life of Soviet Miners," *Report on the USSR* 2, no. 32 (10 August 1990), pp. 10–11.

26. See David Marples, "Turmoil in the Donbass:

The Economic Realities," *Report on the USSR* 2, no. 41 (12 October 1990), pp. 12–14.

27. Teague, "Soviet Workers Find a Voice," pp. 13–15; *Izvestiia TsK KPSS*, no. 5 (1990), pp. 131–132.

28. "Bumerang," *Izvestiia*, 22 May 1991, p. 2. This article, in contrast to the Teague article cited in note 27, says that ten million workdays were lost to strikes in enterprises and organizations in 1990. Perhaps strikes related to ethnic grievances are not included.

29. This discussion of the UFW relies heavily on the article by Elizabeth Teague, "Perestroika and the Soviet Worker," *Government and Opposition* 25, no. 2 (1990), pp. 207–209.

30. Andrei Amalrik, *Will the Soviet Union Survive Until 1984?* (New York: Harper & Row, 1970). See also Helene Carrere d'Encausse, who focuses more explicitly on the national issue in *Decline of an Empire: the Soviet Socialist Republics in Revolt* (New York: Newsweek Books, 1979). Translated from the French edition published in 1978.

Bibliography

Historical Background

Cohen, Stephen F. *Rethinking the Soviet Experience: Politics and History Since 1917.* New York: Oxford University Press, 1985.

Fainsod, Merle. *Smolensk Under Soviet Rule.* Cambridge, Mass.: Harvard University Press, 1958.

Fitzpatrick, Sheila, ed. *Cultural Revolution in Russia, 1928–1931.* Bloomington: Indiana University Press, 1978.

Liebman, Marcel. *Leninism Under Lenin.* London: Merlin Press, 1975.

Medvedev, Roy. *Let History Judge: The Origins and Consequences of Stalinism.* Rev. ed. New York: Columbia University Press, 1989.

Pipes, Richard. *Russia Under the Old Regime.* London: Widenfeld & Nicolson, 1974.

Rosenberg, Suzanne. *A Soviet Odyssey.* Oxford: Oxford University Press, 1988.

Szamuely, Tibor. *The Russian Tradition.* Edited by Robert Conquest. London: Secker & Warburg, 1974.

Tucker, Robert C. *Stalinism: Essays in Historical Interpretation.* New York: W. W. Norton, 1977.

Post-Stalinist Politics Before *Perestroika*

Bialer, Seweryn. *Stalin's Successors: Leadership, Stability, and Change in the Soviet Union.* Cambridge: Cambridge University Press, 1980.

Breslauer, George W. *Khrushchev and Brezhnev as Leaders: Building Authority in Soviet Politics.* Boston: George Allen & Unwin, 1982.

Bunce, Valerie. "The Political Economy of the Brezhnev Period: The Rise and Fall of Corporatism?" *British Journal of Political Science* 13 (April 1983), pp. 129–158.

Gustafson, Thane. *Reform in Soviet Politics: Lessons of Recent Policies on Land and Water.* Cambridge: Cambridge University Press, 1981.

Hough, Jerry, and Merle Fainsod. *How the Soviet Union Is Governed.* Cambridge, Mass.: Harvard University Press, 1979.

Linden, Carl. *Khrushchev and the Soviet Leadership: 1957–1964.* Baltimore: Johns Hopkins Press, 1966.

Politics Since 1985: General

Bialer, Seweryn, ed. *Politics, Society, and Nationality Inside Gorbachev's Russia.* Boulder, Colo.: Westview Press, 1989.

Cohen, Stephen F., and Katrina van den Heuvel. *Voices of Glasnost: Interviews with Gorbachev's Reformers.* New York: W. W. Norton, 1989.

Daniels, Robert V. *Is Russia Reformable? Change and Resistance from Stalin to Gorbachev.* Boulder, Colo.: Westview Press, 1988.

Davies, R. W. "Gorbachev's Socialism in Historical Perspective." *New Left Review*, no. 179 (1990), pp. 5–27.

Gooding, John. "Gorbachev and Democracy." *Soviet Studies* 42, no. 2 (April 1990), pp. 195–231.

Lewin, Moshe. *The Gorbachev Phenomenon: A Historical Interpretation.* Enl. ed. Berkeley: University of California Press, 1991.

Nove, Alec. *Glasnost in Action: Cultural Renaissance in Russia.* Boston: Unwin Hyman, 1989.

Sakwa, Richard. *Gorbachev and His Reforms, 1985–1990.* London: Philip Allan, 1990.

White, Stephen. *Gorbachev and After.* Cambridge: Cambridge University Press, 1991.

Political Institutions and Political Change

Hahn, Jeffrey W. *Soviet Grassroots: Citizen Participation in Local Soviet Government.* Princeton, N.J.: Princeton University Press, 1988.

Lane, David, ed. *Elites and Political Power in the USSR.* Aldershot, England: E. Elgar Publishers, 1988.

Urban, Michael E. *More Power to the Soviets: The Democratic Revolution in the USSR.* Aldershot, England: E. Elgar Publishers, 1990.

Voslensky, Michael. *Nomenklatura: The Soviet Ruling Class.* Translated by Eric Mosbacher. Garden City, N.Y.: Doubleday, 1984 (English edition).

White, Stephen, and Alex Pravda. *Ideology and Soviet Politics.* London: Macmillan Press Ltd., 1988.

State and Society

Alexeyeva, Ludmilla. *Soviet Dissent: Contemporary Movements for National, Religious, and Human Rights.* Translated by Carol Pearce and John Glad. Middletown, Conn.: Wesleyan University Press, 1985.

Hosking, Geoffrey A. *The Awakening of the Soviet Union.* Cambridge, Mass.: Harvard University Press, 1990.

Lapidus, Gail W. *State and Society in the Soviet Union.* Boulder, Colo.: Westview Press, 1989.

Rutland, Peter. "Labor Unrest and Movements in 1989 and 1990." *Soviet Economy* 6 (October–December 1990), pp. 345–384.

Sacks, Michael Paul, and Jerry G. Pankhurst. *Understanding Soviet Society.* Boston: George Allen & Unwin, 1988.

Scanlan, James. "Reform and Civil Society in the USSR." *Problems of Communism* 37 (March–April 1988), pp. 41–46.

Shlapentokh, Vladimir. *Public and Private Lives of the Soviet People: Changing Values in Post-Stalin Russia.* New York: Oxford University Press, 1989.

Teague, Elizabeth. "Perestroika and the Soviet Worker." *Government and Opposition* 25, no. 2 (1990), pp. 191–211.

Zaslavskaya, Tatyana. *The Second Socialist Revolution: An Alternative Soviet Strategy.* Translated by Susan M. Davies with Jenny Warner. Bloomington, Ind.: Indiana University Press, 1990.

The Soviet Economy

Aslund, Anders. *Gorbachev's Struggle for Economic Reform: The Soviet Reform Process, 1985–1988.* Ithaca, N.Y.: Cornell University Press, 1989.

Ellman, Michael. *Socialist Planning.* 2d ed. New York: Cambridge University Press, 1989.

Gregory, Paul R., and Robert C. Stuart. *Soviet Economic Structure and Performance.* 4th ed. New York: Harper & Row, 1990.

Kornai, Janos. *The Road to a Free Economy: Shifting from a Socialist System; The Example of Hungary.* New York: W. W. Norton, 1990.

Lewin, Moshe. *Political Undercurrents in Soviet Economic Debates: From Bukharin to the Modern Reformers.* Princeton, N.J.: Princeton University Press, 1974.

Nove, Alec. *The Economics of Feasible Socialism.* 2d ed. London: George Allen & Unwin, 1991.

Shmelev, Nikolai, and Vladimir Popov. *The Turning Point: Revitalizing the Soviet Economy.* New York: Doubleday, 1989.

The Nationality Issue

Bahry, Donna. *Outside Moscow: Power, Politics, and Budgetary Policy in the Soviet Republics.* New York: Columbia University Press, 1987.

Hajda, Lubomyr, and Mark Beissinger, eds. *The Nationalities Factor in Soviet Politics and Society.* Boulder, Colo.: Westview Press, 1990.

Karklins, Rasma. *Ethnic Relations in the USSR: The Perspective from Below.* Boston: George Allen & Unwin, 1986.

Kozlov, Viktor I. *The Peoples of the Soviet Union.* Bloomington: Indiana University Press, 1988.

Motyl, Alexander J. *Sovietology, Rationality, Nationality: Coming to Grips with Nationalism in the USSR.* New York: Columbia University Press, 1990.

Nahaylo, Bohdan, and Victor Swoboda. *Soviet Disunion: A History of the Nationalities Problem in the USSR.* New York: Free Press, 1990.

Roeder, Philip G. "Soviet Federalism and Ethnic Mobilization." *World Politics* 43 (January 1991), pp. 196–232.

Smith, Graham, ed. *The Nationalities Question in the Soviet Union.* New York: Longman, 1990.

Soviet Foreign Policy, the Military, and the KGB

Colton, Timothy, and Thane Gustafson, eds. *Soldiers and the Soviet State: Civil-Military Relations from Brezhnev to Gorbachev.* Princeton, N.J.: Princeton University Press, 1990.

Gorbachev, Mikhail S. *Perestroika: New Thinking for Our Country and the World.* New York: Harper & Row, 1987.

Hough, Jerry. *Russia and the West: Gorbachev and the Politics of Reform.* New York: Simon & Schuster, 1988.

Jacobson, Carl G., ed. *Soviet Foreign Policy: New Dynamics, New Themes.* New York: St. Martin's Press, 1989.

Knight, Amy W. *The KGB, Police and Politics in the Soviet Union.* Boston: Unwin Hyman, 1988.

Nogee, Joseph L., and Robert H. Donaldson. *Soviet Foreign Policy Since World War II.* 3d ed. New York: Pergamon Press, 1988.

Ulam, Adam. *Expansion and Coexistence: The History of Soviet Foreign Policy, 1917–1973.* 2d ed. New York: Praeger, 1974.

Selected Newspapers and Journals

Current Digest of the Soviet Press (American Association for the Advancement of Slavic Studies).

Journal of Soviet Nationalities (Center of East–West Trade, Investment, and Communications, Duke University).

Kommersant.

Moscow News (Moskovsokie novosti).

Problems of Communism (Washington: Documentary Studies Section, International Information Administration).

Report on the USSR (Radio Free Europe/Radio Liberty, Inc.).

Soviet Economy (Silver Spring, Maryland).

Soviet Review (New York: International Arts and Sciences Press).

Soviet Studies (University of Glasgow).

Soviet Union: Union Sovietique (University Center for International Studies, University of Pittsburgh).

Studies in Comparative Communism (Los Angeles).

Survey (London: Congress for Cultural Freedom).

Index